When Worlds Collide

Colin Harvey

When Worlds Collide

How Video Games Reinvent Storytelling
and Why It Matters

Colin Harvey

Canbury Press

First published by Canbury Press 2025

This edition published 2025

Canbury Press

Kingston upon Thames, Surrey, United Kingdom

www.canburypress.com

Typeset in Athelas (heading), Futura PT (body)

Cover design: Ruby Usiskin

This is a work of non-fiction

ISBN:

Paperback: 9781914487347

Ebook: 9781914487354

Contents

ACKNOWLEDGEMENTS

Gamers of a certain vintage are used to waiting. Back in the heady days of the 1980s games came on cassette and you had to sit and wait while *Manic Miner, Pitstop 2, Ghostbusters* or some other dazzling interactive adventure loaded up. Frequently something would go awry and you'd be forced to rewind the tape, performatively blow the dust out of the deck, and start all over again.

Fitting, then, that this book should have such a long gestation period. Forty years in fact. What started as haphazard noodling with Atari BASIC in an effort to create my own text adventures at the tender age of eleven eventually evolved into an academic career teaching and researching interactive storytelling. This in turn gave way to my current manifestation as a game writer, narrative designer and narrative director. Only now, with all these experiences safely loaded into my middle-aged buffer, do I feel able to share them with the world.

In many ways the book is a love letter to the storytelling potential of a medium which is often misunderstood and misrepresented by the wider culture but which is nevertheless increasingly influential. It's also a salute to the immensely talented professionals who create games and think critically about them, many of whom I've been fortunate to work with and encounter in lots of different contexts. You'll see that some of these individuals have kindly contributed their time and insights to helping me explore the subject from different angles. I've cited many more perspectives from industry practitioners, journalists and academics.

There isn't time and space to thank everyone individually. Instead I'd like to send a hoorah to the various studios I've worked at throughout my career. These include the amazing people at Criterion Studio, as well as colleagues at Ripple Effect, Motive and DICE, all part of the wider Electronic Arts family. I'd also like to express my gratitude to former colleagues at Sony's much mourned London Studio, along with friends and former workmates from Saber Interactive and Rebellion Developments, all the way back to Sony's Team Soho where I got my first freelance gig. These studios are full of passionate people whose perspectives and experiences helped shape the various stories and worlds we built together. Suffice to say, all the views expressed in this book are either mine or the views of individuals based on their own experiences. There are no corporate perspectives here.

Similar gratitude goes to the students and academics I worked with at King's College London, Bournemouth University, London South Bank University and Western Sydney University during my time teaching, researching and leading courses in game narrative and creative writing. Often this support came in the form of inspirational conversations grabbed in corridors or over lunch, as much as formal conference presentations or publications. A special callout, too, for colleagues at the University of the West of England, who made much of the running on this subject before anyone else caught on.

More specific thanks go to the friends and family members who've indulged me over the years. In suitably non-linear order these include friends Dryden Goodwin, Jo Cole, Damien Goodwin, John Grindrod, Rick Porras, Guy Gadney, Chris Elliott, Andrew Dewdney, Cath Dewdney, Jon Dovey, Sharon Stammers, Malcolm Watt, Amanda Renz, Gavin Renz, Sean Ly, Sola Ly, Claire Corbett, Julian Leatherdale, Nod Miller, Joe Lidster, Ian Farrington, Colin Salmon, Rob Salt, Simon Skinner, Paul Jones, Leandro Lima and Andrew Halford. A huge thank you, too, to Martin Hickman and to Gaby Monteiro at Canbury Press for seeing the potential in this book and for all their support in getting it over the finish line.

Most of all I'd like to thank my amazing children Zak and Aphra and my extraordinary friend and partner Anna Reading. The three of you help make sense of the real world and inspire my imaginary ones. (I'm still the best at *Mario Kart*, though).

Finally, this book is dedicated to the memory of our friend Justin Der Gregorian, a beautiful human being who loved games and helped bring so many amazing stories and worlds to life.

Press <START> to begin.

INTRODUCTION

I'm on my own. Much of the warehouse is in shadow, though I can make out a desk and some box files, suggesting the area immediately ahead is being used as a makeshift office. Directly in front of me is a battered wooden table and beyond that is an empty, blue plastic chair. To my right is a white board. There's a green, flickering exit sign too, but since I can't move beyond the table I guess I won't be going through that anytime soon. Peering down, I notice that the table has graffiti carved into it. Seems like I'm not the first person to end up in this position.

There's also something lying on the table. It's a clipboard, with a sheet of paper. With some effort, I pick it up. There's an image of a white man in his early thirties wearing a military uniform, along with various stats, though most details are redacted. The implication is clear – this is me, and I'm a Special Forces soldier. I'm startled by the abrupt rattle and scrape of an ancient lift descending, followed by reverberating footsteps, and the unlocking of heavy security doors. I hurriedly place the clipboard back on the table. The tension builds with each nearing footstep. Eventually a door ahead swings open and a tall black man in a blue shirt enters.

It turns out he is a CIA agent called Carson and I'm an SAS soldier called Ryan Marks. What follows is the beginning of an interrogation, with Carson listing the charges I face: 'terrorism, conspiracy – more murders than we can even count.' The next thing I know we're fading down and everything goes black. A mortar explodes. When we fade up I'm standing by a partly destroyed wall in a desert. A truck goes past me on the left but the wall provides sufficient cover for me to go undetected. I'm in a warzone and we've flashed back in time. I'm full of anxiety but I try to play the part of the Special Forces soldier. Ahead of me is a battle-scarred building with an underground entrance. Seconds later I'm storming into the building, dispatching enemy assailants, rescuing my buddy and escaping in a hair-raising car chase.

Sony's London Studio released *Blood and Truth* – a virtual reality video game – in 2019 for the PlayStation VR system. Aside from the sequence I've just described, the game is primarily set in contemporary London, since not only is Ryan an SAS soldier, he also happens to be the son of an infamous East End gangster. When Ryan's dad drops dead, he finds himself having to defend his family from a takeover bid by a rival set of gangsters. Ryan is recruited by the mysterious Agent Carson, a CIA operative played by the film and TV actor Colin Salmon. *Blood and Truth* is far from subtle but that's the point. It's a roller-coaster ride which puts the player 'inside an action movie.'

As with many VR games, for reasons I'll explore in due course, my presence in this world is conveyed by a pair of hands, in this case two caucasian hands consistent with the fact that the main character is a thirtysomething white guy. I can move my hands, clenching and unclenching them, and even use the fingers and thumbs to create a thumbs up or give someone the 'bird', all thanks to the VR controllers. The hands are my avatar throughout the game, my means of locating myself but also the chief way I interact with the world. It's weird having hands and not a body, but it's something I adjust to.

I can talk with some authority about the game's story and fictional world as I was intimately involved in its creation, both as a screenwriter and narrative designer. Game storytelling is something I've long been obsessed with, ever since I won my first computer – a stately Atari 800 boasting 16K of memory – back in 1983 in a *Daily Express* competition to 'Design A Home of the Future'. From that point onwards I started experimenting with choice-based stories akin to the 'Choose Your Own Adventure' books I was also reading at the time. My obsession would later evolve into an academic interest in interactive narrative and in due course a job as a professional writer and narrative designer working in the game industry.

Virtual Reality is just one flavour of video game. There are plenty more offering all kinds of experiences. Some games have little or indeed no narrative content, like the tessellating genius of *Tetris* or the hypnotic *Beat Saber*, another VR game. But most have stories, or at least fictional scenarios. Some stories are tightly woven into gameplay like *The Last of Us* games, the revived *God of War* games and *Ghost of Tsushima*. Some, like the satirical *Fallout* series, utilise narrative systems to help build the fictional world and enable immersion. Some are sprawling sandboxes in which the player can explore and experiment to their heart's content, like *Grand Theft Auto, Red Dead Redemption 2* and *Cyberpunk 2077*. Some are designed around choices the player makes, like the *Fable* franchise and *Detroit: Become Human*. A thriving indie sector gives us extraordinary flights of creativity like *Papers Please, Everybody's Gone to the Rapture* and *The Cult of Lamb*.

Many are collaborative and connected. The long-running *World of Warcraft* invites players into a vast fantasy realm which they can explore and where they can undertake adventures together. *Fortnite, League of Legends* and *Overwatch* pitch players against each other in colourful combat, though each have carefully constructed worlds boasting complex lore. As well as connecting players, these games are increasingly part of wider connected universes that stretch into other media like novels, films, television shows and comics. In global terms games are now bigger than the music and film industries combined.

Game storytelling is fundamentally about managing the collision of two worlds. On the one hand there's the world of the player, the real world in which we're sitting or standing, where we have romantic and familial relationships, where we work, pay taxes and carry out domestic chores. On the other hand there's the virtual world of pixels and polygons with infinite possibilities – a domain that one moment could be full of breathtaking spectacle and in the next intimacy and emotional insight. The role of video game storytellers and world-builders is to fuse the real world and the fictional world together, to tell stories through game controllers and keyboards, to immerse players in a world of make-believe. And like the games themselves, we come in all shapes and sizes, a mixture of writers, narrative designers, world-builders, scenarists and story choreographers.

This is a book about this most contemporary of storytelling forms, its challenges and potential, and what it means for how we think about storytelling more generally. It's about the techniques and tropes that games borrow from other narrative media, including some approaches that date back millennia. It's about the things that game storytelling does differently, the ways in which it takes those ancient techniques and reinvents them. It's about the wholly new approaches required for a medium that's often trivial but should never be treated as such.

Along the way, I draw not only on my own first-hand experiences as a game storyteller but those of fellow narrative professionals working in the field. I also deploy a range of academic and theoretical perspectives from game studies, literary and narrative theory, film studies, theatre studies and screenwriting theory, in what's known as a comparative media approach. I use these to frame various contemporary and historical game examples. Such theories can be forboding and abstruse, but hopefully I've done this in a way which is friendly and not off-putting to the general reader. The intention is an exploration that's informative, discursive and reflective.

My hypothesis is simple – that this newest and most compelling of art forms is fundamentally changing how we tell stories. And I'm going to show you how – and *why* – it matters.

1.
GAMES VERSUS STORIES

At face value, games and stories have a lot in common. Both have a beginning, middle and end. Stories are told using characters that we listen to, watch or read about. Lots of games feature characters of one kind or another – ones we play as and ones we encounter along the way. In a game someone wins or loses, or maybe there's a draw. The same is true of stories. Characters might succeed or fail, or at least come to the end of their 'arc'. Irrespective of whether they're thrillers or romances or science fiction tales, stories require conflict to drive them. Games are also powered by a struggle, either between the players themselves or between the player and the game. Both games and stories can delight, frustrate and surprise. It's not surprising that the two forms should have collided so frequently throughout their history, creating all manner of extraordinary hybrids.

At first glance, contemporary video games epitomise this fusion. The original *The Last of Us* (2013) game tells the story of Joel, a man whose daughter dies tragically and must learn to be a father again, all set against the backdrop of a terrifying spore-based infection that has created a living dead-infested apocalypse. *The Last of Us* and its sequel are expertly crafted, and have justly won many awards. They look beautiful and feature cinematic elements and tightly woven gameplay. To all intents and purposes they're interactive stories. It makes sense that these particular games have transferred so successfully to television, in an adaptation that has been praised by critics and fans alike.

Looks can be deceptive, though. For all their shared features, games and stories are also very different in fundamental ways. Human or anthropomorphic characters are an essential condition of all storytelling. Every story, irrespective of medium, features characters we can empathise with, or which are intended to provoke an emotional response. This is as true of children's animations featuring talking cars and radio soap operas depicting an everyday story of country folk as it is of blockbuster movies, abstruse literary novels and West End plays. We watch, read and listen to characters as they go on journeys and adventures through whatever fictional world the storytellers have chosen to fabricate. Characters are our way into the story.

The same is not necessarily true of games. For every game that uses characters like *The Last of Us, Destiny* or even the board game *Cluedo*, there are many others that don't. Counter-based games like Drafts and Go don't have any characters, and neither do many commercially and critically successful video games. *Tetris* is an obvious example, in which the player must fit falling shapes together to create solid lines that then magically vanish. Simply put, we don't *need* characters for games, they're not integral in the way they are for stories. When games do feature characters, it's arguably a superficial, additive component. Chess pieces aren't characters in the sense we would understand from storytelling – they are counters capable of specific functions set by the rules of the game.

Nonetheless, many contemporary video games do feature characters and stories of varying degrees of sophistication. Popular culture is packed with examples: Pac-Man, *Tomb Raider*'s Lara Croft, Mario the plumber, Sonic the Hedgehog, *Halo*'s Master Chief and *The Legend of Zelda*'s Link, to name just a handful. They emerge beyond the boundaries of the game world to populate lunch boxes, comics, movies, television shows, transforming into plushies and action figures, often woven into everyday life in all manner of ways. Cortana, the female AI from the science fiction epic *Halo*, went on to become the voice of Microsoft's virtual assistant, and cropped up in many software applications, far removed from her fantastical origins.

Sometimes stories are expertly integrated into gameplay like the majestic *Ghost of Tsushima* or the satirical *Fallout* games. In other games, the story components are added after the fact to help rationalise the actions of the player and provide context. Games have unique attributes, just as other kinds of storytelling have their own tropes and techniques which clever storytellers seek to exploit to their advantage, sometimes choosing to subvert expectations as well as reinforce them.

Television is often talked about as an intimate medium, whereas movies are renowned for their ability to convey a sense of scale and sweep. The novel affords psychological insights into characters that dramatic media may struggle to convey. By dint of their interactive and immersive qualities, games are good at things that these other media struggle with, whether it's giving a player the ability to make a moral choice and experience first hand the consequences, or the chance to inhabit a completely different persona in a living and unpredictable imaginary world.

Irrespective of the medium, a well-told story has impact precisely because it's well-told. The storyteller controls how and when information – about plot or characters – is revealed to us. A good story leverages its structure and its pacing to gradually unfurl itself to us, in a way which is driven by the skill and artistry of the storyteller.

Every scene in a screenplay serves a dramatic purpose, every action in a theatre play tells us about character, and perhaps also plot. All storytelling is in some sense collaborative, and we're working with the storyteller to understand the story being told to us.

This is particularly true of games, which are collaborative in the most explicit sense because of their interactive nature.[1] Most obviously this takes the form of gameplay, though it also includes configuring the game's settings. For a game to progress, something is required of the player. It may be touching keys on a keyboard, manipulating a game controller or moving a Virtual Reality headset. But the player has to do something. In a video game or other kind of interactive experience, control is awarded to the participant. Which means that video game storytellers, unlike their opposite numbers in television, film, novels, theatre and radio, have to cede control. And with that, come all sorts of implications that make video games fundamentally different to these other media.

Not that older kinds of storytelling are somehow passive. If you've ever jumped at a horror movie or cried when a much cherished character dies in a long-running television drama you'll get the point. At both a philosophical and physiological level, our bodies are constantly in flux, which means that our understanding of stories, irrespective of medium, is constantly active and changing. And that includes our response to 'bubblegum' Hollywood blockbusters and soap operas like *Eastenders*. We can make value judgements over whether something is inherently trivial and a waste of time but no medium is really passive.

Games are different because they're *needy* in a way this other media isn't. They require very specific and explicit forms of interaction on

---

1 I'm aware there are many examples of interactive novels, stage plays and films. Don't worry, I'll get to those.

the part of human users. And because human users get things wrong, games are designed to accommodate these errors. In contemporary games, if you die you might respawn, perhaps going back to an earlier point when you chose to save your progress or the game automatically did it for you. In older games you were often given a finite number of lives, and when your last life was expended the game was over. What game developers want, of course, is for you to restart the game, to keep coming back for more despite – or maybe *because* – of your humiliation. It's what US academic Sherry Turkle describes as 'holding power'[2], the ability of games to keep you transfixed, not in spite of your mistakes but because of them, because you want to fix them.

Many contemporary games involve exploration and to some extent experimentation. They encourage you to wander around environments, finding your own way, trying out different routes, uncovering clues, encountering extraordinary characters, stumbling across moments of unexpected spectacle or surprising intimacy. For most kinds of linear storytelling, such ambulatory moments would be anathema – sure we might get a quick montage of a journey or a series of connected actions, but on the whole they want to cut straight to the chase. A Hollywood producer friend of mine derides scenes in which a character travels from one location to another as 'shoe leather'. Such elements are the mainstay of many video games. They are the chief mechanism through which we explore the fictive world we've created. Understanding the differences between sequential storytelling media and video game storytelling is vital to understanding the latter.

In 2001, when Games Studies first began as a formal discipline to be taught and researched in universities, it was fixated on the

---

2 Turkle, Sherry [1984] (2005) *The Second Self - Computers and the Human Spirit.* London: The MIT Press.

relationship between storytelling and gameplay. Helpfully, the academics involved divided themselves into two distinct camps. Simply expressed, narratologists or narrativists believed that video games could be analysed with theories adapted from other story-focussed disciplines like Literary Studies, Film Studies and Theatre Studies. Ludologists, meanwhile, argued that games were rule-based and experiential and that applying theory from these other fields missed the essential qualities of games. For academia, the row was unusually passionate, although some later claimed it all arose from a misunderstanding encouraged by the gaming press.

These days the academic dispute has subsided but the fundamental problem of resolving the differences between games and stories hasn't gone away. Within the industry, we talk about 'ludonarrative dissonance'[3], an idea coined by Clint Hocking, video game designer/director and veteran of LucasArts and Ubisoft. The concept refers to the disjuncture between the intentions of gameplay and the intentions of story within a video game. Hocking uses the example of *Bioshock* (2007), considered by many a classic of the medium. Set in 1960, the player assumes the role of Jack, whose plane is downed over the Atlantic. As the only survivor of the crash, Jack makes his way to a mysterious lighthouse and then uses a bathysphere, a capsule lowered from a ship, to descend to a city beneath the waves created by a fictional industrialist called Andrew Ryan. The city is called Rapture, and our first glimpse of the grandiosity of its art deco design remains one of the most spectacular in video game history.

What's intriguing about *Bioshock* is that thematically the whole game is concerned with the nature of free will and agency, as espoused by Andrew Ryan, the principal villain. The character of Ryan is clearly heavily influenced by libertarian philosopher Ayn

---

3 It might elicit groans, but we still talk about it.

Rand, author of *The Fountainhead* (1943) and *Atlas Shrugged* (1957). Rand formulated the theory of Objectivism, founded on the idea that there is only one objective reality and that certain moral truths exist independently of human knowledge, or indeed our ability to perceive them. For some, Rand is a shining beacon of libertarianism, for others a grim recipe for a world in which only the strong prosper, with all that connotes. The fictional Andrew Ryan espouses similar views, and the player encounters them throughout their exploration of Rapture.

At points in the game the player is given the ability to choose which path to follow, consistent with the thematic concerns of the game. Along the way the player will encounter Little Sisters, young girls who have been genetically altered and brainwashed into reclaiming a substance that grants superhuman powers to the player-character. The player can choose whether to kill the Little Sister in question and take all of the genetic material, or release the Little Sister from her conditioning. If the player chooses the more compassionate approach, they'll receive less genetic material. Eventually, however, the player has no choice but to help a character called Atlas in leading a revolt against Andrew Ryan. The game's need to channel the player through the story has reasserted itself.

It's a prime example of ludonarrative dissonance: while the game-player may want to take one path, the game itself has chosen another. The term has proven influential, informing much subsequent debate about the relationship of story and play in games. Central to this discussion is whether ludonarrative dissonance is something to be avoided at all costs, or in fact a key feature of games that can be leveraged to make gamers think about their actions inside the fictional world they've chosen to inhabit.

Another oft-cited example of ludonarrative dissonance occurs in the *Uncharted* series. These are intricately constructed, highly successful games developed by the studio Naughty Dog for PlayStation and PC platforms. A modern day take on Indiana Jones, the player assumes the role of Nathan Drake, a handsome, wise-cracking explorer engagingly voiced by Nolan North.[4] *Uncharted*'s gameplay involves lots of derring-do in the form of climbing, dodging, solving fiendish puzzles and, crucially, killing people. Lots and lots of killing people. 'Cut scenes' – cinematic interludes within the game which deliver the bulk of the plot – don't ever account for this bloodshed, instead concentrating on Drake's all-round charm and likability.[5]

But as the academic Frédéric Seraphine points out, some games actively lean into the nature of the gameplay in an effort to ensure a more synergistic approach between story and interactivity. Seraphine cites the example of *Grand Theft Auto IV* (2008), which tells the story of Niko Bellic, an ex-soldier from Eastern Europe who has come to America to locate the individual who betrayed his army unit years earlier but finds himself embroiled in a seething criminal underworld. As Seraphine observes, the psychotic behaviour of the player during gameplay – killing, maiming, stealing – is deliberately aligned with the psychotic behaviour of the main character during the cut scenes. By mirroring Bellic's actions, ludonarrative dissonance is therefore minimized.

Arguably the phenomenon is not limited to games. The climax of the *Hawkeye* television show on the streaming service Disney+ culminated in a battle between the two lead characters – Clint Barton and Kate Bishop, played by Jeremy Renner and Hailee Steinfeld – and an enemy gang known as the Tracksuit Mafia. In the course of the

---

4 A ubiquitous performer in games and something of a legend amongst players and developers alike.

5 This didn't stop PlayStation Studios from making a 2022 movie based on the *Uncharted* series starring Tom Holland, which effectively functions as a loose prequel to the first game in the series.

confrontation on an ice rink, any number of these gang members are injured, probably maimed and almost certainly killed. Yet the demands of the plot require Kate Bishop's villainess mother Eleanor be arrested at the scene for the murder of a character from earlier in the series – the fact that a massacre has happened several feet away being of little apparent concern to the New York Police Department.[6]

Musicals provide another obvious example of dissonance. Suddenly breaking into a song and dance number in real life would, at the very least, raise eyebrows, and might possibly result in your being hauled off for various observations and interventions by the authorities. In the context of *Singing in the Rain* (1952), *Seven Brides for Seven Brothers* (1954) or *La La Land* (2016), we accept that these songs are expressing the inner feelings of the characters, advancing the plot, or simply entertaining us. For the most part we accept the dissonance, because our expectations of musicals have led us to anticipate that characters can and will break into song and dance routines in a way which is generally not found in real life – or indeed other genres.

For games, the contradictions between gameplay and storytelling are baked into the medium, not just specific genres like the adventure story or musical, as is the case with these other media. Throughout their history, some game developers have sought to approach the tensions directly, conjuring ingenious solutions. Many other developers simply ignore ludonarrative dissonance. Often, it falls to game storytellers to retroactively 'fix' games by stitching together the various elements in a way that makes sense for players.

---

6 Douglas Adams, creator of *The Hitch-Hiker's Guide to the Galaxy*, talks about exactly this phenomenon in relation to the cop show *Cannon*, in which subsidiary characters are indiscriminately killed without so much as a by-your-leave. As a response to this, and with his trademark absurdist élan, Adams created the character of a sperm whale whom he then makes us care about, immediately prior to killing it.

This constant need to bridge the gap between storytelling and gameplay means that over time the games industry has evolved specific roles to tackle the problem. In 2006, Stephen Dinehart was asked by the game developer and publisher THQ to write a job description for an individual who could create the game's story and manage the integration between the narrative and gameplay. When THQ were subsequently unable to find anyone to fit the bill, they hired Dinehart himself, and he became the first 'narrative designer'. Twenty years later, narrative design is a recognised craft in its own right, often expressed in terms of aligning the player's experience with the player-character's experience.[7] Given the never-ending debates concerning the relationship between storytelling and play in video games, it's perhaps inevitable that the exact parameters of what constitutes narrative design should remain a topic of heated debate.

Narrative design in the strictest sense is inherent to all storytelling, whether it's plot design, act design or determining character biographies and motivations. Depending on the storyteller's particular process and the context in which the creation of the narrative is happening, this might be a heavily structured, formalist exercise or something that's much more freeform and explorative. In other words a screenwriter tasked with creating an episode of a long-running television series would probably have a much stricter remit than, for instance, someone creating a stage play that they hope to sell to a theatre, though the latter has its own structural rules too. In terms of game storytelling, it's perhaps the looseness of the term that contributes to frequent misunderstandings within the industry. Nevertheless, experienced storytelling practitioners are able to point to a high level version of the narrative design term as it relates specifically to video games.

---

7 More of this later.

Veteran game writer and narrative designer Andy Walsh defines it this way: 'In its purest form (without the 20,000 different ways companies define it) narrative design is the art and craft of understanding story spaces in interactive media. This requires an understanding of the technology, game and narrative genres, along with the capabilities of the art, audio, AI teams and the demands of game design. When narrative design works well it allows the writer (or the writer's work if the skills are separated) to marry into a single experience avoiding the terror that is... ludo-narrative dissonance (cue the sound of lightning and evil cackling, or player frustration and the hurling of games controllers)'.

As Walsh alludes to, a recurrent complicating factor is that studios define narrative design very differently. It's easy to see why developers need distinct approaches based on the specific project. A particular kind of campaign-led game[8] with carefully curated set piece encounters that move in and out of gameplay is liable to need a considerable amount of integrated narrative design from the very beginning of development and throughout the process. Whereas, on some projects narrative design happens after the fact, with narrative designers retrospectively adding story elements.

Some bigger games might contain a variety of gameplay modes that require different techniques; what works for multiplayer might be quite different to what works for single player. Ultimately most projects involve some combination of preparatory story work which evolves into ongoing input and culminates with frenetic last-minute fixes as deadlines loom. What this suggests is that narrative design needs to be an organic and adaptive craft, able to modulate to the

---

8 That's a single-player, story-based experience like *The Last of Us* or *Ghost of Tsushima* (though both games have different modes).

needs of the project and requirements of the studio, rather than a prescriptive set of rules.

Narrative designer Anjali Shibu highlights the disparities between studios around the term: 'If you ever see the title Narrative Design, it can mean very different things from studio to studio. I personally would define Narrative Design as the space where you tune how the story and gameplay interact and therefore engage the player. Most often, it's about conversations with various teams to find new ways to engage the player... seamlessly integrating consequences for their actions, implementing pipelines and systems, getting them to work well with each other, and getting the timing for any line spot-on!'[9] Another veteran game writer, Antony Johnston, sums it up pithily: 'No two narrative designers are the same, because no two projects are the same'.

As a result, the narrative designer role can differ massively from studio to studio and even within studios. A studio might employ various ranks of narrative designer from junior to lead, alongside game writers, which also come in a number of distinct flavours depending on an individual's experience and expertise. Some narrative design roles are skewed towards writing, which can include everything from the main screenplay to in-game dialogue, collectible documents and on-screen text, while others will be much more technical, perhaps involving an individual going inside the game engine and setting up 'hooks' for game dialogue or moving around art assets. There are numerous other roles we might describe as 'story' or 'world-adjacent'.

In my career I've done a lot of these different roles, all under the baggy heading of storytelling. I've been a contract writer, a freelance story designer, a narrative designer, a staff writer, lead writer and

---

9 Interpersonal skills, the ability to listen as well as champion your own perspective, are essential – though rarely discussed – qualities for narrative designers.

narrative director. I've created scenarios and written pitches based on fragments of gameplay design. I've worked on projects with extremely sophisticated narrative ecologies, including processes and pipelines familiar from more established industries like film and television, such as Writers' Rooms, table reads and audience testing. But I've also worked on projects in which none of these things have been in place, in which story development has been ad hoc and driven by creative whim rather than focussed direction. The maturity and sophistication of the studio's internal culture can be a big factor in its approach to storytelling and worldbuilding.

With all this in mind, determining the distinctions between narrative design and writing is often tricky. Narrative design frequently merges with writing, with many narrative designers writing and, conversely, many writers carrying out narrative designer duties. Another seasoned writer, Kim MacAskill, provides a useful indication of where the distinction might lie based on her experience: 'The best way I would separate a writer from a narrative designer is in looking at a mission. A narrative designer will tell you what dialogue trigger types are needed before they've even written a line of dialogue (damage taken, health needed etc), whereas a writer may not be expected to work this out, simply they are prescribed types of lines required (often by a designer) and then proceed to write the dialogue accordingly.'

A more abstract but still potentially useful way of differentiating the roles might be found in ideas of temporality and spatiality. As Andy Walsh suggests, 'narrative design is the art and craft of understanding story spaces in interactive media'. In other words, video games are explorable spaces in a way that makes them distinct from other non-participatory media, and narrative design is the means by which this story is delivered. Invariably, though, a lot of games incorporate story sequences which are time-based – temporal – in the sense that once activated they can't be stopped or interfered with.

To this end, a lot of game writing involves telling a portion of the story in a way which is essentially sequential in nature. Most obviously we see this in cut scenes, those extended interludes which look the most like film and television. Historically such cinematic sequences haven't involved any interactivity, though these days it's not unusual for developers to introduce elements of participation to ensure the player feels more involved in proceedings. These kinds of interactivity aren't necessarily sophisticated, and might simply involve a particular button press or set of actions[10] from the player, as we see in the likes of Naughty Dog's *Uncharted* games and Santa Monica's *God of War* series. In such contexts the available options for the player are extremely limited and the results correspondingly confined, the wrong choice often resulting in a fail condition or meaning the game won't progress until you've done the right thing.

Other kinds of scripted scenes might offer more in the way of branching, allowing the player to choose their actions and causing something to happen in the game world as a result. From a technical viewpoint a sequence like this would probably sit within the game engine, and the implications of the player's decision carefully managed. Cut sequences and scripted sequences are still the 'forward-facing' part of the story for lots of games, and the ones upon which game critics and fans judge the game's narrative.

But as Walsh notes, narrative design is mainly concerned with the organisation of the story in spatial terms. In exploring an abandoned castle in a *Zelda* game or the streets and buildings of a baroque, beautifully realised alternate reality in the *Dishonored*

---

10 Though they are inevitably complex to implement from a development standpoint.

games, we might encounter an artefact or document that tells us more about this world, like a fragment of a diary or a discarded letter. The spatial placement of such objects might be intended to intrigue, reward or otherwise immerse the player, and is a task that falls to narrative design. Similarly, narrative design might work with environment artists to request specific elements to abet storytelling or worldbuilding. Inside the game's editor, invisible 'trigger volumes' can be set up which when entered by the player activate a specific piece of dialogue or other kind of narrative event.

For instance, I worked on an open world game that used a 'hub and spoke' structure in which the player could battle adversaries and then return to their base of operations to reload their weaponry, recharge their shields, store and examine their collectibles, etc. During the exploratory elements the player could trigger different cut scenes in any order, meaning they received the story in a non-linear way – but the scenes themselves were inherently linear. In shaping the experience, I had to think about the unfolding story in an overarching way which was driven by spatiality, but the cut sequences themselves effectively played out as mini movies with a distinct start and end point.

Another key way for narrative design to convey story is through the game's mechanics, the ways in which the player interacts with the game and how the game responds. A good example is *Ico* (2001), a masterpiece of a game in which the player controls the eponymous character, a little boy who must guide a girl called Yorda so together they can escape a castle. The game's central, story-inflected mechanic is this hand-holding and the challenges it poses for Ico and the player as you negotiate multiple puzzles and obstacles. Such a mechanic is intrinsic to the game, the story and the world.

With that in mind, it's unlikely that expensive and time-consuming *bespoke* mechanics will be created to fulfil a highly specific narrative purpose, no matter how much certain members of the dev team might desire this. The emphasis on systems is echoed in Antony Johnson's comments: 'To me, that's narrative design in a nutshell: the art and skill of deciding how to convey narrative to the player within a game, and designing the systems necessary to achieve the desired experience and effect. That still leaves a lot open to interpretation, which is to be expected with any kind of interactive design.'

The role of the player in all this is of course critical. Games are an explicitly participatory medium, and as we'll see it's this that constantly redefines how we understand storytelling and worldbuilding. For narrative and experience designer Yasmeen Ayyashi, the collaborative element of narrative design is integral to the craft. 'Narrative design is a practice that extends beyond traditional verbal or textual storytelling,' she suggests, 'to the design of experiences in which a story unfolds through the interplay of (physical or virtual) space, objects, elements, and audience engagement, over time. It can encompass various formats of physical and digital reality... to construct "worlds" that are co-created by designers and participants.'

Like the ludology-narratology debate that began in academia and the subsequent discussion of ludonarrative dissonance inside and outside the industry, conversations about narrative design and its exact definition are often impassioned and heated. The sheer diversity of game projects and studios' disparate approaches to thinking about story mean that narrative design is always liable to take different forms depending on the context. Some projects are story-driven, in which narrative design is necessarily fundamental and calls the shots, while many other projects are driven by gameplay, in which narrative is retro-fitted as a way of making sense of what the player is doing. Many more games are a compromise between these approaches. There is no 'one size fits all' solution, nor should there be. The role of game storytellers – the broad term I'll use going forwards – is to make sure they're using the right approach for the particular project.

Nevertheless, it is possible to identify high level commonalities based on the unique experiences of practitioners working in the field. To me, narrative design or direction in its broadest sense is at least partly about managing the interrelationship between the spatial and temporal components of the game's story. This will be important going forwards in understanding how game storytelling is shaping other modes of storytelling. As we'll see, rapid technological and cultural developments will mean that narrative design is going to have to evolve in all sorts of intriguing ways.

2.
PRECURSORS

Interactivity is the key attribute that makes game storytelling different to other kinds of storytelling. It can take any number of forms depending on the nature of the game. It might be the difference between the player taking the route through the dark forest or up the mountain path. It might mean deciding whether to kiss a character or murder them, join a quest with fellow players or leap on the back of a dragon and travel to a far flung location for further adventures. The player's ability to intervene in the narrative, to change things, is something the game storyteller has to constantly anticipate and plan around. For developers of all stripes, it's hard work to engineer such scenarios but immensely rewarding when you succeed.

The logic of interactivity disrupts the flow of the story in video games. Again this can take many different forms, depending on the kind of story being told, the nature of the fictional world being explored, and the type of interaction. Plot elements may play out in different ways, the order in which the player comes across specific characters may change, and the player may encounter or miss story elements. In other words, interactivity is inextricably linked to non-linearity. Suffice to say, this makes game storytelling a complex and challenging pursuit, in ways markedly different to that of more traditional media.

For one thing, interactivity fundamentally changes the audience's relationship to the story. 'Interactivity is a shortcut to immersion,' says game writer Antony Johnston. 'When story choices are put in our hands as players, we can't help but be drawn into the narrative and put ourselves in the place of the character facing those choices. As writers we have to keep that in mind and write accordingly, hopefully in a way that keeps player and character decisions in sync – or, at least, minimises dissonance.' Narrative director Karen Hunt is similarly effusive: 'On the condition that it's done well... a well designed interactive story experience makes the story much more emotional.'

Most novels, films and television shows are fundamentally *sequential* in nature, in that they tell a story from beginning to end. Such stories require the audience to consume the narrative in a particular way through watching, reading or listening. With the exception of video games, stories that incorporate interactivity tend to exist very much outside the mainstream, and are often experimental and challenging. We can place interactive films, participatory theatre and branching novels in this category. In letting you choose your path through the narrative they are necessarily non-sequential, and can be consumed in multiple different ways. Fortunately, there's a diverse and instructive history of interactive narrative that we can look to.

Probably the earliest example of interactive storytelling is that of oral storytelling. Gathering around a campfire to tell tales is common from culture to culture, and we see traces of it all around in everything from joke-telling to gossip, from songs to improvisational drama. Oral narrative forms are often collaborative, involving an exchange of ideas that shape the course of the story. The roleplaying game *Dungeons and Dragons* (1974-), in which a 'Dungeon Master' steers the story of the game in concert with the players, responding to their actions and rolls of the dice, sits within this tradition. In a modern context, digital connectivity has enabled collaborative storytelling in the form of games like the long-running and hugely popular *World of Warcraft*, more of which later.

The novel offers other kinds of precedent for both non-linearity and interactivity. *The Life and Adventures of Tristram Shandy, Gentleman* was published in nine volumes from 1759 to 1767. The book is told as a stream of consciousness by the eponymous anti-hero. Along the way Sterne explores the terminology around sexual practices, insults, military life, religion, politics and philosophy. This is all told in a manner which is highly discursive and humorous, not to mention exceptionally playful. It's not for nothing that *Tristram Shandy* is often described as the 'ultimate shaggy dog story'. In the course of the novel we encounter many colourful characters, including Tristram's father and mother, the choleric physician Dr Slop, the chambermaid Susannah and the parson Yorick,[1] who will go on to feature in another of Sterne's novels.

Sterne was 'meta' before the term had ever been coined, let alone abused. In the guise of Tristram, he constantly interrupts his own narrative, addressing the reader directly, sometimes telling them to go back and read the preceding chapter or calling out specific points they might have missed. Sterne also plays with the typography of the text. At one point a character crosses himself, and we get a symbol to represent this action, or the icon of a pointing hand is used to highlight something important. When a character dies, the scene is immediately followed by two pages of entirely black ink. The digressions pile up, creating a sense of a non-linear narrative, though for the most part the story is resolutely sequential in nature.

---

1 Yes, that Yorick.

Where *Tristram Shandy* departs from this most obviously is in its use of footnotes, which require the reader to either break away from the main narrative, returning once they have read the footnote, wait until the chapter has finished and double-back, or simply ignore them.[2]

In fact, most kinds of storytelling utilise some form of non-linearity. Often it serves the storyteller's intentions to jump around in terms of how they're conveying the story, perhaps using flashbacks to reveal a character's past experiences and actions to clarify their current behaviour in the dominant, 'present' mode of the story. Journalist Steven Poole, author of the book *Trigger Happy* (2000)[3], an important early discussion of game culture, utilises the terms *synchronic* to describe the present story and *diachronic* to describe the back story. For some genres, the disclosure of the diachronic story is a fundamental structural moment towards the end of the narrative, expressed as a flashback. In a detective story it might be the point at which the killer's identity is revealed, in a romance it might be the point where one character reveals their love for the other character. In stark contrast, the soap opera is a form in which continuous time is privileged over jumps backwards and forwards in chronology – as a rule everything moves forwards in one direction.

Flashback and flashforward techniques are used routinely in movies, television series, theatre and novels, to the extent that audiences are extremely familiar and comfortable with the techniques involved. Generally the context for these jumps in chronology is immediately clear or soon becomes apparent, and can even be assisted by captions such as 'Two years earlier'. Sometimes, though, such context is denied to us, at least in the short term. Quentin Tarantino's movies *Reservoir Dogs* (1992) and *Pulp Fiction* (1994) offer prime

---

2 Best not to ignore them.
3 Poole, Steven (2000) *Trigger Happy - The Inner Life of Videogames*. London: Fourth Estate

examples of this approach. On first seeing *Pulp Fiction*, for instance, I was baffled when Samuel L Jackson and John Travolta's characters suddenly appear wearing volleyball gear having previously been dressed in black suits and white ties, Tarantino's uniform for hitmen and gangsters. The change in appearance isn't explained at the time, and it's only as the film progresses that we start to understand we've witnessed a time jump. It's the movie's non-linear structure that provides the explanation in a surprising and satisfying way.

Another technique is that of repetition, of the kind we see in Harold Ramis' romantic comedy *Groundhog Day* (1993), in which Bill Murray's acerbic weatherman is forced to repeat the same day over and over until he learns to be a better person acting out of genuine motivations. This conceit has been used multiple times since in genre films like the science fiction movie *Edge of Tomorrow* (2014) and the horror movie *Happy Death Day* (2017). In each of these, scenes are replayed with key differences as the protagonist tries to escape the time loop.

In a similar fashion, the exploratory nature of video games means that players often revisit spaces, experimenting until they solve puzzles, overcome obstacles or defeat enemies. It's only then that they'll be allowed to progress to the next part of the story. This kind of repetition is an inevitable component of games as disparate as *Elden Ring* (2022), *Prince of Persia: The Sands of Time* (2003) and the *Fallout* series (1997-). The so-called 'roguelike' genre even makes repetition the primary game mechanic, forcing the player to undergo the same gameplay sequence over and over until they succeed.

A variation on this approach is to retell the same event from different perspectives. The New Testament gives us differing perspectives on the same events courtesy of the Gospels. In a similar vein, the legendary Japanese film-maker Akira Kurosawa's *Rashomon* (1950) shows a murder from multiple different perspectives throughout the course of the film. In the context of digital storytelling, the American academic Janet H Murray[4] takes this approach and frames it as a structure known as a 'Violence Hub'. This is a particular kind of 'hub and spoke' formation with a violent event at its centre. The user or player is then able to decide which perspective they want to view on the event in question. Though similar to *Rashomon* in plot terms, the interactive component makes it quite different to Kurosawa's movie, in which he determines the order in which the story is revealed to us.

This is a critical point. There's a huge difference between those stories designed for sequential media that employ jumps in time as part of the narrative but which remain fundamentally sequential. Tom Stoppard's theatre play *Arcadia* (1993) tells two stories set hundreds of years apart but set in the same house. At its climax, characters from the past and present era are present on the stage at the same time without registering one another, and the parallels between the two strands are made explicit.

Douglas Maxwell's 2002 play *Helmet* adopts the structure of the fighting video game *Tekken* to tell and retell the relationship between two men - a shopworker and a customer - in a Glaswegian video game shop. We watch as the same disputes play out with different outcomes, the strength of the character's argument reflected in the power meters rendered on either side of the stage, just as you would find in *Tekken* itself. Though each of these examples play with chronology, they remain fundamentally sequential because of the established parameters of the medium. In contrast, interactivity allows for all kinds of exotic narrative structures far removed from the straight lines of sequential media like film, television and theatre.

---

4 Academic Janet Murray seminal book *Hamlet on the Holodeck* (1997) remains insightful and prescient almost thirty years after it was first published.

Another significant moment in the development of interactive storytelling occurs towards the later half of the twentieth century. The Oulipo Movement gave the world multiple works intended to challenge established narrative codes and conventions. Created by the writer and publisher Raymond Queneau in 1960, Oulipo was a loose gathering of French writers who employed mathematical and other constrained writing techniques. Oulipo's full title was *Ouvroir de littérature potentielle*, which translates as 'workshop of potential literature', because its members believed that these self-same limitations actually afforded freedom.

Queneau's own *Cent Mille milliards de poèmes* – published in 1961 and known in English as *A Hundred Thousand Billion Poems* – necessitated the involvement of mathematician Francois Le Lionnais. The book consists of ten sonnets, each line printed on a separate strip. Since the individual sonnets possess the same rhyming scheme and the same rhyme sounds, each can be combined with other sonnets in multiple ways to create new poems. Another key work to emerge from the movement was Georges Perec's *Life: A User's Manual* (1978), a novel written using Perec's 'story-writing machine', which referred to a series of constraints generated by the application of lists and corresponding grids akin to Sudoku squares.

For video game storytellers managing the relationship between gameplay and narrative, not to mention multiple, complex technological constraints, this approach is bound to strike a chord. Just like the work of the Oulipo movement, video game storytellers must constantly anticipate the choices of players and the vagaries of chance, reconciling these eventualities with the capabilities and limitations of the game hardware and software. A line of dialogue might only trigger if a particular set of conditions have been met, or a secret doorway might only reveal itself if the player has carried out a particular task in the required way. Game writers and narrative designers must shape their stories to accommodate a player encountering an event, character or location at a specific moment, but they must equally make allowance for the player completely missing this element of the story.

The Oulipo movement searched for literary precedents, alighting upon reversible poems from third century China and even word puzzles hidden within the Psalms. A particular point of influence was Argentine writer Jorge Luis Borges' 'The Garden of Forking Paths', a baroque, multi-layered short story first published in 1941. The story begins with the account of a delay to a British attack during the First World War, and suggests that the statement of a Chinese professor called Yu Tsun will make sense of the delay. We then follow Yu Tsun as he goes to visit an individual who turns out to be researching the work of the professor's ancestor. The ancestor in question had supposedly created a labyrinth and a novel, but it turned out that this was one and the same thing. The Forking Paths of the novel refer to multiple different outcomes. As a result Borges' story, though itself sequential, has proven hugely influential on much thinking around branching storytelling.

For academia, how we understand and analyse interactive and non-linear stories has been a subject of ongoing debate. Perhaps the most useful tool for approaching these kinds of stories in all their myriad forms is that of the 'ergodic', as explored in the book *Cybertext: Perspectives in Ergodic Literature* (1997), written by the noted academic Espen Aarseth. The term originates in mathematics and physics, 'ergon' meaning work and 'hodos' meaning path. Aarseth uses it to describe those kinds of literature which require 'non-trivial effort' to read or, as Aarseth frames it, 'traverse'. In other words, in ergodic literature we have to work out which path to follow, constantly reassessing our decisions. The concept's applicability to games and interactive storytelling is far ranging.

For instance, branching narrative is a key ergodic form and a variety of story structure commonly associated with video games. Players are presented with decision points and the choices they make determine which route they'll take through the subsequent story. For a medium like video games and other related kinds of story-driven interactive media, the ability to make choices is fundamental, and the thing that differentiates the medium from established sequential kinds of storytelling. Though there are technical constraints on branching that I'll talk about in subsequent chapters, we still see it used in all manner of video games, since it's a key way of immersing players in imaginary worlds.

A strand of children's literature called Choose Your Own Adventure books are a useful point of reference here. Perhaps not accidentally, these novels coincided with the height of the arcade boom in the 1980s and spawned many imitators. As the title suggests, readers would be given options as to which path to travel through the book, with more sophisticated versions introducing an element of chance through the use of a dice. These books are the epitome of Aarseth's ergodic storytelling, requiring the reader to work at solving the plot, with the protagonist's fate often in the balance. For this reason, young readers like me would often keep our finger on the page where the decision point occurred, then change our minds if the outcome wasn't to our liking.

Choose Your Own Adventure books and their imitators remain hugely influential in terms of thinking about branching narrative and have spawned lots of related works. Kim Newman's 1999 novel *Life's Lottery* translated the idea to that of an adult novel, allowing readers the ability to choose their own gender and make crucial life choices, then watching those decisions play out. For instance, accepting a cigarette behind the bike sheds might have consequences much later in the story.

The interactive television episode *Bandersnatch* (2018) is similarly influenced by such branching stories. Part of Charlie Brooker's *Black Mirror* anthology of nightmarish fantasies founded around technology, the drama is set during the 1980s and tells the story of a young game programmer trying to turn a decide-your-own-destiny style book into a video game. His path through the story is, of course, decided by you, in true branching narrative fashion. Again, this is a potential candidate for an ergodic television show, alongside Brooker's follow-up *Cat Burglar* (2022), an interactive cartoon in the style of Tex Avery.

Recalling the pioneering approach of *Tristram Shandy* some two hundred years earlier, other literary works of the digital age have explored the power of interactivity and non-linearity in storytelling and worldbuilding. Mark Z Danielewski's debut novel *House of Leaves* (2000) is focussed around a fictional documentary movie and told through a handwritten monograph, letters and footnotes, techniques frequently utilised by video games. JJ Abrahms and Doug Dorst's 2013 novel S. utilises comparable techniques. The novel contains two stories, presented in distinct ways. On the one hand the book is framed as a library book telling the story of *The Ship of Theseus*, written by the mysterious unknown author VM Straka. At the same time, handwritten notes in the margins provide a metacommentary, as two students try to work out who the author really is but also the true meaning of Straka's story. In addition, supplementary materials like postcards, photocopied articles and letters are physically contained within the book and help to advance the story between the students.

As well as stories that want to be games or exhibit game-like qualities, there's an equally illustrious tradition of games that want to be stories. Most scholars believe the first board game to be Senet, an Egyptian creation from 3050 BCE, which means it predates even the dynastic era. The game comprises a board of thirty squares, arranged in three rows of ten, and two distinct sets of pawns. A set could be made from ceramic, ivory or wood, or even made from a combination of these materials. Unfortunately, for some reason the Romans didn't like playing Senet, and the actual rules of the game have been lost to history, a phenomenon some contemporary people – particularly parents of small children – will be familiar with. Interestingly, by the time of Egypt's New Kingdom in the sixteenth century BC, the pawns have started to become recognisable as either dogs or humans with dog-shaped heads.

As I mentioned in the first chapter, a prerequisite of all stories is that they should contain human or anthropomorphic characters. On this basis, it would be hard to argue that games like draughts, backgammon and *Tetris* are stories. Equally, though, the inclusion of human or anthropomorphic characters is not sufficient to constitute a story. For instance, many card games feature human characters or characters imbued with human traits but it would be a stretch to describe a game of cards as a story in the sense we would generally understand. Arguably what the picture cards in a deck do achieve, however, is to set a fictional theme and tone for the game. The royal cards – the King, Queen and Jack – are suggestive of courtly antics, and the powerplays we would associate with such a setting. Fictional scenarios are important to think about in the context of game storytelling, even if they aren't stories in their own right.

Chess, the earliest accounts of which date back to the seventh century, gives us the familiar scenario of a battle, along with the two rulers conducting the contest and their respective armies. When we begin a game of chess, there is no story, only the potential for a story. Thanks to the terminology used to frame the various pieces on a chess board, when we start to move them, we start to create the story. Individual character motivations are absent of course. Rather, the pieces on the board are conduits for the desires and impulses of the two human players. 'Queen takes Rook', is a statement full of subtext, in the sense that it speaks to the strategy of the player who has undertaken the manoeuvre.

Context can be supplied in other ways beyond the inclusion of human or anthropomorphic characters. For instance, *The Mansion of Happiness*, a board game that first appeared in 1843, featured a strong moral message rooted in Christianity, and which informed the way the gameplay was framed. Players used 'virtue' spaces to advance themselves around a track, while 'vice' spaces would send them backwards. Slightly later, lithographer Milton Bradley produced *The Checkered Game of Life* (1860), his first such effort, and one which would lay the foundations for a mighty gaming empire that still exists today. The game tasks players with travelling through life from young adulthood to retirement, and achieving goals such as completing college, getting jobs and having children. In common with *The Mansion of Happiness*, there is a strong moralistic component, in which players progress and succeed by landing on 'good' squares. The more familiar modern version of the game was published in 1960, and reimagined many of its core elements for contemporary players.

Indeed, this is another aspect games share with stories – both evolve along with their surrounding culture and society. Fascinatingly, although the contemporary version of *Monopoly* is associated with the accretion of money and property, the original version was developed by the American game designer and feminist Lizzie Magie to explain the single tax theory of Henry George. Again, *Monopoly* doesn't contain humanistic characters – instead offering up avatars in the form of a dog, top hat, iron, etc – but the scenarios presented are sufficiently recognisable as to spur storytelling as players try to out-do one another.

The conflictual element at the root of games is perhaps most evident in those games themed around war, and which continue to prove popular today, both in the context of video games, their tabletop cousins and activities like paintball. HG Wells, whose work would go on to influence video games in other ways, created *Little Wars* in 1913. It outlines a set of rules for a miniature wargame to be played with infantry, cavalry and artillery, along with a cannon that fired projectiles and could be used for knocking down enemies. Wells was a well-known pacifist, and the book contains many philosophical points about the nature of war. In many ways *Little Wars* is the template for the war and fantasy tabletop games that would later follow. Its influence can be seen in the rule books of contemporary games like *Dungeons and Dragons* and the *Warhammer* fantasy and science fantasy games published by Games Workshop, the latter of which has become a hugely successful transmedia franchise.

The arrival of digital technology in the form of game consoles and home computers served to automate some of the processes involved in these older analogue forms. At the same time, a parallel evolutionary track emerged in which a more serious, literary mode of interactive storytelling developed, again in the tradition of *Tristram Shandy*. It's another hybrid form, in which the computer and the novel have intertwined, creating the medium of electronic literature, otherwise known as Interactive Fiction (IF) or hypertext novels. In 1992, Robert Coover, a novelist noted for his metafictional work and a key advocate of electronic literature, even wrote an essay for the *New York Times* entitled 'The End of Books'.

It was a (knowingly) premature judgement, of course, but by this point the field of IF had started to thrive with fascinating works of art. Michael Joyce's *afternoon, a story* appeared in 1987, and tells the story of a man who witnesses a car crash and subsequently comes to realise his wife and child may have been involved in the accident. The novel was written using the hypertext authoring system Storyspace, created by Eastgate Systems, and allows the reader to choose their own path. On repeat readings it's possible to choose different paths, thus leading to a markedly different experience. Unsurprisingly, Espen Aarseth dedicates considerable effort to discussing the ergodic characteristics of *afternoon*.

Often mentioned in the same breath as *afternoon* is Stuart Moulthrop's *Victory Garden*, which was also written using Storyspace. The story is a complex network of links which the reader navigates through. Set during the 1991 Gulf War, there is no obvious protagonist, though the character of Emily Runbird may be the closest the story has to a central focus. Runbird was a soldier but it's never entirely clear whether she's been killed or not. In his academic writing, Moulthrop would subsequently champion the idea of 'configuration' as a way of understanding the process of human-computer interaction, a concept which chimes with Aarseth's idea of the ergodic.

Geoff Ryman's novel *253*, otherwise known as *Tube Theatre*, is another non-linear work that uses hypertextual links. Originally created as a website in 1997 and later published as a print edition in 1998, *253* tells the story of a train full of passengers on a Bakerloo Line tube train travelling between the Embankment and Elephant and Castle stations on 11 January 1995. The title refers to the number of passengers the train carries if everyone is sitting down and including the driver. *253* is particularly useful when considering relationships between characters who can be encountered in any order, a trait of many video games.[5]

Ultimately, both the genuinely 'ergodic' stories I've mentioned and those stories which are technically sequential but choose to experiment with chronology in radical ways can give us clues about how to treat storytelling in an interactive and non-linear medium like video games. Non-linearity means players may encounter story

---

5 This is a work I've returned to at numerous points in my career.

elements out of order or have to repeat experiences over and over again until they've solved an aspect which allows them to progress. It can also refer to varieties of branching narrative where the player gets to choose which path they'll take, even though once the choice is made they'll experience something that feels fundamentally linear. As we'll see in subsequent chapters, the effect of interactivity and non-linearity is to reimagine storytelling in time and space.

The impetus towards interactivity in some strands of storytelling and conversely towards narrative on the part of some games, reasserts the commonalities between games and stories that I discussed in the opening chapter. As I mentioned, though, this doesn't mean stories and games are the same, and the tensions will continue to challenge game developers and storytellers as well as offering them opportunities. When games began as a commercial medium, they gave us scenarios to contextualise gameplay and fire our imaginations like *Asteroids*, *Pac-Man* and *Space Invaders*. Contemporary games give us similar opportunities to create our own stories through gameplay choices but they also give us authored stories to unlock and discover. How these elements fuse together is crucial to the craft of game storytelling and worldbuilding, and key to the medium's power to evoke emotion.

Intrinsic to these enduring tensions has been the evolving technology through which we play games, from the earliest arcade machines and home consoles to the digital connectivity which informs every aspect of our contemporary lives. Different games require different approaches to storytelling rooted in their hardware and software. To understand how these diverse approaches have arisen, we need to understand the role of the machine in this most technological of storytelling forms.

3.
NOT ROCKET SCIENCE

It's often been said that cinema is unique as a medium because it brings together so many other artistic disciplines, from storytelling to art direction, from set design to acting and music. The same, however, is true of contemporary video games, which similarly fuse together multiple artistic and technological crafts and practices. There's a key difference though. While production processes and the grammar of film-making have changed to incorporate editing, sound recording, colour film and digital processes, the act of *watching* a film has remained largely the same throughout its history. In contrast, interacting with a video game can differ from game to game, and sometimes even within a game. Each time we boot up a new adventure, we have to learn how to interact all over again.

It's certainly the case that many games use the same approach to certain kinds of interaction, like pressing 'X' to fire a weapon or pulling the left trigger to accelerate a vehicle. But modern game controllers offer a multitude of possibilities for interaction, depending on different combinations of button presses and joystick manipulation. The representational world we experience as players, our power over cause and effect in this world, are driven by these interactions. They determine whether we succeed or fail, and whether we unlock the story and progress to the next plot point, encounter a new character or gain access to a new vista. This is why most games have a tutorial element to help players understand how to manipulate their avatar through the environment in question.

As a result, game technology and game storytelling have evolved together. While we're constantly asking players to adapt, game developers are constantly adapting too. We're continually thinking of new ways of enabling players to explore and experience our worlds and stories. Not that we necessarily succeed, at least not in the sense of always creating something new. More often than not we emulate techniques used by another game and reconfigure it for a new context, or bring together approaches from disparate games and combine them in new ways. In a similar vein, we're often heavily influenced by other popular media. Games constantly reimagine set pieces from successful movies and place the player in the midst of the action.

A sense of originality often arises precisely from the ways in which gameplay drives the images we see and sounds we experience, especially if we haven't encountered this particular combination before. In his breathless 1982 non-fiction book about early video games[1], the novelist and essayist Martin Amis describes exactly this interplay. While talking about the classic side-scrolling science fiction game *Defender* (1981), he discusses the strategy for dealing with 'Baiters', green flying saucers which drop bombs on your spaceship: 'Don't necessarily spray your shots: try firing in a continuous jet and hope he slips into it... But the Baiter is a bitch: emitting bombs and sharp little grunts, it hovers above or beneath you, and tries never to give you a clear shot.'

---

1 Amis, Martin (1982) *Invasion of the Space Invaders*. London: Hutchinson. Possibly embarrassed by the book, Amis let it go out of print until 2018.

For Amis, *Defender* has 'the best mythology', which might seem surprising for a game that seems so crude and simplistic, especially when viewed in the light of the dense worldbuilding we see in the likes of the *Final Fantasy* (1987-), *Fallout* (1997-) and *The Witcher* (2007-) franchises. But while early video games seem tame and unsophisticated by modern standards, the impulse towards storytelling, and the solutions those pioneering developers came up with, say something important about the nature of this medium.

You could even say that this impulse typifies the form from its inception. *Spacewar!* was created by Steve Russell and fellow academics at MIT in 1962 for the gigantic PDP machine, and is often described as the first fully formed video game. Two players control rocket ships called the 'Needle' and the 'Wedge' and must fight each other with their missiles, or force their opponent into the gravity well of a nearby star. You don't have to look hard to see where their inspiration was coming from. In the real world, the Space Race between the US and the Soviet Union was well under way, a sort of technology-meets-propaganda subplot of the Cold War which at that point the US was widely perceived to be losing.[2]

Real world preoccupations and concerns were visible in other kinds of popular culture of the era, often transformed through the lens of science fiction B-movies and their televisual equivalents. That games should also want to reflect – or distort – these concerns speaks to their early storytelling and worldbuilding potential. Few games were wholly abstract – even *Pong* (1972) was framed as a game of tennis, and indeed exists in a tradition that stretches back to the experimental *Tennis for Two* from the 1950s. And while there is clearly a strong tradition of games as simulation – from aeroplane

---

2 Earth's first artificial satellite was launched by the USSR in 1957, and Soviet Cosmonaut Yuri Gagarin was the first man in space in 1961.

simulators to train and even fishing simulators – games' potential for the fantastical has long provided inspiration and narrative framing. From *Spacewar!* through *Space Invaders* (1978), *Missile Command* (1980), *Galaxian* (1979), *Galaga* (1981), *Tempest* (1981), *Defender* and *Robotron 2084* (1982), games have long exhibited a fascination with science fiction, particularly in terms of invasion and threat narratives. With crude graphics and limited sounds and music, however, the ways in which these narratives were framed were critical to their success, even if that framing happened *outside* the game itself:

> **Asteroids surround you.**
>
> **Trapped far from home, your embattled spaceship hurls toward its doom. You are caught in the center of a gigantic cloud of asteroids. You have no choice. You must pulverize all the asteroids in your path with your photon cannon – if you are ever to save yourself and your ship.**
>
> **From the *Asteroids* manual for the Atari 400/800 (1979)**

In *Asteroids* the player is tasked with piloting a stubby little spaceship around a field of asteroids to the tune of a steadily increasing beep. Hitting the asteroids with your laser fire makes them smaller, and hitting those same asteroids another time makes them smaller still until you can finally destroy them. Collision with an asteroid of any size is lethal of course; and in certain modes your fellow player might be an adversary or ally. At first glance there seems to be a colossal gap between the grandiose expectations outlined by the above scenario and the actuality of the game but it was enough to spark my excitement. If anything, the game's abstract appearance left room for my mind to invent scenarios.

Arguably external framing devices like the over-excited text contained in game manuals and the vibrant, illustrated exteriors of arcade machines are important indicators of the urge on the part of developers to situate their games in bigger fictional universes. In fact, the packaging art of Atari games by the likes of Chris Kenyon and George Opperman were works of beauty, promising heady, adrenalin-fuelled thrills and excitement (you can study them to your heart's content in Tim Lapetino's magnificent coffee table book, *Art of Atari*). As a kid these external elements were critical in activating my imagination, and seeing this particular style of illustration is enough to trigger profound nostalgia in me.

What I'm describing here can probably be best conceived in terms of 'paratexts', identified by literary theorist Gerard Genette to describe material which sits outside of the main text but which informs and extends our understanding of that primary text, in this case the video game itself.[3] At the time *Asteroids* was released, when technical limitations meant story material inside the game was necessarily limited, paratextual material like box art was essential for helping sell the game's scenario, in the process exciting and intriguing the player. Paratexts from this era can be seen as foreshadowing the complex transmedial networks from which many contemporary franchises are constructed, which I'll explore more thoroughly later in the book. It also recalls the fictional scenarios I mentioned in the previous chapter in relation to pre-digital games that featured story components but which weren't in themselves stories – for instance, a game of chess that provides the narrative ingredients for a battle of wits but which lets the players themselves determine the specifics of that battle.

---

3 We can also view them as 'extra-diegetic', which means sitting outside of the game's diegesis or storyworld. This is something we'll return to in due course.

Beyond the explicitly linked material like the box art and instruction manual, it's important to note the extent to which games are influenced by other kinds of media, not just other games. The first game I ever owned was *Star Raiders* (Atari 1980) for my Atari 800. Unfortunately, the manual was missing, so it took an awful lot of experimentation to try and understand what I was meant to be doing. That I was piloting a space fighter through a 3D starfield in search of enemy spaceships to fight was pretty obvious from the outset, and over time I discovered that I could dock at friendly starbases.

Even without a guiding manual like the one I had for *Asteroids*, the influences on the enemy spaceships were easy to see: one type looked like the TIE fighters from *Star Wars*, another type looked like the ships from *Star Trek*, and the starbases were strangely reminiscent of the 'basestars' (ahem) from the original, disco version of *Battlestar Galactica*. Suffice to say, none of these references were officially sanctioned by the IP holders in question. Years later I interviewed Doug Neubauer, the creator of *Star Raiders*, for *RetroGamer* magazine who admitted – a little sheepishly, I thought – that my assessment of these influences was totally accurate. (Interestingly, the sequel *Star Raiders 2* started out as an official tie-in to the movie *The Last Starfighter,* an association that was later abandoned).

Just as now, the limitations of the available technology heavily influenced the shape of games and their storytelling. *Colossal Cave Adventure* is another significant early example of the storytelling urge. It appeared in 1976 and sends the player-character on a heroic quest through a variety of different dungeons in a manner redolent of Tolkien and the fairy stories that in turn informed him. *Adventure* – as it later evolved into – even became the subject of the first PhD to explore video games from an emotional and cultural standpoint. In her doctoral thesis from 1985, a researcher at the University of California called Mary Ann Buckles analysed *Adventure* using the theories of the renowned Russian folklorist Vladimir Propp. Years later, Espen Aarseth chose to quote from Buckles' thesis extensively in his book *Cybertext*.

The storytelling impetus is apparent across the medium. Sometimes it's obvious, as in the case of the text-based adventures which proliferated in an era when computer processors struggled to convey convincing graphics. An early example of this was *Zork* (1977), an interactive story itself inspired by *Colossal Cave Adventure*, which would spawn four sequels. The original *Zork* began life on the PDP-1, just like *Spacewar!*, and its creators would go on to form the American game developer Infocom. In *Zork*, the player is situated in a *Dungeons and Dragons* style fantasy realm. By inputting commands like 'Go North', the player could navigate their way around the world. By typing in instructions like 'Get sword' they could interact with the world.[4]

Throughout the 1980s, the Massachusetts-based Infocom developed and published text-only games in a wide variety of genres beyond sword and sorcery. These included more fantasy adventures like *Wishbringer* (1985) and *Spellbreaker* (1985), science fiction escapades like *Planetfall* (1983) and its sequel *Stationfall* (1987), and thrillers such as *Deadline* (1982) and *The Witness* (1983). Infocom also worked with the novelist Douglas Adams to produce a version of his *Hitchhiker's Guide to the Galaxy* (1984), the comedy science fiction adventure which began life as a BBC radio series before evolving into a series of novels, a TV series and eventually a film.[5] In common with the source material, the game was hilarious to play, although the lateral humour

---

4 Nick Monfort's book *Twisty Little Passages* (2005) provides a fascinating overview of interactive fiction, including a thorough examination of *Zork* and Infocom's work more widely.

often meant solving the various puzzles was impossible without the assistance of cheat sheets.

As so often in the history of storytelling, the limitations of the medium were the engine for creativity. Text-only adventures of this era were able to harness the power of the written word to the power of interactivity. Even as a kid with extremely limited programming abilities, I was able to create my own crude text-based branching adventures. However, I quickly discovered the innate challenges of this genre, too. Just like the Choose Your Own Adventure-style books with which such games share a close affinity, the need to constantly branch the story depending on the player's input means that plot strands proliferate. To some extent this can be eased by dovetailing strands, but without an adequate plan such stories can soon become unmanageable. Mapping these kinds of story out becomes crucial, again speaking to the inherently spatial nature of video game narrative.

The Infocom games stood out because they were brilliantly conceived, well-structured affairs with increasingly sophisticated language parsers and a comprehensive understanding of how to handle branching narrative. They were also extremely well written, immersing players in beautifully described worlds populated by expertly crafted characters. Not all text-led games of this era were exclusively text-based, however. Melbourne House adapted JRR Tolkien's *The Hobbit* (1982) and then its epic three-part sequel *The Lord of the Rings* (1985/87/89) into text-led games that also featured multiple colourful graphics. Both were well received by critics and fans alike, an especially impressive feat given the high expectations of Tolkien fans.

The Melbourne House graphics were necessarily crude, given the processing constraints of the era. Advances in memory size would start to change this, however. While text-only games continued to emerge, examples like *The Pawn* (1985) were able to incorporate increasingly detailed, beautiful illustrations which took advantage of the computing power offered by the new generation of machines, as typified by the Commodore Amiga and Atari ST. Probably the best known text-driven game to emerge in the 1990s was *Myst* (1993), which also included illustrations and a degree of branching at the conclusion of the story, offering up three different endings.[6] The game's popularity spawned a number of sequels.

For amateur developers in the UK the 1980s were a golden period. Sir Clive Sinclair's ZX Spectrum was one amongst a number of machines that transformed the way in which games could be made and, crucially, published.[7] Thanks to the home computer keyboard and the ability to save programs onto cassette, games could be created in people's homes and distributed via mail order. Bedroom coders, often working alone or in small groups, were able to stretch the possibilities of the hardware to create new games, often in the arcade tradition. Many featured a distinctively British, surreal sense of humour rather than complex storytelling, though once again the scenarios were sufficient to grab the imagination. Matthew Smith's *Manic Miner* (1983) and *Jet Set Willy* (1984) proved hugely popular, as did Jeff Minter's *Attack of the Mutant Camels* (1983) and its sequels.[8]

For all that the technology of the period served to democratise the creation and distribution of games, there were still technical problems

---

6 For the longest time – at least until game studies coalesced into a formal academic discipline – *Myst* seemed to be the only game that scholars would analyse, probably because it so closely resembled an interactive book.

7 My wife worked in the Spectrum factory in the early 1980s and tells stories of Sinclair's son traversing the factory floor in a C5 (Sinclair's much derided electric car akin to a giant motorized slipper) with a bullhorn, through which he shouted at the employees to work harder. According to her, it didn't work.

8 In the early noughties I interviewed Minter for *Edge* magazine – his email replies included multiple bleats and baas, consistent with his love of camels, llamas and sheep.

to overcome. As detailed by Francis Spufford in his book *Backroom Boys* (2004), the creators of the video game *Elite* for Acorn's BBC B machine were faced with a particularly knotty challenge. Released in 1984, *Elite* is a space and combat trading game, its entrepreneurial spirit the embodiment of the Thatcherite zeitgeist. The game was one of the first to utilise wireframe graphics, giving it a minimalist, abstract feel. An accompanying novel by science fiction writer Robert Holdstock entitled *The Dark Wheel* (1984) provided fictional context for the *Elite* universe, demonstrating the ways in which paratexts were becoming increasingly sophisticated.

The challenge faced by *Elite*'s creators David Braben and Ian Bell was how to concertina an expansive universe for players to explore into the available memory. To do this, they utilised the Fibonacci Sequence, a mathematical formula that enabled a vast play area to be created afresh each time the game was booted up. Rather than building a constant universe with bespoke planets that never altered, the equation meant that a procedurally generated universe would pop into existence for each new play session, giving the game inbuilt replayability. Comparable techniques are deployed in contemporary games such as *No Man's Sky* (2016), bringing with them similar challenges for storytellers.

Expansive universes don't necessarily equate to immersive universes because they're different every time the game is booted up. Not only is this hard to write for, but guaranteeing player investment in the fiction is therefore challenging to achieve. Arguably the text-based games of this early period were capable of much more dense worldbuilding than their graphically-oriented cousins because of the limited visual capabilities of the technology. To this end, there was often a quid pro quo between the sophistication of the representation of the world and the characters inhabiting it.[9]

The more graphically sophisticated the game, the more difficult it became to implement meaningful interactivity. *Dragon's Lair* (1983) amply demonstrates the point. Groundbreaking for its time, it was effectively an interactive film on a laser disc, available to play in arcades. However, the hugely sophisticated Disney-level style of the animations placed severe limitations on how the player could interact with the game, offering them the ability to react to events but little else.

However, this trade-off between the technical capabilities of the medium and the need to immerse players led to all manner of interesting hybrid forms. *The Secret of Monkey Island*, developed by LucasArts and published in 1990, is a point-and-click adventure heavily influenced by the *Pirates of the Caribbean* (at that stage a theme park ride rather than a movie franchise) and the fantasy-themed pirate novel *On Stranger Tides* (1987), written by Tim Powers. *The Secret of Monkey Island* tells the story of Guybrush Threepwood, who wants to be a pirate, as he declares in his opening line. The player is able to choose from a range of interaction types which operate in tandem with the world with the use of a cursor. With this interaction system, the player can enable Guybrush to 'Look at' a poster, or 'Walk to' and 'Open' a door. Certain actions trigger short, linear, non-interactive sequences, akin to the animated cut scenes utilised in later games.

The combination of a simple but appealing visual look together with puzzle-based gameplay would prove alluring and other point-and-click adventures soon followed. *Broken Sword: The Shadow of the Templars* (1996) sent the player on a globe-trotting adventure akin to

---

9 As we'll find out, these remain ongoing challenges for those working in the field of emergent storytelling.

Indiana Jones, in which real historical events are interwoven. The game benefitted from a distinctive visual style created by animators from Don Bluth Studios who had previously worked on *Dragon's Lair*, and a score by Barrington Pheloung, a composer noted for his work on prestige television shows like *Inspector Morse*. It was followed by *Grim Fandango* (1998), a gloriously conceived point-and-click adventure set in a retro-futuristic version of the 1950s. Unfortunately *Grim Fandango* was a commercial failure, and led to LucasArts stepping away from the genre. Point-and-click games didn't vanish completely – *The Wolf Among Us* (2013), *Papers Please* (2013) and *The Excavation of Hob's Barrow* (2022) are notable recent examples – but at the time other technological developments were bringing new genres to the fore.

As computer and console processing power developed, so too did the possibilities of storytelling. Outside of point-and-click adventures, games were able to offer more complex versions of the parser system pioneered by the early text adventures, combined with much greater visual fidelity. *System Shock* (1994), set aboard a space station in a cyberpunk-themed future, is a first-person action-adventure game. The player sees the events through the eyes of the unnamed hacker trying to access files concerning Citadel Station, before being whisked to the station itself. At the time of its release, *System Shock* was praised for its combination of action and puzzle elements, its story and immersive world.

As with many other games, *System Shock* handed on many of its key facets to successor titles. *Deus Ex*, an action roleplaying game that appeared in 2000, was created by Warren Spector, who'd been a producer on *System Shock* and is occasionally referred to as the Steven Spielberg of games. A science fiction story set in 2052, *Deus Ex* follows JC Denton, an anti-terrorism agent, as he attempts to uncover a complex, multi-layered conspiracy. One of the game's key features is its dialogue tree, which allows the player to choose which line it would like Denton to say to the Non-Player Characters (NPCs) he encounters in the *Blade Runner*-esque environment.

Text games and point-and-click adventures were designed for computer systems featuring keyboards. After all, this was the era of the ZX Spectrum, Commodore 64 and BBC B, and subsequently the 16-bit Atari ST and Commodore Amiga. Consoles hadn't entirely vanished – the Nintendo Entertainment System, Super Nintendo Entertainment System and Sega's Genesis were all prominent during this period. But storytelling in console games tended to be simpler, with notable exceptions like *The Legend of Zelda* (1986) and *Final Fantasy* (1987). It was the arrival of Sony's PlayStation console in the mid-1990s which would change things dramatically, in every sense of the word.

The new console would prove transformative for all sorts of reasons. Sony had never before created their own hardware. Keen to enter the market but nervous to go it alone, they originally began collaborating with Nintendo as early as 1988 with a view to jointly creating a console. For various reasons the deal collapsed, but undeterred Sony moved ahead with their own plan. The PlayStation was revolutionary because of its dedication to three-dimensional games using polygons, rather than the pixels and 'flat' graphics that had dominated games up until this point. The console also broke new ground with its controller, which provided two 'thumbsticks', a development that would be emulated by many subsequent controllers.

The emergence of more powerful technology required imaginative, new solutions to the challenge of integrating gameplay and story. *Half-Life* is a first-person shooter from 1998. The player assumes the role of scientist Gordon Freeman, one of the all-time great video game characters. You control Freeman as he explores the Black Mesa Research Facility following a scientific experiment that's gone wrong, in the process discovering that aliens have invaded. Among many other things, *Half-Life* is notable for its use of scripted sequences to convey specific plot points, scenes of high drama that would play out in-game, thus retaining the player's sense of immersion. Up until this point this technique was largely unheard of, but it would become a mainstay of subsequent games, from *Gears of War* (2006) to *Uncharted* (2007-2022) to *Call of Duty* (2003-).

Half-Life and its spiritual successor *Portal* (2007) were both developed by Valve and neatly demonstrate the ways in which games and their constituent elements can be successfully remixed to offer distinct experiences. A puzzle-platform game, *Portal* is technically set in the same universe as *Half-Life*, a measure taken to reuse art and environment assets.[10] The player controls Chell, a silent protagonist, who is aided in her mission by an Artificial Intelligence that directs her through the environment and monitors her life-signs. Chell is tasked with navigating a series of puzzles using the Aperture Science Handheld Portal Device, effectively a gun that creates portals the player can step into and emerge from. Though the game is short, it gathers its own narrative momentum to deliver an experience that feels emotionally satisfying as well as engrossing to play.

Outside of the arcade, console and home computer markets, developers continued to explore other kinds of technology in terms of their gaming potential. An obvious but under-discussed example is that of mobile gaming, which accounts for a huge slice of the gaming market. Nowadays we tend to think of mobile gaming in terms of phones, but the roots extend further back. The British and New Zealand electronics manufacturer Grandstand produced a range of portable devices in the 1970s and 1980s, including *Munchman* (1981), a variation on *Pac-Man*, the side-scrolling shooter *Scramble* (1982),

---

10 Marc Laidlaw, a *Half-Life* writer brought in to finesse the connection with the *Half-Life* universe, was opposed to this as he felt it made both universes feel smaller.

and *Caveman* (1982).[11] Nintendo transposed many familiar games and characters from the arcades to their Game and Watch handheld devices released from 1980 to 1991, including *Donkey Kong* (1982) and *Mario Bros* (1983). The arrival of *Tetris* in 1989 turbocharged the release of Nintendo's Gameboy, which revolutionized the video game marketplace.

These days, mobile phones offer a hugely popular means of encountering games, particularly for the large slice of the market known as 'casual' gaming. Early mobile phone games boasted fairly simple fare like *Snake* (originally known as *Worm*) and the casual game tradition continues with the likes of *Angry Birds* (2009) and *Fruit Ninja* (2010) as well as conversions of popular arcade classics such as *Space Invaders* and *Pac-Man* (1980).

As with other technology, mobile games which seek to integrate storytelling need to be attuned to the particular strengths of the medium. For instance, the elegant isometric puzzles of *Monument Valley* (2014) are 'wrapped' by a light touch approach to story in which the central character Ida is on a quest for forgiveness. Rather than being a fully worked through story or world, the minimalist approach is intended to provide atmosphere, and according to Lead Designer Ken Wong is more akin to a music video than a book or a movie.[12] This is born out in the use of introductory text to each level and murals on the walls. Periodically the character of Ghost appears to give hints about the history of Monument Valley.

More recent years have seen the re-emergence of Virtual Reality technology as a means of providing a fully immersive experience. There is huge variation in the sophistication of the different technologies occupying this particular gaming space, ranging from

---

11 Outside of the arcades, these devices were the main way myself and my friends encountered digital games.
12 Nicer Tuesdays (Storytelling) : Ken Wong on Youtube.

extremely expensive, high-end systems to much simpler kits that are designed to incorporate mobile phones. As a result, the experience for the player can vary significantly, but as with other examples I've discussed, the more effective story-led games utilise the apparent limitations of the medium to their ultimate benefit.

Many of the more recent crop of VR games are sequels or extensions of existing franchises. These include *Half-Life Alyx* (2020), *The Walking Dead: Saints and Sinners* (2020) and *Batman Arkham VR* (2016). The last of these is firmly set in the well-established Rocksteady version of the Batman universe, and lets the player utilise multiple different kinds of gadget. In one sequence the player touches the required keys on a grand piano and suddenly finds themselves descending into the Batcave beneath the mansion. The experience successfully captures the potential for spectacle that VR affords, allowing the player to look around themselves as well as up and down as the vista unfolds.

Beyond specific pieces of hardware, probably the most transformational technology relates to the Internet. Faster and more reliable broadband connections have transformed contemporary gaming, allowing players to team up with each other across the world. Fantasy games like *Ultima Online* (1997) and *World of Warcraft* (2004) led the charge, creating vast imaginary realms for players to explore together. As I'll look at in subsequent chapters, the storytelling skills required for these Massively Multiplayer Online Roleplaying Games (MMORPG, to give them their clumsy abbreviation) are complex and evolving. These and other varieties of multiplayer gaming require established storytelling techniques borrowed from other media but also original approaches. Such games are social and highly collaborative, and storytelling and worldbuilding needs to accommodate this.

Not that video games were ever the solipsistic activity of lore. Although there was probably – *definitely* – some truth in the stereotype of the solitary teenager in their bedroom, in actual fact a lot of the surrounding culture of video games was always heavily social. There were the arcades, of course, their adolescent devotees so energetically essayed by Martin Amis back in 1982. But the playground was the place in which games were discussed and swapped, and after school we would go to friends' houses to explore the cooperative and competitive delights of *Pitstop II* (1984), *Beach Head II* (1985) and *Chop Suey* (1985).

Video games have always existed at the nexus between technology, commerce and culture. It would take a different book to list all the ways in which new developments have impacted how games handle narrative. Nevertheless, a recurring characteristic is that technical limitations have often been a source of creative inspiration. As with other storytelling media, working around such constraints can often lead to lateral thinking and ingenious solutions. As we've seen, this can take any number of forms. In the early days it might have meant coming up with a fictional scenario designed to excite and provoke the imagination, ably supported by paratexts like box art or tie-in media like comics. Alternatively, technical constraints might have dictated the design of a character or a specific line of dialogue, all the way to a complex piece of worldbuilding that explains why a particular game mechanic exists. This aspect of creativity hasn't changed.

Irrespective of software, hardware or genre, the most successful of games understand their primary concern should be the player, and the need to place that player in the midst of the action. This might mean letting them steer the path of the story or activating the story, either alone or in collaboration with others. To this end, the cleverest, most adept game storytellers are akin to engineers, who understand the power of the technology available to them, but also the ways in which structure can be deployed to enable player agency. In the next chapter I'll explore what it means to make something happen and watch the consequences unfold – and why this, more than anything else, is so crucial to the medium of the video game.

4.
CAUSE AND EFFECT

The Georgia-Russia border, 2009. You're Gary 'Roach' Sanderson, an SAS Sergeant. As part of Taskforce 141, a multinational special forces unit, you and your squad have battled through multiple hazardous missions. Now you're hunting down Vladimir Makarov, ruthless leader of a Russian ultranationalist group. It turns out Makarov wasn't at the safehouse you headed for, but you have at least secured lots of useful intel. Now you've moving toward your extraction point, where your superior Lieutenant General Shepherd has arrived to rescue you and your fellow soldier Simon 'Ghost' Riley. Except that, in a startling reversal, Shepherd shoots both you and Ghost dead.

Another time, another place. It's 1274, the Japanese island of Tsushima. You play Jin Sakai, a samurai tasked with protecting Tsushima against the rampaging Mongol hordes. Throughout, you've been able to choose whether to play honourably according to the Samurai code, or employ dishonourable stealth tactics to assassinate opponents. Now, at the conclusion of the game, you are faced with the ultimate decision. Because of your actions, the Shogun considers you a threat to the stability of the island and has instructed your uncle, Lord Shimura, to kill you in a duel. However, you have bested

Shimura and now hold his fate in your hands: kill him and let him die honourably, or let him walk free, but in disgrace. Either way, you are now an enemy of the Shogun.

Another time, another reality. It's 1492 in the Forgotten Realms, a *Dungeons and Dragons* fantasy land. Having created your own character or group of characters, you've joined with a party of adventurers who are either pre-existing NPCs or real, online players. One of your early tasks presents itself at a place called Emerald Grove, where a group of druids have been helping some Tieflings, humanoid creatures descended from humans and demons. However, relations between the druids and the Tieflings have soured, and the situation is complicated by attacks from goblin marauders. You can choose among a number of options, including helping the druids and Tieflings to make peace, wiping out one side or the other, attacking the goblins or siding with them. There are immediate consequences from your actions, such as having a romantic liaison with a particular character, but also long term ramifications.

Three very different video games with three different approaches to cause and effect. In *Ghost of Tsushima* (2020), the ability to choose whether to kill your beloved uncle and mentor Shimura is only possible because of interactivity. As a player, we get to decide on the ultimate outcome of the protagonist Jin's journey. In plot terms the choice you make won't affect anything – the Shogun remains your enemy either way. But, in a complex exploration of the relationship of duty and love, the game lets you decide how the relationship with your uncle ends. Equally, in the case of *Baldur's Gate* 3 (2023), your choices in Emerald Grove have both short and long-term consequences for how the game's story will play out. Again, this is a kind of storytelling which is unique to the video game medium, in which your actions cause effects and influence the course of the story.

But in *Call of Duty: Modern Warfare 2* (2009) we see something different – the removal of agency. When General Shepherd turns on you and Ghost, it's a shock precisely because you've come to trust this character. It's the kind of twist that movies, television shows and novels have been doing with greater or lesser success for as long as these media have existed. But it's even more impactful because as a player you don't have any control over events, all you did was complete the preceding section of gameplay as required. Nevertheless Roach, the character you've invested hours in is killed, and there's nothing you can do about it.

Agency, as defined by academic Janet H Murray in her seminal book *Hamlet on the Holodeck* (1997) is the ability to take meaningful decisions in an interactive context. In a video game, agency can take multiple guises depending on your viewpoint. The key word in Murray's definition is 'meaningful' but we can interpret that in multiple different ways depending on the context. Making a choice in a video game that leads to the player's demise is an obvious example of agency, but so is blasting aliens that would otherwise overwhelm and kill us. As with so much else of the discussion around video game storytelling and worldbuilding, context is absolutely paramount.

Dr Alison Norrington, Founder and Creative Director at Storycentral Ltd., explains the centrality of agency to the experience in these terms: 'Engineering agency in game contexts is one of the most crucial – and challenging – elements of interactive storytelling. It's about giving players the sense that their choices, actions, and decisions have a meaningful impact on the world, the characters, and ultimately, the narrative. When players feel like their actions truly matter, they become emotionally invested, and that's when the game *experience* transcends simple gameplay and becomes something memorable and deeply engaging.'

Agency is important because that's how we experience the real world, or like to think we experience the world, or would prefer to experience the world if we could. We live our lives taking decisions in the hope that the outcome in each instance will be that which we desire. Such actions might be self-interested or altruistic, selfish or generous. When we feel agency has been taken from us, we're understandably angry. When we witness or experience something over which we have no control and are reduced to a feeling of helplessness, we're similarly upset.

By extension, as a mirror to human life – no matter how distorting that mirror might be – storytelling is similarly founded in ideas of cause and effect.[1] The difference is that in life we generally take measures to mitigate surprises and shocks. In storytelling we want to be surprised. We want twists like Shepherd's betrayal, no matter how emotionally painful they might be. In a medium supposedly founded on agency and the ability to affect events, having that power wrenched away is all the more intense.

Aristotle knew the importance of cause and effect. In his study of dramatic theory *Poetics*, he argues that for a story to be a story it must have all the requisite elements. In other words, if something is missing we'll feel dissatisfied – a cause must have an effect. Equally, as sophisticated consumers of all kinds of stories, we might feel hard done by if we can guess where the plot is going. The Russian playwright Anton Chekhov famously suggested that if we see a gun in a drawer in Act One then we expect it to be used later in the play – but clever audiences will necessarily expect something clever to be done with it. This is why sophisticated contemporary audiences so intensely dislike *deus ex machina* when they appear. The term

---

1 In his 1967 classic *The Sense of An Ending*, literary theorist Frank Kermode suggests that fictional endings are a method used by writers to understand and contain the linear course of life.

derives from Greek drama and literally describes the descent of a god character on a platform who 'resolves' the story, irrespective of what came before. For the Ancient Greeks it was a perfectly valid way of resolving a drama. For us, not so much.

Causality on its own isn't enough. A plot, as defined by EM Forster, the novelist and critic, is precisely concerned with cause and effect, but it's not simply a sequence of events that follow one another. As Forster says: 'The King died and the Queen died' isn't a plot. However: 'The King died and the Queen died of grief' is a plot, because it gives us a reason *why* the Queen expired.

The poet TS Eliot is similarly interested in cause and effect because of the ways in which it can supply emotional insight. In his essay 'Hamlet and His Problems', he develops the concept of the 'objective correlative' to describe a group of elements or objects, or chain of events which collectively and systemically show emotions and which in turn are intended to 'evoke' emotions in the audience.

In the essay, Eliot explores the apparent absence of an objective correlative in Shakespeare's *Hamlet*, and specifically how it relates to the titular character. Eliot makes the point that Lady Macbeth's state of mind as she is walking in her sleep is conveyed by provoking in the audience a series of emotional responses, so that when Macbeth reveals her death it makes perfect sense – in other words, the objective correlative is fulfilled. Eliot argues that in stark contrast, Hamlet's emotions have not been adequately established by previous events, to the extent that Shakespeare falls back on madness – or at least ambiguity over his madness – to help explain why Hamlet behaves as he does.[2]

---

2 It turns out Hamlet has a lot to teach video game storytellers – which is why we'll keep coming back to him.

Other kinds of storytelling attract their own versions of the same or similar phenomenon related to causal relations. The screenwriting guru Robert McKee talks about causality in terms of 'set ups' and 'pay offs', and other theorists have their own versions. For McKee, the set up embeds something earlier in the story which the audience forgets about and is then sent back to rediscover at the conclusion. The point is that this relationship is ironically charged, so that the action of remembering provokes a sense of revelation or insight. This is what we see with Chekhov's gun – ideally we notice it on a subconscious level and then promptly forget about it, recalling it only when it reappears in a startling way.

These same discussions are as applicable to many games as they are to other storytelling media. Games with any kind of evolved storytelling require plots to function in a way which ultimately makes sense, even though the game's structure might mean that said plot is delivered to us in a non-linear way. Equally, choices taken by the player might mean that a particular plot strand plays out in a certain way and another strand is completely ignored. Games need the cause-and-effect of set-ups and pay-offs, too, though again the game's structure might mean that these are experienced differently for different players.

For the purposes of this discussion, let's start at the beginning. The game *Halo: Combat Evolved* (2001) starts with a spectacular, lengthy cut sequence. Set against an ethereal, choral soundtrack, a vast spaceship hangs in the stars. Inside the ship, on the command deck, a senior officer looks out at the void. The image of a holographic female appears and informs him of the imminent approach of hostile forces. Suddenly alarms are ringing and the crew are racing to their posts. The opening is deliberately reminiscent of the epic science fiction movies that are a mainstay of popular culture, immediately evoking the start of *Aliens* (1986) and the military aesthetic of *Starship Troopers*

(1997). This beginning serves to establish the genre of the game and hook us with a moment of high drama and intrigue, akin to those movies it references.

Our perspective shifts and suddenly you're looking out of a high-tech suit while a crewman runs through a series of tests. He instructs you to look left and then right, up and then down. Once you've achieved this you step out of the containment unit and onto the deck. All around you, the emergency is continuing. The enemy has boarded. Nevertheless, your objective is to regroup with your Captain and evacuate the ship. En route you encounter the hostile alien species – the Covenant – and battle is joined. You must quickly work out how to fight them.

Learning how to play the game and how its central mechanics work – understanding the relationship between cause and effect – is a key aspect of video game development. As a result, tutorials are often built into the fiction of the experience. Commonly, User-Interface design[3] is used to explain or reinforce the player's actions and help them understand what's required of them. As *Halo* demonstrates, a non-playable character might be included to help guide the player in as seamless a way as possible. Very often multiple strategies are employed to 'on board' the player into the world of the game and its mechanics. Games must not only set up the plot and fictional universe, but also how the player interacts with this story and world.

This approach of separating out an introductory cut scene from tutorial elements is a recurrent feature of many games. On *Sniper Elite 4* (2017), we made the decision to disconnect the game's Inciting Incident – the key event that kicks off the events of the plot – from the tutorial element. Instead, the game opens with an overview of the

---

3 Graphical or textual overlays that facilitate player configuration of the game's mechanics, settings and features.

world situation in 1943, then moves to show a mysterious new type of Nazi missile destroying a ship off the coast of Italy. Our hero, Karl Fairburne, is washed up on the coast of a fictional island San Celini, where he must investigate the missile. From the beach onwards, we integrate tutorial mechanics into the player's progress, introducing an easy-to-overcome assailant while maintaining the fiction of the adventure.

As a rule, it's a good idea to throw players into the action as rapidly as possible. After all, this is an interactive medium, rather than a feature film or television show. *Spider-Man 2* (2023) does this expertly, in the process bringing together two different versions of Spider-Man, Peter Parker and Miles Morales. The player is immediately tasked with making their way through the city to tackle the Sandman, a gigantic villain menacing New York City. The game seamlessly integrates the mechanics of swinging through the city with firing webs, climbing, etc with important story exposition. This is all the more remarkable given that the player's perspective switches between Parker and Morales on a number of occasions. The effect is exhilarating and satisfactory, creating an immediate bond between the player and the two characters, and once again immersing the player in the world of the game.

Another technique which often features in the opening sequences of games is to show the location in which the game takes place, and in this way foreshadow gameplay events. *Grand Theft Auto: San Andreas* (2004) begins with a montage of shots of the city, reminiscent of the film and televisual examples the game is riffing off, but also giving the player previews of the game space they'll be exploring for themselves very soon. It's a foreshadowing technique we've seen used before in cinema and television shows, but reimagined in the context of the game medium. This reinvention of well-established tropes from other media is something games excel at, and another way in which cause and effect manifests itself.

Sometimes the influence of other media is absolutely explicit. While *Indiana Jones and the Great Circle* (2024) tells a new story in the life of the eponymous, swashbuckling hero, it begins with a retelling of the famous opening of the original *Raiders of the Lost Ark* movie from 1981. This approach carries multiple benefits for the developers of the game. On the one hand it serves to stitch this new instalment into the existing canon. Through inhabiting the role of Indy the player is able to experience first-hand the famous temple, including interactions with obstacles and traps reimagined for an interactive context, as well as exchanges with well-known characters, culminating in the escape from the enormous rolling boulder. At the same time, the player understands that they must enact the role familiar from the movie, in the process learning the game's specific mechanics.

The culmination of the game story is equally important. The endings of games obey the same logic as other storytelling forms, particularly that of certain genres of popular cinema. Many campaign-driven video game endings tend to be bombastic affairs, aping the Hollywood blockbusters to which they're most obviously indebted. For instance, the first *Halo* ends with a chaotic escape through an exploding spaceship on a Warthog, a highly manoeuvrable military vehicle. It's a suitably spectacular ending to an epic game and the first instalment in what would become an immense franchise with a complex mythology. But *Halo* has a definitive, single ending, unlike *Ghost of Tsushima, Myst* or the *Star Wars* game *The Force Unleashed* (2008), all of which feature multiple different endings.

According to Robert McKee, the climax of a classically structured story is the point at which the Controlling Idea wins out against the Counter Idea, and the true meaning of the story is expressed. The two endings of the *Blade Runner* movie illustrate the point. The film adaptation of Philip K Dick's science fiction novel *Do Androids Dream of Electric Sheep?* remains a masterpiece of storytelling and film-making, but its genesis was not without problems. In 1982, when executives saw Ridley Scott's original cut of the film, they found it too ambiguous. As a result they demanded a number of cuts be made to the film and that the ending should be changed. Since lead actor Harrison Ford – who played main character Rick Deckard – was still under contract, they brought him back and recorded a Chandleresque narration to provide additional context and render the film's meaning less unclear.

As a result, the first released version of the movie sees the human Deckard and his lover, the android Rachael, flying off happily together away from the city and into the countryside,[4] accompanied by Ford's explanatory narration. However, about a decade after its original release, Ridley Scott's original cut was discovered in the basement of an LA cinema. This version retained the original ambiguous elements, including the ending, which suggest that Rick Deckard is himself an android. Over subsequent years Scott perfected his original vision, and this latter version has become the dominant one, to the extent that Denis Villeneuve's 2017 sequel *Blade Runner 2049* is much more of a sequel to the director's cut of *Blade Runner* than the version that was originally released in 1982. The point is that the different endings of the film completely changed the movie's meaning , i.e. its Controlling Idea.

Changing endings is one thing of course, and something that we associate with games because of the branching possibilities of the medium. But as I said earlier, agency in a game environment can take many different guises depending on how we define it. At the most fundamental level we expect a player character to be able to traverse – walk, run, swim, drive – through an environment, consistent with

---

4 Using spare footage from the opening of Kubrick's *The Shining* (1980).

the design of the fictional world. We also expect to be able to interact in other ways, from talking to other characters to dispatching hostile monsters. In the broad sense all of these activities might be viewed as storytelling, in that they exist inside and affect the fictional world or universe.

The ability to intervene in the fictional world of the game means that structure and agency are intrinsically linked. In addition to any linear elements they might include, games utilise space in a way which is fundamentally different to that of sequential media.[5] Interactivity manifested as gameplay often means being able to explore an environment. Often the player can choose the order in which they undertake tasks or quests, or in the case of 'side-quests' ignore them completely. Open world games in particular offer huge opportunities for non-linear exploration and experimentation. This has colossal implications for thinking about how meaning is structured and delivered to the player.

This is the purpose of narrative design and why it's so critical to many contemporary video games. As we saw in Chapter 1, narrative design can have different emphasises depending on the particular project and studio's requirements. But one of narrative design's primary roles is to stitch together the spatial elements associated with exploring the environment with the more temporal aspects of storytelling, like conversing with a character you encounter in the world, or triggering a cut scene because you've entered an abandoned temple. I've already identified the enduring popularity of single player, campaign-led games such as *God of War* (2018), *Control* (2019), *Horizon Zero Dawn* (2017) and *Dishonored* (2017), in which beautifully

---

5 Murray identifies multiple varieties of spatial structure afforded by interactive narrative, including the 'Violence Hub' I mentioned in Chapter 2.

crafted stories are woven into intricately designed, wholly immersive fictional worlds.

At the same time, various kinds of multiplayer game are also hugely popular. *Overwatch* (2016), *Destiny* (2014) and the all-conquering *Fortnite* (2017) are perhaps best known for their frenetic combat. But each of them also feature deceptively complex fictional universes and have developed their own approaches to ongoing, seasonal storytelling. Many franchises like *Grand Theft Auto, Red Dead Redemption, Halo* and *Cyberpunk* combine campaign-led narrative strands with online sandbox environments, and boast regular narrative updates. Many of these game storyworlds are vast narrative ecologies, demanding a constant stream of content from teams of writers and narrative designers.

While each of these games will have vastly different approaches to the concept of agency, the importance of making the player's actions in the imaginary world feel meaningful are primary concerns for each. Alison Norrington identifies the temporal aspect intrinsic in allowing this to happen: 'For agency to feel truly meaningful, the consequences of a player's actions need to echo across time. Whether a player's choices impact the immediate plot or stretch far into the game's future, the sense of lasting change helps solidify their agency. Games like *The Witcher 3* or *Detroit: Become Human* excel at giving players the sense that their actions ripple through time, affecting the world and people they encounter.'

This is the aspect of games which makes them distinct from most other storytelling forms and which enables agency to take place: they remember. Video games can make a computational note of the actions you take, and change the story or world based upon those choices. This is true of *Baldur's Gate 3, Red Dead Redemption, Cyberpunk 2077*, and any number of other examples. From saving your progress through the design of your character, from the path you take to the characters you encounter and how you react to them, from the weapons and equipment you carry to your achievements in the game, all can be remembered and utilised accordingly. The outcomes of multiple remembered decisions create an increasingly complex experience, but at root the principle is extremely simple.

Fittingly for a discussion of memory, let's step back in time 40 years. Like a lot of my friends I would type in programs from books and magazines like *Computer and Video Games* (1981-2004) and *Atari User* (1985-1988) into my Atari 800, my first computer. These programs were mainly games, and I would often experiment with the variables in the code to see the results. This helped give me the confidence I could write my own text-based game, akin to the kind released by the game studio Infocom during this period. My experiments were haphazard and crude to say the least, but I quickly realised I could create a scenario in which the player finds a sword and is offered the chance of picking up the weapon or leaving it. If they chose to grab it then SWORD=1, but if they left it in place SWORD=0. Later on they might meet a bellicose dragon and the program would check to see if SWORD=1 or 0, allowing the player to battle the creature or end the game prematurely as the dragon's dinner. Hey presto, the computer has memorised the player's decision and used that to modify their experience.

When I was creating my simplistic branching story as a kid, I soon discovered that to make the game more interesting and immersive I had to give the player more choices, but for these to be meaningful choices these different branches had to have different outcomes. The obvious problem with this is that the branches quickly proliferate. In text-only adventures like the original Infocom games, this was less of an issue, but for other kinds of game it's a big potentially a big problem. Since cut scenes are expensive to make, developers understandably don't want to put a lot of time and effort into constructing pathways and outcomes that players aren't going to encounter because they chose a different path. Non-gamers often assume that contemporary games feature lots of this kind of decide-your-fate style branching but lots of genres don't engage in this structure for exactly these reasons.

Remembering is vital to video games because of their non-linear structure. The game needs to know where you've been and what you've done. It needs to know whether you've picked up that sword or hidden a gun in a drawer. I might plant a bomb in *Spy Vs Spy* (1984) to blow up my opponent or drop a banana skin for a competitor to skid on in *Mario Kart* (1992). In *Grand Theft Auto V* (2013), I might shoot a police helicopter out of the sky that crashes into cop cars and causes each of them to explode in turn, or get my eponymous cheeky bird to steal the groundsman's hat in *Untitled Goose Game* (2019), thus causing him to run after me, remonstrating.

This is an intrinsic way in which video game storytelling extends and reshapes more established storytelling techniques. Irrespective of medium, an audience's understanding of a plot is dependent on them remembering crucial elements so that the ending possesses the intended emotional impact. In a traditional storytelling context, the reveal of a pay-off requires an audience to recall an element to see its importance. As memory machines, games can remember the actions of the player, shaping the story and world accordingly, supplying set-ups and pay-offs in different ways depending on the game's structure and approach to non-linearity.

We can see this as a recurring characteristic of video games – the ways in which the medium constantly reinvents what we know about storytelling. Games often challenge our expectations, even when we think we know exactly what we're going to get. In the next chapter, I'm going to look at another crucial aspect of games borrowed from other media, but which games playfully subvert – genre.

5.
GENRE TROUBLE

Video games come in all shapes and sizes. From *Pong* to *Grand Theft Auto 6*, from *Donkey Kong* to *Fallout*, this has always been a diverse medium. And though games are clearly art, they are also commerce. As a result, publishers are constantly seeking ways to market their products to us, and genre is a key method for doing this. Just like movies, television shows, theatre plays and novels, games are packaged and presented in terms of genres we recognise – science fiction, fantasy, horror, thriller, sports and many more – that bring with them a whole host of expectations. But that's only part of the equation. Despite appearances, genre is another key way in which video game storytelling differs from these other media.

Genre as a way of categorising stories is far from a new phenomenon. In *Poetics*, Aristotle identifies distinct techniques for artfully implementing tragedy, comedy, the epic, dithyrambic poetry (meaning wildly passionate writing or speech) and phallic songs. Many subsequent writers and thinkers have tried to create their own genre classification systems. According to the contemporary academic John

Frow[1], these include the Roman theoretician Quintilian, English poet Philip Sidney and the German writer Johann Wolfgang von Goethe. A key later figure in the theorisation of genre is Mikhail Bakhtin, the Russian literary theorist. Bakhtin sees genre as inherent to language and propounds the idea of the *dialogic*, suggesting that genres are the result of ongoing interactions between people and the language forms they use – everything from spoken speech to newspaper articles and novels.

In the 20th Century, genre became a way of marketing books to audiences, a practice which was also adopted by the cinema industry. Indeed, such is our familiarity with genres in other media that we're quickly able to identify their codes and conventions, whether they're explicitly marketed that way or whether they're embedded in the narrative itself. While we know that cowboys, horses and iconic locations like Monument Valley are suggestive of the Western, we also know that rocket ships, aliens and robots are associated with science fiction. This is as true of fundamentally sequential storytelling media like the novel as it is of television, film and radio. Advertising and marketing furnish us with expectations which we expect to see satisfied.

Despite being published almost half a century ago, the key work in terms of film genre theory remains Will Wright's book *Six Guns and Society* (1977). Wright makes the case for the mythical status of the Western, arguing that recurring elements, from repeating iconography to common situations, enable the genre to retain its contemporary relevance. Since we're long past the heyday of the filmic Western – let alone the hugely popular Western novels that preceded it and for a time lived alongside – this may seem surprising, but for a key point in cinema's early evolution, it was the dominant genre.

———————

1 Frow, John (2015) *Genre*. Abingdon: Routledge

Not that a genre that works in one medium necessarily prospers in another. There haven't been many Western-themed video games, compared to other high profile genres. An early example, *Custer's Revenge* (1982), remains infamous for reasons I'll explore later in the book. Probably the best known recent example of a Western game is Rockstar's *Red Dead Redemption II* (2018), the third entry in the *Red Dead* series. The game is a sprawling action-adventure set in a fictionalised version of the Wild West. *Red Dead Redemption II* includes much of the iconography we would recognise from the Western genre, as handed down from the films of director John Ford and actors Gary Cooper and John Wayne.[2] The soundscape, often comprising specific musical tropes like the mouth organ, is an equally important method for conveying genre characteristics.

Of course, the lack of Western games might be down to their diminished popularity as a cinematic genre, far removed from their heyday. Musicals are another interesting example. Though Hollywood is no longer dominated by the genre, there's still clearly an ongoing audience, as the Bollywood film industry suggests and as the thriving theatrical scenes of London's West End and New York's Broadway also indicate. As well as occasional breakout hits like *La La Land* (2016), the genre has found a home on television thanks to the likes of shows like *Glee*, and has permeated other non-musical genres such as fantasy (*Buffy the Vampire Slayer*) and science fiction (*Star Trek* and *Doctor Who*).

Not to say that there haven't been many highly successful video games in which music is a key component of gameplay. Dance games have long been a feature of arcades, from *Dance Dance Revolution*

---

2 Sergei Leone's 'spaghetti Westerns' like *A Fistful of Dollars* and *For a Few Dollars More* are fascinating precisely because they were filmed in Italy and Spain rather than the US and so lack the iconography we would recognise from the classic Western tradition – no Monument Valley, for instance.

(1998) to the *Just Dance* series (2009-2024) and its sequel. Other kinds of rhythm game, in which the player has to manipulate the controller in time to the musical score to progress the game, include *Frequency* (2001) and its sequel *Amplitude* (2003). There's also the hugely popular *Guitar Hero* series (2005 onwards) and Sony's *SingStar* series, a Karaoke-style game which required players to sing-along with well known standards like Petula Clark's 'Downtown' and Carl Douglas' 'Kung Fu Fighting'.

These games aren't totally lacking in narrative, which is often supplied under the guise of a 'career' mode encouraging a player to work their way through the music or entertainment industry. For instance, *The Beatles: Rock Band* (2009) features a story mode which allows players to play their way through the history of the band. But often the narrative of music games is simplistic, or little more than a scenario used to frame gameplay. In *Frequency* (2001) the player controls an avatar called FreQ down an octagonal tunnel, and in *Amplitude* (2003) the player is tasked with controlling a 'beat blaster ship'. In the hypnotic *Rez* (2001), the player must guide a hacker into a malfunctioning AI system, the avatar evolving as you progress. Conversely, in the eccentric but captivating *Vib-Ribbon* (1999), the player must stop Vib the rabbit from devolving into something that's very much not a rabbit.

There are therefore no readily apparent game mechanic reasons as to why the musical wouldn't translate to the video game medium, and the popularity of sing-a-long events like *The Rocky Horror Musical, The Sound of Music* and *Mamma Mia* suggests an appetite for playful, interactive engagement involving more sophisticated narratives than is currently the case with most music-focussed games. However, the games industry is exceptionally risk adverse, preferring to emulate tried and tested genres – notably sports, science fiction and fantasy, war and crime – rather than strike into new territories.

Some commentators have argued that this conservatism has led to a narrowing of genres, with developers releasing numerous sequels to an existing successful product – though there are often good reasons for wanting to use the same game engine and update the gameplay and audiovisual look of a game rather than expanding into completely new territory.

By comparison, sports and simulation have proved enduringly popular, probably speaking to the natural affinity these genres share with video games. This makes sense since soccer, tennis, racing games, train simulators and fishing simulators are primarily concerned with rules rather than storytelling.[3] Science fiction, meanwhile, has been a mainstay of the medium since *Spacewar!* and has prospered ever since thanks to blockbusters like *Space Invaders, Portal, Deus Ex* and more recent examples like *Destiny* and *Starfield*. The reasons why certain genres dominate over others are partly cultural, speaking to the wider context in which they're produced. But there are other formal reasons why some genres lend themselves more readily to video games than others.

Importantly, unlike their opposite numbers in other media, games are not just operating on a representational level. As I've already discussed at length, the interactive component of games, the ability to intervene in the story and world, is an obvious point of distinction. This interactivity is afforded in all sorts of different ways by the hardware and software being utilized, and the ways in which game developers exploit these limitations to facilitate their creativity. In other words, games are understood through their gameplay and the technological means by which that gameplay is activated as much as they're understood by their audiovisual characteristics. The *Red*

---

3 Incorporating narrative into these genres is, as a consequence, a particular challenge for game storytellers though there have been some great examples over the years.

Dead games are Western themed action adventures. *Doom* (1993) is a science fiction themed first-person shooter. Game genres need to be understood in thematic, tonal but also *technical* terms.

As the academic James Newman tells us, the game review magazines of the mid to late 1980s used genre as a primary way of differentiating game types from one another.[4] In fact, as he points out, genre categories that still exist such as shoot 'em ups and beat 'em ups were first identified in the pages of these magazines.[5] It's significant, though, that these genre classifications were defined as much by the nature of the interaction as by the thematic dressing used to contextualise that interaction. This isn't to necessarily suggest that one element is more important than the other. It's just good to know whether we're shooting zombies or beating them up.

In fact, academics have wrangled with genre classifications for some time. In a key early intervention, Mark Wolf uses interactivity as the main determining factor in differentiating game types.[6] In response, Aki Järvinen argues that genre is a poor way of understanding games, suggesting instead that they should be viewed in terms of their audiovisual perspective and the techniques they employ.[7] As with so many aspects of games, applying consistent frameworks is rendered challenging by the ways in which games and the concomitant technology evolve, and by the fact that different types of games cross-pollinate to create new types.

---

4 Newman, James (2004) *Videogames*. London: Routledge
5 The Oxford English Dictionary suggests that the descriptor 'shoot-'em-up' was first applied to particular kinds of film and literature in the 1950s.
6 Wolf, Mark (ed) (2001) *The Medium of the Videogame*. Austin: University of Texas Press
7 Järvinen, Aki (2004) 'Gran Stylissimo: The Audiovisual Elements and Styles in Computer and Video Games in Mäyrä, Frans (ed) *CGDC Conference Proceedings*. Tampere: Tampere University Press

Of course, these complexities don't bother the games industry. Genre is used extensively in all sorts of ways. This ranges from the ways in which games are conceived and pitched by developers both internally and to external partners and publishers, all the way through to the marketing and distribution of the finished project. Game publishers understand that genre is crucial to setting expectations and making sure that their products are targeted at the correct audiences. This might mean appealing to an existing fanbase or extending to new demographics, or maybe doing both. Suffice to say, the mechanisms and processes for enabling this, particularly at the AAA end of the sector, are as sophisticated as any other entertainment industry.

Within the industry, genre is often articulated through discussions of theme and tone but also through game mechanics. This will often involve looking at previously published examples within the same genre and analysing these games' characteristics to see what can be learned from them. This might mean adopting mechanics from different titles and recombining them in new ways. It might equally mean putting distance between the planned project and competitor titles. Plotting on a spectrum or chart where the game sits in relation to other titles or franchises is a common technique for understanding where similarities and commonalities lie. Game storytellers, whether they're narrative director, designer or writer, are often intimately involved in this process.

Dr Alison Norrington, Founder and Creative Director at Storycentral Ltd., frames it this way: 'The key thing to understand is that while games share many foundational elements with traditional media genres, the way these genres translate into games is heavily shaped by the interactivity and agency that gaming allows. As someone who specialises in both transmedia storytelling and interactive experiences, I think of this translation not as a mere copy-paste of genre conventions, but as a reimagining of familiar themes, tropes, and narrative structures within the unique framework of games.'

Such insights can be vital in understanding how a particular game deploys genre techniques. For instance, horror has worked very successfully in media ranging from novels and films to theatre and radio. The same is true of video games. A well-wrought horror game is able to place players directly inside the story, building suspense until moments of genuine horror are shockingly delivered. The long-running *Resident Evil* series has a history of manipulating players according to the conventions of the genre. The original *Resident Evil* features a jump scare involving rabid dogs leaping out at the player, while the VR mode of *Resident Evil 4* builds tension by having the player approach an abandoned log cabin in early evening sunlight, strikingly reminiscent of the original *Texas Chainsaw Massacre* movie (1974).

Horror is an instructive genre to look at in terms of video games. To be successful, horror stories need to generate a strong sense of immersion, which may be why the genre lends itself so well to games. After all, the affective response – the feeling it's intended to provoke – is contained in that descriptor 'horror'. Clearly, as with any of the other genres I've so far mentioned, genre-specific techniques need to be reinterpreted for a medium driven by interactivity. In the case of horror, this means working out how to engineer suspense but also how to deliver shocks and scares along the way through gameplay.

For Norrington, horror is an example of a genre that translates particularly effectively into the video game medium: 'In games like *Silent Hill 2* or *Resident Evil 7*, the player's direct control over the environment heightens this tension. The sense of vulnerability is amplified because the player doesn't just watch the horror unfold – they are part of it. The use of first-person perspective or limited resources (like ammunition or health) further increases that feeling of unease, allowing the player to experience the horror as a participant rather than an observer.'

Just as with other video game genres, horror games come in many different forms. *The Excavation of Hob's Barrow* (2022) is an intricately constructed point-and-click adventure developed by Cloak and Dagger Games. The player controls the character of Thomasina Bateman, a Victorian antiquary who has travelled to the town of Bewlay in the north of England to unearth the burial mound of the title. In common with much older point-and-click adventures in the mould of the *Monkey Island* games, the player must talk to various members of the community, in the process unravelling the terrible truth at the heart of the village.

The game is an example of folk horror, the name of the sub-genre popularized by the British writer and performer Mark Gatiss. *The Excavation of Hob's Barrow* sits in a popular cultural tradition that can be traced through the novels of Dennis Wheatley and films like *The Wicker Man* (1973) and *Blood on Satan's Claw* (1971). Thanks to simple but elegant visuals, *The Excavation of Hob's Barrow* very successfully evokes the sense of disquiet and creeping dread associated with the genre. This is partly achieved through the sound design, which utilises the noise of the windswept moors, including the rustling of trees, tweeting of birds and isolated sounds like a solitary dog barking. Even the pub in which Thomasina stays eerily creaks as she crosses the floorboards. This approach is augmented by appropriately disturbing music designed to underscore moments of tension or drama.

The slow uncovering of the truth which typifies the genre irrespective of medium fits the point-and-click mechanic surprisingly effectively. As well as finding out what's really occurring in Bewley, while we're guiding Thomasina we uncover more of her own tragic backstory, another approach employed by folk horror and gothic stories more broadly. This is conveyed by flashback sequences to the

Bedlam-like institution in which her father was incarcerated years earlier. A further disturbing technique is to include sudden close ups of key characters, at odds with the distanced visual approach of the bulk of the game. These startling close-ups are created by John Inch, and according to the game's designer Shaun Aitcheson, supply an 'uncanny "otherness".'[8] Fascinatingly this approach might be seen to harken to the cinematic folk horror genre and its use of jump scares, rather than something commonly employed in the technical genre of point-and-click games.

A useful point of comparison is offered by the game *Alan Wake 2* (2023). From a thematic standpoint the game starts off as an example of folk horror, albeit in a North American context, though it contains striking similarities with its English cousin. As with *The Excavation of Hob's Barrow* and other non-game examples of folk horror, the protagonist is initially tasked with uncovering what's really happening in the rural location. This time it's Cauldron Lake, a fictional location in the mountains of Washington State in the US. As the game progress it assuredly moves away from folk horror and takes some major twists of the kind beloved of the innovative developer behind it, the Finnish studio Remedy. The technical genre of the game is quite different to that of *The Exploration of Hob's Barrow*, since *Alan Wake 2* is a survival horror game played from a third person perspective.

You awake as a naked man on the shores of Cauldron Lake in the dead of night. You stumble through the undergrowth away from some unknown terror, plagued by occasional horrific flashes of an unknown creature. The agency you experience is limited and ultimately goes nowhere – you're soon captured by people in terrifying masks. Now powerless, you spend the subsequent cut scene watching

---

8 An Interview With Hob's Barrow Designer Shaun Aitcheson (dreadcentral. com)

as the character you controlled is horrifically disembowelled by these same masked people. We switch to the opening credits as a car makes its way along a freeway and through the beautiful forests of Bright Falls, the larger area in which the game is set, a sequence redolent of the opening of Stanley Kubrick's adaptation of Stephen King's horror classic *The Shining* (1980). The car is driven by Saga Anderson, an FBI Special Agent, who is accompanied by her colleague Robert Nightingale. The pair of you have been sent to investigate this crime and a series of related ritualistic killings in the vicinity. Upon arriving you assume control of Saga and begin your investigation.

Alan Wake 2 features a 'mind place', a clever story and gameplay device that situates you in the room of a hunting lodge where you can review the clues you have so far amassed.[9] Such safe areas are common to lots of games and allow for important gameplay activity to take place, though they can often be a challenge to integrate from a narrative perspective as they tend to disrupt the flow of the story. Making this location an imaginary one in the mind of the main character is a lateral solution to the problem of removing the protagonist to a different location for the purposes of gameplay.

The game's mechanics and visual presentation make it experientially very different from the point-and-click approach of *The Excavation of Hob's Barrow*, with *Alan Wake 2* borrowing heavily from horror cinema tropes but also the survival horror tradition in which it sits. Despite their aesthetic and mechanical differences, both games are adept at creating a sense of unease with occasional forays into outright shock and horror. In a sense, production of genre material for games might be seen as an exercise in *adaptation*, in which developers take the existing tropes of a genre and convert them

---

9 Echoes here of the memory palace employed by Benedict Cumberbatch's version of the eponymous detective in the BBC's *Sherlock*.

into game mechanics and structures that exploit the potential of the medium.

Recalling Aki Järvinen's point, the key distinguishing factor between *The Excavation of Hob's Barrow* and *Alan Wake 2* is perspective and how it's implemented. Our third person control of Alan Wake and Saga Anderson is immediate, as we pilot them through the game environment uncovering clues. Thomasina Bateman's movement is slower and more deliberate, as we search for the kind of interaction we want her to engage in. Indeed, perspective has been the element that has differentiated genres for a long time, and its evolution is woven into the development of gaming technology. We've moved from the top down and side perspectives that characterised early arcade games, through isometric viewpoints and side-scrolling, arriving at different varieties of first and third-person perspectives.

From a development standpoint, the connections between genre expectations and the limitations of the available technology are sometimes less visible but no less significant. On the VR game *Blood and Truth* we wanted the Agent Carson figure to walk behind the player-character, our version of a classic crime genre trope in which the detective or cop circles the suspect to intimidate them. We achieved this, but in doing so we were acutely aware that the tethered nature of the Sony VR headset – the cable connecting the headset to the console – meant that players would struggle to turn to look at their interlocutor.

The dominance of certain genres in the video game market owes a lot to how well the genre in question translates to an interactive medium. For instance, action-based genres tend to transfer very well because action is synonymous with interactivity. Similarly, genres which include strong elements of mystery, along with the unearthing and eventual solving of clues, seem a particularly good fit. This probably accounts for the popularity of detective-based games, as well horror and thriller stories with mystery-style plots. For instance, Sam Barlow's *Her Story* (2015) puts the player in the position of a police investigator trying to piece together the story behind the disappearance of a man. Set in 1994, the player is presented with an old-style computer desktop, from which they can access various folders including a searchable database of police interviews with the missing man's wife, played by Viva Seifert. Thanks to its non-linear mechanics and lack of a distinct authorial voice, the approach very successfully reinvents the detective story for an interactive medium.

As we've seen, other games wear their influences much more explicitly. As James Newman has observed, games are a highly 'intertextual medium', meaning that they constantly remediate iconography, themes and ideas from other media. A horror game like *The Quarry* (2022) is clearly rooted in the teen-based slasher and supernatural movies that began with the likes of *Friday the 13th* and *Halloween* back in the 1970s. *The Excavation of Hob's Barrow* feels like it has a wide range of folkloric influences, including ones which are literary and televisual as well as filmic, but it also draws real world inspiration from Hob Hurst's House, a Bronze Age barrow in Derbyshire.[10] As we've seen, these influences can reach into gameplay as much as the audiovisual elements the player encounters as they journey through the virtual space.

Another challenge for larger contemporary games lies in the decision to include different kinds of 'technical' genre within a single game title. For instance, a single player mode following a fairly linear plot might be used to introduce the game to a wider audience, with the idea that the ongoing version of the game will be primarily multiplayer in nature. This means that ultimately the single player

---

10 What Is Folk Horror, Really? An Interview with Leading Horror Devs (escapistmagazine.com).

mode must satisfy players by providing a story that's resolved, while at the same time leaving enough threads dangling to continue the story into multiplayer mode, in which narrative components tend necessarily to be more exploratory and embedded in worldbuilding.

There are other factors to consider too. Games are ritualistic activities. Players generally expect to operate controllers in specific ways to achieve their intended outcome in the game, perhaps pressing the trigger button to fire or manipulating the left joystick to move and the right to control the camera. As I discussed in the preceding chapter, these configurations can change from game to game, which is why tutorial elements exist to teach a new set of rituals. Once we've learnt the controller combinations, repeated usage means we become faster and faster. Learning the rituals of a new game is part of the challenge but also the pleasure of the experience.

Genre, too, is similarly ritualised, which might also go some way to explaining why most games fall into some pre-existing genre. From the way the game is presented to us, either through marketing, reviews, articles, the box or menu iconography, and the way the game frames itself, we'll likely approach the game with some understanding of its language. We know the codes and conventions of particular genres and either expect them to be fulfilled or subverted as appropriate. We know, too, that games necessarily interpret genres in their own ways, consistent with a wider syntax developed by video games over six decades. In the next chapter, I'll explore this storytelling grammar in more detail – and as our discussion of genre showed us, it's all a question of perspective.

6.

THE GRAMMAR OF GAMES

For a novella written some ninety years ago, Stanley G Weinbaum's *Pygmalion's Spectacles* is extraordinary. It relates the story of Dan Burke, a man who encounters a mysterious scientist character called Ludwig while out walking in New York. Ludwig entices our hero back to his hotel room, where he proceeds to demonstrate a new piece of technology he has been working on: a Virtual Reality headset. Ludwig convinces Dan to put on the headset and enter the immersive world created by the technology. In the course of his experience, the Dan falls in love with a wholly convincing young woman he encounters in the imaginary realm. As he knows he must, our hero eventually takes off the headset and returns to the real world. When he tries to find Ludwig a second time it's without success. He can never see the woman he loves again.

Weinbaum describes with gobsmacking accuracy something very close to a contemporary VR experience. From the description of the headset to the peculiar dissonance the VR user feels between the audiovisual world surrounding him and the physical world of the hotel room, Weinbaum's predictive powers are uncanny. In an age long before the digital, it is really only the specifics of the technology

Weinbaum describes that jars, rooted as it is in an extrapolation of chemical photography. Otherwise, the mechanics of VR are brilliantly anticipated, its profound effect upon the story's hero superbly wrought. Somehow, Weinbaum understands the language of a medium that hadn't been invented.

VR is just one instance of digital storytelling for which a new grammar is required. The spread of home computing technology and subsequently mobile technology and connectivity constantly requires users to learn new storytelling techniques. Specific video game platforms need players to interact in specific ways, while genres of game are constantly evolving their own grammar. With notable, important exceptions – some of which I've already discussed – sequential media remain largely unchanged. On the whole, novels, films, television programmes, radio plays and theatre plays are consumed through time, from beginning to end. We know there are exceptions, and digitality has increasingly transformed how we consume some stories. But the dominant mode is from start to finish, even if the story's creator chooses to tell the story out of sequence.

As I explored in the preceding chapter, perspective is integral to discussions of genre. Indeed, franchises are often associated with a particular perspective, such as *Halo*'s first-person shooter viewpoint, to the extent that fans can become apprehensive when a franchise spreads into a new genre, as was the case with *Halo Wars*, a real-time strategy game released in 2009. Similarly, some gamers will have expectations regarding perspective when a beloved franchise transfers to the game medium. This was the case with MachineGames' *Indiana Jones and the Great Circle* (2024), which during gameplay employs a first-person perspective rather than the third person some fans desired, since they wanted to see themselves fully controlling the iconic hero of the title.

The different modes available to game storytellers have a huge impact on the viewpoint of the player-character, since this is how the story is understood. Most novels and short stories are told from a first-person perspective, in which events are perceived from a specific character's viewpoint, or a third person, omniscient point of view, the so-called 'Voice of God' who knows and relates everything. The second person perspective – 'You did this,' or 'You went here,' is much less common in conventional forms of prose. Jay McInerney's 1984 novel *Bright Lights, Big City* is a notable example, and uses the approach to tell the story of a young writer caught between his respectable daytime life as a fact checker and his debauched, drug-addled nightlife.

The literary theorist Gerard Genette – he of the 'paratext' I talked about in Chapter 3 – also coined the idea of 'focalisation' to describe the perspective through which the story is presented, and the restrictions inherent in this. Genette identifies internal focalisation to describe stories that emphasize an individual's inner thoughts and feelings, external focalisation for stories driven by actions, behaviours and settings, and zero focalisation to describe the omniscient, God-like variety mentioned above, in which there are no restrictions. Arguably different genres lend themselves to different kinds of focalisation – a gumshoe thriller of the kind written by Raymond Chandler might be much more interested in external action than a more literary novel.

If we extend the conceit from prose to other kinds of storytelling, we might similarly make the case that a medium like radio is better at psychological insight than visual media, because of its ability to centre the protagonist experience with the listener. Movies and television shows will often portray events from the perspective of one or two protagonists, though the extent to which actual Point-of-View (POV) shots are employed are liable to be limited, depending on the intention of the storytellers.[1] In fact, in terms of film and television language, it would be difficult to differentiate a first perspective from a second perspective, since both could plausibly use POV.

In game terms, second person is a staple approach of the Infocom-style text adventures discussed in Chapter 2, again echoing the mode used by their close cousin Choose Your Own Adventure books. More broadly, games and Interactive Fiction necessarily position the user as 'You', in the sense that 'You' must participate in the story to advance it. It's the precise nature of that interaction which dictates the extent to which a participant feels immersed in the world of the game or IF story, whether it's something that drives the plot or which is located much more at the character level.

Gaming technology, game engines and genre considerations offer opportunities but also place constraints on the kind of games that can be made, the kind of stories that can be told and the worlds that can be built. A game that works brilliantly on a console won't necessarily translate to mobile phone. Strategy games like the hugely successful *Total War* (2001-) series set in different historical epochs during different campaigns are designed for personal computers rather than consoles. If we talk about a grammar of games, therefore, it's one that must accommodate diverse dialects attuned to the strengths of specific gaming platforms, software and genre. A player's perspective, their place in the action, will necessarily be determined by all of these interrelating factors.

Cut scenes – often described as Full-Motion Video (FMV) sequences or cinematics – are a primary tool of the video game storyteller. Historically they have been non-interactive, akin to mini films, often employing similar techniques of composition and editing to tell a

---

1 There are obvious exceptions such as ensemble pieces like *Magnolia* (1999) and *Pulp Fiction* (1994), as well as genres like soap opera.

crucial part of the game's story. Cut scenes have a multitude of uses. They can be employed to set the scene or establish worldbuilding fundamentals, as well as advancing the plot and supplying character development. They're also frequently used to establish objectives for players and reward them when these objectives are fulfilled, but also to introduce new devices for the player to utilise in gameplay, or new environments for them to explore.

A cut scene following a battle with a mighty foe – a boss at the end of the level – might show the creature collapsing and dying, as in the elegiac Japanese game *Shadow of the Colossus* (2005). Alternatively, the player might be rewarded with the destruction of an important enemy surveillance site, as in multiple stealth-based war and espionage games like the *Sniper Elite* (2005-) or *Splinter Cell* (2002-2013) franchises. A longer cut scene might begin by rewarding the player but swiftly move on to setting their next series of objectives.

As with other storytelling elements, cut scenes can be deployed in various contexts depending on the particular structure of the game in question. However, the expense, time and effort involved in creating cut scenes means that they're often concerned with delivering exposition vital to the player's understanding of the story, information that's too important to risk being lost if it's communicated through other storytelling mechanisms or if it can't be guaranteed the player will even encounter them. For this reason, cut scenes are often tasked with the heavy-lifting of story and worldbuilding, constituting the spine of the so-called 'Critical Path' or 'Golden Path' of the game that the player must traverse.

Writing for the online magazine *A Critical Hit!*, Kate Willaert identifies *The Sumerian Game* as not only the first narrative game, but also the first game to feature an unskippable cut scene.[2] *The Sumerian Game* was created by a schoolteacher, Mabel Addis, in 1964 – arguably making her the first game writer – and is a text-based resource management game designed to teach basic economic theory. The cut scene elements were added when Addis revised the game in 1966, and consisted of taped audio lectures using slide projections in which Addis explained new concepts that had been introduced in the preceding gameplay sequence.[3] Another, less sophisticated example of an early cut scene is arguably the sequence in *Pac-Man* (1980) which follows successful completion of a series of mazes. In this brief interlude, a ghost chases after the titular hero from one side of the screen to another, only for the ghost to then be chased by an outsized version of Pac-Man back the other way.

Cut scenes have lots of obvious advantages. In their most conventional, non-interactive form they are akin to mini movies and obey the same rules of composition and cutting. The director of such a sequence can therefore control what the player is seeing and hearing during this sequence. This means that essential information about the world of the game, about the plot, the characters and what's required of the player can be delivered without having to worry about the player missing anything. While many players prefer to skip such sequences no matter how artfully they've been implemented, lots of players enjoy watching these scenes so they can learn more about the world they're inhabiting.

Lengthy cut scenes are most readily associated with the work of Hideo Kojima. His long running *Metal Gear* (1987-2023) series of stealth games is renowned for using exceptionally long cut scenes to deliver its complex plot. More recently, Kojima's open world action

---

2 The Sumerian Game: The Most Important Video Game You've Never Heard Of – A Critical Hit! (acriticalhit.com)
3 Ibid.

game *Death Stranding* (2019) also featured extended cut sequences featuring a stellar cast of actors led by Norman Reedus. Some players and critics relish this approach but for others extended portions of non-interactivity feel contrary to the spirit of video games, at odds with a medium which should be first and foremost participatory in nature.

To this end, there exist many different kinds of interactive sequences. The names given to such sequences can differ from studio to studio, their grammar and the means of their implementation jealously guarded. This means that certain studios possess a distinctive authorial approach to how they conceive of and execute interactive sequences, a vocabulary that might extend across multiple titles. These in turn often speak to a distinctive aesthetic and to specific processes and pipelines used to bring this aesthetic to life. The nature of a game's mechanics but also its look and feel often relate to the specifics of the game engine used to execute it. Nevertheless, when a game's approach is critically and commercially successful, other studios will look to see how and why it worked, borrowing ideas and interpreting the creative ambition and mechanics to their own ends.

For instance, Santa Monica-based Naughty Dog pioneered its approach to interactive storytelling with its hugely popular *Uncharted* games, and then extended and evolved its methods with the apocalyptic fantasy franchise *The Last of Us*. Often this takes the form of scenarios in which the game will not progress unless the player has interacted in a specific way. *Uncharted 4: A Thief's End* (2016) begins with an exhilarating boat chase in which the main character Nathan Drake must fight off attackers and then take control of the boat itself. When another boat crashes into your boat, Nathan is sent hurtling into the water. We then find ourselves in a flashback sequence to Nathan's Catholic school where he's being scolded in a cut scene by one of the nuns. After the nun leaves, young Nathan sees a signal from elder brother Sam.

In order to rendezvous with Sam, the player needs to climb out of the window and navigate along the rooftops. Here we see another good example of where the terminology used to describe games can become confusing. Throughout Nathan's journey across the rooftops, the player can choose to go the wrong direction, eliciting responses from Nathan like 'No, not that way.' In this sense, then, gameplay is allowing for non-linearity. But in plot terms, the game requires that you guide Nathan in a very particular way through the section. When you climb back into the building, you'll need to hide in order to eavesdrop on the nun talking to her male colleague about you. Again, it's possible to not hide, triggering a short cinematic in which the nun catches you and leads you away by the ear, but you'll immediately be placed back at the beginning of the eavesdropping section. The expectation is that you'll carry out the required set of actions in order to progress. So non-linearity is present at a granular level, but it doesn't mean that the story itself is necessarily non-linear at this point.

In a similar vein, the more recent *God of War* games expertly integrate varieties of in-game cinematic into the wider experience, seamlessly moving between such sequences and gameplay. The beginning of *God of War* (2018) puts the player in the role of the mythical warrior Kratos and requires you to cut down a tree which you must then tow down the river to the location of your cabin. You soon discover the chopped log will form part of a pyre for your recently deceased wife. The events are largely linear, but only unfold as you accomplish specific actions. Giving you this agency fuses you with the character of Kratos and also his son Atreus, helping to implicate you in their grief and thereby bond with the duo.

Other, stylized techniques are available and often used as scene setting devices. *The Legend of Zelda: The Minish Cap* (2005) for the GameBoy Advance includes an opening sequence that sets up the story of the world using stained glass window images. The approach quickly and effectively establishes the game's backstory in a manner in keeping with the style of the game. The *Witcher 3: Wild Hunt* (2015) meanwhile uses hand-drawn imagery to provide a prologue to the game, though the game's cut scenes and in-game cinematics are very sophisticated. In a similar vein, the *Call of Duty* games use motion-graphic sequences to brief players on missions, in addition to premium cinematics. From a production standpoint, such techniques are much more flexible than cut scenes requiring performance capture, since they tend to be stylized and driven by audio and feature limited animation, if any. If elements of game design change, then it's far easier to change motion-graphic sequences than expensive cut scenes.

Aside from cinematics, venturing through video game space, whether it's a side-scroller or more modern games exploiting the Z-axis, means exploring fictional worlds. These are the milieu that we walk, hop, swim, drive or fly through. The design of these environments and their ability to convince us they are genuine play a central role in immersing us in the game, no matter how fantastical the realm in question actually is. Environmental storytelling surrounds us, beckoning us ever onward, providing clues or raising questions that as players we want to answer.

US academic Henry Jenkins sought to outline a variety of different approaches to video game storytelling in a useful essay on 'Narrative Architecture', published in 2004.[4] His categories include 'Embedded Narrative', which describes what's more familiarly known as

---

4 Jenkins, Henry (2004) 'Game Design as Narrative Architecture' in Wardrip-Fruin, Noah and Harrigan, Pat (eds) (2004) *First Person: New Media As Story, Performance and Game.* London: The MIT Press.

'Environmental Storytelling'. In this approach, writers and narrative designers will work with artists to construct explorable environments which tell the player something about the world around them. This might take the form of, for instance, an ancient, broken-down temple or an abandoned village in a contemporary warzone.

To this end, game writers and narrative designers work closely with colleagues in environmental art to populate these realms with elements which help articulate the worldbuilding of the game in such a way that it equips the player with a sense of place. Environmental storytelling builds on the context provided by level design, helping to establish the history and context of the world. In terms of the built environment, this means establishing the purpose of the architecture we're traversing, whether it's a Siberian base in *TimeSplitters 2* (2002) or an eighteenth century watermill in an idyllic, rural location in A *Plague Tale: Innocence* (2019). Often the art team will be inspired by real world locations, even if it's heavily fictionalised. For example, it makes sense that an enemy base might be located on the site of a much older building or groups of buildings, since historically it was a good defensive position.

Ideally the game's story will be largely locked before environmental art engages fully with worldbuilding, though inevitably this isn't always possible. In the case of *Blood and Truth*, for instance, the table in the warehouse in which the player-character Ryan Marks is interrogated by CIA Agent Carson is festooned with graffiti. In earlier versions of the narrative this table was in a different location and featured a piece of graffiti declaring one character's love for another. In the final version of the story, these characters had become brother and sister so the graffiti was no longer relevant and had to be removed (otherwise we'd be telling a *very* different kind of story).

While making our way through these environments, we're liable to be encouraged to pick up objects along the route. From Sonic the Hedgehog's obsession with golden rings to the treasure Harry collects in *Pitfall* (1982), collection has been the primary aim of many games throughout the evolution of the medium. Indeed, acquiring such objects is often the main objective of the player and for game designers the chief method of controlling the player's progression through the game. Unless you've acquired all the diamonds in *Boulderdash* (1984), for instance, you won't be allowed to move to the next level. When we're talking explicitly about 'collectibles', though, we might be talking about something far more sophisticated.

Collectibles are generally optional objects that a player can choose to acquire. While ideally these objects are consistent with the established worldbuilding of the game, they don't necessarily need to be involved in storytelling per se. For some completist players, however, acquiring all of the collectibles may be an additional goal on top of finishing the level and ultimately completing the game. Collecting, too, is a broad description for the actual interactive action involved in acquiring the object – for instance, while in some games you might simply pass through an object to collect it, in others you might need to shoot or smash the object for it to become one of your possessions.

Other kinds of collectible are more obviously connected to storytelling or worldbuilding. A prime example are collectible documents, which can take many forms depending on the wider fictional context, including letters, diary entries, memoranda and even poetry and songs. Such documents can serve a range of purposes, some of which may be story or world-focussed, and others of which may be more concerned with gameplay. Some documents may be standalone, while others may be linked, building up their own mini-story once they're all brought together.

For example, *Sniper Elite 4* (Rebellion 2017) is a World War Two game set during the Italian campaign in 1943 in a series of fictionalized locations. While the game features a main narrative strand told through a limited number of cut scenes, the story is enlarged by a complex ecology of collectible documents dotted throughout each of the environments. 'Last Letters' are a category of such documents which can only be accessed once the player has frisked the body of a dead enemy. Inspired by the real-life phenomenon of soldiers writing letters to their loved ones in the event of their deaths, Last Letters are intended to give an insight into the character of the deceased individual and the wider context of the war, or at least this fictional version of the war.

I designed and wrote these letters to elicit particular emotional responses from the player. Many will make the player feel validated in killing the individual, since the letter in question reveals they were enthusiastic proponents of Nazism and its wider aims. Other Last Letters might reveal that the deceased individual was a young conscript, ripped from his family, scared and missing home. A subsequent YouTube tribute to the letters created by fans frames them as though they're real (complete with melancholic soundtrack), with an array of commentators articulating their varied emotional responses.[5]

Often these documents speak to the location in which the particular NPC is located, and might even refer to specific elements in the environment designed to reinforce the story outlined in the documents. For instance, in one mission in *Sniper Elite 4*, the player can follow a bread-crumb trail of connected documents that lead to the catacombs beneath the Monastery. Here the player will find abandoned children's toys and food, along with documentation that

---

5 Sniper Elite 4 | Last Letters Home (youtube.com)

confirms the Abbot of the Monastery was helping children escape from the Fascists. Importantly, the toys and food were pre-existing art resources which could be re-used in this context to add an additional environmental storytelling element to the narrative communicated by the documentation.

While most documents featured in the game are optional to collect, some are integrated into the main narrative of the story – the aforementioned 'Golden Path' – meaning the player must locate and retrieve them to progress beyond a specific point. These include a letter written by the leader of the Partisans, which is located in a café in the fictional town of Bitanti, the site of a battle between the resistance, the Nazis and their Fascist allies. Uniquely for the game, this particular document is voiced by the character in question, the audio serving to emphasize its importance. In addition, the player is sometimes required to seek out and retrieve various kinds of intel, including blueprints and, in the follow up sequel DLC (Downloadable Content) missions set in Germany itself, scientific formulas connected to the Nazis' atomic programme.

Frequently there's a puzzle element involved in acquiring collectibles, even if the primary mechanic of the game is, for instance, action or shooting-based. In the *Uncharted* series, as well as exploring and fighting enemies, the player must also solve a variety of puzzles to uncover collectible items, including crucial documents. More broadly, collectible documents act as clues in many different games, including the *Tomb Raider* franchise. Retrieving these documents can be part of the main story line or contained within side quests, depending on their relevance to the main plot, or whether they're more about expanding the game's worldbuilding.

Elements which exist within the fiction of the world and can be heard, seen or otherwise experienced by the characters within the story can be understood as 'diegetic', a term borrowed from film and television studies. Everything from the broader environment to interactable objects, dialogue and characters themselves can be understood as diegetic. Other elements are 'non-diegetic', existing outside of the fictional framework of the story and assisting the player in their emotional understanding of the game or their progression through it. For instance, music emanating from a radio which a character can hear is diegetic, whereas music on the game's soundtrack designed to influence how the player feels about the game is non-diegetic.

Sometimes elements of game grammar can fall into either of these categories or both. Many games feature a User-Interface (UI), an overlay providing critical information related to gameplay. UI can provide all manner of context related to gameplay but also narrative. This might include the amount of ammunition the players have left or important stats related to their health or strength. The multiplicity of ways in which UI can be deployed means that it can play a crucial role in developing the story and in worldbuilding. Many combat-themed games feature a Heads Up Display (HUD) giving vital information to the player but which we assume is also visible to the player-character, and so can be understood as diegetic. Other UI elements allowing the player to configure how they interact with the game, such as controller options, sound levels or visual brightness, should be viewed as non-diegetic.

A key example to talk about here is maps. Since many games are exploratory, maps can be critical for locating a player spatially within an environment. A map might help situate the player and enable them to more effectively navigate the environment, as in the *Grand Theft Auto* games. Of course, it's entirely possible to find a map as a collectible and use this as a navigational tool in the same way you'd use a map in real life, as in *Wolfenstein – The New Order* (2014). The difference is that a map that's part of the UI design can be dynamic, specifically locating the player in the world of the game, akin to how GPS works on mobile phones.[6]

Different kinds of gaming technology necessitate different storytelling approaches. Again, perspective tends to be at the forefront of this discussion. As a medium, VR doesn't lend itself to cut scenes in a way comparable to more conventional, flat-screened games. VR games necessarily require a consistent Point-Of-View or otherwise risk not only disrupting the immersion of the player but also undermining the player's comfort (motion-sickness is a perennial problem for VR users). As a result, the editing and compositional techniques associated with cut scenes, themselves borrowed from sequential media like cinema and television, aren't available to VR storytellers in the way we find in other kinds of game.

There are ways of fudging this problem. The science fiction shooter *Farpoint* (2017) begins with a sequence in which two astronauts are presented as talking on a 2D plane in a fashion familiar from lots of real broadcasts. The 2D plane gradually becomes bigger, with the camera's POV being forcibly 'moved' by one of the astronauts to show a view through a portal. The POV then transforms to show the interior of a cockpit which builds around the player to become fully encompassing. The player has been elegantly relocated without ruining their sense of immersion.

The *Farpoint* example happens at the beginning of the game. With the right level of creativity, it's possible to achieve a comparably seamless transition in the midst of gameplay. *Resident Evil 4*'s VR mode includes a sequence in which the player comes across an old video cassette. Inserting the cassette into a video player causes the perspective to shift to that of the camera operator so that the player

---

6 In *The Tough Guide to Fantasyland* (1996), famed novelist Diane Wynne Jones observes that arcane maps in fantasy books are always unerringly accurate, which is not at all the case with arcane maps in real life.

is suddenly inhabiting the terrifying flashback sequence and learns more about prior events. The technique is a clever way of maintaining immersion while providing important exposition.

The cinematic and televisual technique of cutting between different action sequences is clearly not viable in the context of a consistent POV. In *Blood and Truth*, we got around this problem by having the player stumble across a security office containing a bank of CCTV screens. The player is tasked with tracking down the character Keach so they can interrogate them. Pushing buttons on the controls allows the player to switch camera perspective to follow Keach's movements through the hotel. The player-character's own voice reinforces the correct decisions of the player.

Scene changes are also challenging for VR. On *Blood and Truth* we faded to black as a means to manage the transition from one scene to another so as not to disrupt the player's engagement but also a means of loading in a new location. Since entering and exiting doors is a major component of *Blood and Truth*'s gameplay, it's possible to imagine using this in a less literal way, akin to *Resident Evil*'s time jump with the video camera. For instance, the player could open a door and find themselves in the midst of their twenty-first birthday party, having flashed back in time. As with the *Resident Evil* example, this would be a consistent, immersive and imaginative way of supplying exposition through action.

Without the ability to cut, other possibilities present themselves. Some VR games utilise an on-the-rails technique, similar to the approach used by ghost trains at funfairs where the player's locomotion forwards is fixed and obstacles or other elements spring up. In *Blood and Truth* this is used in a fashion redolent of the arcade and console classic *Time Crisis* (1995), in which the player has to shoot the baddies as they pop up. It's possible to imagine a more narrative-inflected sequence, however, akin to the famous *Goodfellas* (1990) scene in which Ray Liotta's Henry Hill character takes his fiancé to a restaurant. The sequence is shot as one extended tracking shot, following Henry and his partner's path through the kitchen and to a prominent table, encountering other characters along the way. An equivalent VR sequence would constitute an immersive and engaging way of conveying exposition to the player.

The Wolves in the Walls (2018) uses an array of innovative transitional techniques to move the player-character through the story. An adaptation of a story originally written by Neil Gaiman and illustrated by Dave McKean, it places the player in the shoes of a young girl called Lucy, who can hear the wolves in the walls, even though her family can't. Rather than using cuts to transition between environments, the scenery magically transforms around the player, which with the help of sound and music creates a seamless immersive experience that's simultaneously beguiling and often startling. The scene transitions in *The Wolves in the Walls* aptly demonstrate the curious ways in which VR is, in many regards, closer to theatre than film in terms of how it's conceived, produced and experienced.

Despite the limitations imposed by technology and genre, there are a multiplicity of storytelling mechanisms developers can employ. None of these exist in splendid isolation, however, but rather as part of a complex ecology. Some are far easier to implement than others. A cut scene is a costly, logistically challenging and time-consuming affair probably involving performance and motion-capture, whereas in-game documents are easy and flexible to create and execute. Environmental storytelling is crucial for helping the player to inhabit the fictive world the development team have conjured up. The game's soundscape is another vital way of providing storytelling and worldbuilding, and doesn't necessarily require visual referents to succeed – for instance, the fictional radio stations in the later

Grand Theft Auto games and *Just Cause 3* (2015) provide hilarious worldbuilding context.

As we've seen, game storytelling is very often smoke and mirrors, intended to fool the player into believing they have agency when this isn't necessarily the case. As with any magic act, a big ingredient in the success of this is perspective. Who that perspective belongs to and who we encounter along the way are critical components in the game storytelling mix. As with so many other aspects of video games, many of the established storytelling rules around character still apply but many others are thrown into flux. In the next chapter, I'll explore how games give us fictional characters to interact with – by making us fictional too.

7.

CHARACTER DEVELOPMENT

It's October 2004. I'm at the Proud Gallery in London's Camden Town with a bunch of smart and savvy undergrads from the innovative[1] new Game Cultures course at London South Bank University. We're here to see an exhibition called *Alter Ego*, put together by photo-journalist Robbie Cooper. Its purpose is to explore the relationship between players and their online personae. To this end, Cooper has curated an exhibition of thirty players' avatars taken from MMORPGs (Massively Multiplayer Online Role-Playing Games), juxtaposed with photographic portraits of their actual selves and short essays in which they talk about this relationship. It's another vivid example of the ways in which the real and virtual worlds intersect.

Cooper was inspired to create the exhibition after talking to a divorced CEO. The man revealed that when his marriage ended he'd begun using the online fantasy game *Everquest* (1999) to maintain contact with his children. While the actual interactions were pretty banal, they afforded him a crucial way of maintaining contact.[2]

---

1 I can say this with confidence as I'm the one that set it up.
2 Alter Ego: Portraits of Gamers Next to Their Avatars – The Marginalian (themarginalian.org)

Cooper was sufficiently intrigued by the nature of this connection between the real and virtual worlds, as expressed through people's avatars, to put together the exhibition and a subsequent book, with digital cultures writer Julian Dibbell providing the foreword and Tracy Spaight interviewing the participants.

Broadly speaking, the players they talked to divided into two distinct categories. Some wanted to recreate a version of their real life self in the virtual realm. Others were clearly more interested in the power of the virtual to let them role play, to perform a different identity – or perhaps a part of their identity they have to keep hidden or in check. In an article about the London exhibition for BBC Online, journalist Jo Twist talked about a participant named Kelly, who considered herself shy and insecure in real life but wanted to experiment with a more outgoing personality in *Everquest*.[3] Chalmaine, another participant, is photographed with her two small children, while her avatar shows a character called Jova Song, a slim young woman wearing hardly any clothes. Elsewhere, another set of images depict Jason's real world persona and his virtual version. In the real world Jason has muscular dystrophy – he's wheelchair-bound and breathes with a respirator. In *Star Wars Galaxies* (2003), Jason wears an armour of silver similar to that of the infamous bounty hunter, Boba Fett.

In the midst of all the blasting of alien creatures, robbing of banks and stealing of dragon's treasure, self-expression remains an integral aspect of much online gaming activity. *The Guardian*'s video game editor Keza MacDonald talks about this at length in the documentary myself and producer Alex Mansfield made for BBC Radio Four about the Metaverse.[4] MacDonald, a long-time player of

---

3 BBC NEWS | Technology | Virtual gamers reveal themselves (news.bbc.co.uk)
4 Archive on 4 - The Origins of The Metaverse - BBC Sounds (bbc.co.uk/sounds)

games, recounts how she was able to express herself as a young gay woman in virtual environments. This aspect of gaming and virtual realms has a surprising and noble heritage, one that goes back to the very first digital worlds. It's a vital, transgressive component of game storytelling and worldbuilding which is under-discussed, and which I'll return to when I look at worldbuilding in a more focussed way.

As the *Alter Ego* exhibition demonstrates, allowing a player the ability to create their own avatar means they can bring aspects of their own identity to that character. Player identification is seen as a fundamental component of immersion. Having a character that the player designs themselves means they'll feel invested and want to keep returning to the virtual world. Many games encourage players to purchase items which will further strengthen their bond with their character (as well as filling the coffers of the game company). Games like *Fallout 4* (2015), *Starfield* (2023) and *Age of Conan: Unchained* (2008), let players create personalised characters from pre-existing templates. The more advanced character modification systems allow players to adjust the gender of the character, body types, skin colour, size and shape of facial characteristics like lips, eyes, and hair. The approach is redolent of playing with Barbie or GI Joe[5] style characters, changing their clothes and equipment as required.

Avatar-creation also comes with its own specific set of challenges. By definition, such a player-created character lacks the biography we might find in an avatar that's been defined for us. There's none of the sophistication we find in expertly wrought characters like Miles Morales, Ellie from *The Last of Us* or more recent versions of Lara Croft. As a result, the avatar's motivation will be generic, applicable to any version of the character the player can create. In many ways this is the antithesis of what novel-writing and screenwriting guides tell

---

5 *Action Man* as he was known in the UK.

us about creating characters, the need to think through every facet with precision and extraordinary detail. Though as we'll see there are other philosophies of character and story creation which subvert these norms and which are equally important to consider.

There are precedents for such an approach in other media. The academic Farah Mendelsohn identifies Dorothy from L Frank Baum's original novel version of *The Wizard of Oz* as an example of a 'grace'[6], a character whose role is to act as a catalyst. Rather than going on any sort of emotional journey themselves, such a character exists to enable other characters in the story to go on their own emotional journeys. We see the same phenomenon with licensed fiction like tie-in comics and novels, in which writers are tasked with keeping legacy characters intact and putting them back in the creative toy box afterwards. Only the writer's original characters, free from the shackles of the licensor, are allowed their own journeys.

In fact, adaptation and transmedia storytelling often rely on opportunities to play as existing characters we might recognise from other media. In *Indiana Jones and the Great Circle*, for instance, we get to take on the role of Harrison Ford's archaeologist hero, whose mannerisms, attitude and back story we're likely familiar with from the movies.[7] In a similar vein, we can assume the role of Jodie Whittaker's version of the Doctor in the *Doctor Who* game *Edge of Reality* (2021), bringing our existing knowledge of the character from the television show to bear. In these instances, the games benefit from the heavy lifting carried out by the media that's already established

---

6 Mendlesohn, Farah (2008) *Rhetorics of Fantasy*. Connecticut: Wesleyan University Press

7 For a player of a certain vintage, being able to wander around a virtual museum with a virtual version of Denholm Elliott – the late great actor from *Brimstone and Treacle* (1976), *Trading Places* (1983) and *Defence of the Realm* (1986) – is kind of extraordinary.

these characters in the cultural landscape. Our pleasure as players lies in role-playing these characters and bringing to bear our pre-existing knowledge of how they behave.

An alternative technique for certain kinds of multiplayer game is the 'roster' approach, in which the player gets to choose which character they want to play as. In the *Overwatch* (2016, 2023) games the player can select from a range of Heroes, each with their own particular skillset and back story. The equivalent in *League of Legends* (2009-) are Champions, though it's now possible to create your own playable character as well. The appeal of a roster from a development perspective is that this obviates the need for a character creation tool. The danger is that unless the player connects with a particular character that they're less likely to feel emotionally invested in the game. As the *Alter Ego* project demonstrates, the ability to create your own character can lead to a strong level of investment in that character.

What a pre-existing roster of characters provides are the recognisable faces of a game, identifiable and iconic fictional individuals full of cultural and commercial potential. This can be particularly useful for helping to market the product, but can also help with merchandising like action figures or other character-based products like Funko toys. In a commercial sphere more and more driven by broader franchise considerations, specific characters and iconography can be used for other storytelling purposes in comics, animation and other kinds of tie-in material. For instance, the hugely successful animated spin-off *Arcane* (2021-2024) features the characters of Vi and Jinx who originally appeared as Champions in the *League of Legends* game. When game storytellers are creating characters, we are increasingly tasked with thinking about their appeal outside of the game – something I'll return to when we reach the subject of transmedia storytelling.

Avatars fulfil a formal function in video games in which they link together different modes of the game. To this end, the Australian academic Julian Holland-Oliver has described the player avatar as a 'dynamic suture' (2001),[8] an extension of the idea of suturing that film editing borrows from surgery, in which shots are stitched together to create meaning. A dynamic suture refers to the way in which gameplay sequences and cut scenes are stitched together by the moveable player-character, managing the relationship between the two. When Lara Croft steps from a gameplay sequence into a cut scene or vice versa, she is our focal point through which the transition is smoothly managed. The message is clear – gameplay and cut sequence occur in the same fictional world, the same diegetic space.

But as the *Alter Ego* exhibition explored so admirably all those years ago, something else is going on in terms of the complex relationship between players and the characters they control. Our ability to manoeuvre a player-character around an environment, choosing which path to take and how to interact with elements within that world, affects our connection with that character as well as our understanding of that world. Often avatars are discussed in a similar fashion to that of the protagonist, but for game storytellers the ability to control their actions adds another important dimension to how we conceive and build the player-character. Avatars are not just protagonists in the sense we would understand from movies and TV shows – they're something more. As players they fictionalise us, allowing us free passage to another realm.

Which isn't to say that we can't utilise existing theories rooted in sequential storytelling, we just need to be careful how we go about it. In 1949, writer and academic Joseph Campbell published *The Hero*

---

8 From comments made by Holland-Oliver during his presentation 'The Similar Eye: Proxy Life and Public Space in the MMORPG' at the Computer Games and Digital Cultures Conference in Tampere, Finland in 2002.

With a Thousand Faces. It's a book of comparative mythology in which he explores repeating motifs between different hero stories found in world mythology but also religious, spiritual and literary texts. Campbell identified a structure he called the *monomyth*, and outlined the path the central character – the hero – must take. Following a call to adventure, the hero departs the ordinary world and travels into a fantastical domain where he faces all manner of extraordinary challenges, eventually achieving a definitive, substantive victory and then returning to the ordinary world where he can share his good fortune with others.

The Hero With a Thousand Faces has proven hugely influential over the years, most famously on the film-maker and creator of *Star Wars*, George Lucas. A documentary series called *The Power of Myth*, in which journalist Bill Moyers talked to Campbell about his work and ideas, proved an unexpected hit on American television in 1988 and led to a further book of the same name. Screenwriting theorist Chris Vogler took Campbell's ideas and applied them to various movies like *Pulp Fiction* (1994) and *Four Weddings and A Funeral* (1994).[9] Other theorists have rallied against what they see as the limitations of Campbell's approach, seeing it as a kind of straitjacket on creativity.

As with other media, Campbell's structure can be of use for certain kinds of single player video game story, providing as it does a functional framework, though in my experience developers are more likely to view Campbell through the prism of George Lucas, specifically the original 1977 *Star Wars* movie. As the PhD researcher Mary Ann Buckles discovered in her attempt to apply Vladimir Propp – another structuralist – such formulae have limited applicability. Arguably Jeff Gomez's 'Collective Journey', an approach which

---

9 Vogler, Chris (2020) *The Writer's Journey: Mythic Structure for Writers*. California: Michael Wiese Productions

foregrounds collaborative and participatory techniques rooted in the networked, digital era, is of more use for understanding cooperative and multiplayer gameplay modes.[10]

Reconciling interactivity and agency in relation to existing storytelling paradigms is the big challenge. Screenwriting guru Robert McKee uses the relative activity or passivity of the protagonist to differentiate types of story. According to McKee, the active single protagonist is a key element of the classical or arch plot favoured by Hollywood, whereas the passive protagonist is more characteristic of the minimalist plots employed by art house cinema. At face value, because a player's avatar is by definition always active within the game environment then we should regard the player-character as the embodiment of the protagonist. As we've seen, though, agency is to some extent in the eye of the beholder – McKee's approach, as with others, would therefore need to be carefully applied to the game context.

Game storytellers employ all manner of techniques to align the player's journey with their character. A common approach is to begin with the player-character suffering from severe memory loss. This makes a lot of sense, since when the player picks up the controls to a new game they won't necessarily understand anything about the setting, story or indeed how they're expected to navigate through the world of the game. It makes sense to align the player with the avatar by making them equally unaware of the realm they're about to enter, and the adventure they're about to undertake.

There are many highly inventive examples of this technique in action. Often, the player-character's amnesia will form a central component of their ultimate goal. In *Planescape: Torment* (1999), the player controls The Nameless One, an immortal character who wakes

---

10 Collective Journey (blog.collectivejourney.com)

up on a mortuary slab. In the course of the game, set in a *Dungeons and Dragons* world consisting of several planes of existence, he must discover why he died and why he's immortal. Similarly in the game *XIII* (2003), which emulates the graphical storytelling approach of the Belgian comic it's based on, the player must control a secret agent trying to uncover his own identity.

A key element player-characters and protagonists share is in the need to accomplish goals. For influential theatre practitioner and theorist Antonin Stanislavski a character's goal in terms of a scene can be understood as their 'objective', whereas their ultimate goal through the course of the story is their 'super-objective'.[11] Player-characters are similarly defined by objectives within gameplay. To a greater or lesser extent these are determined by gameplay, and can range from mundane – collect foodstuff to feed yourself – to much more elaborate, such as defeating the dragon guarding the treasure. Objectives might be split into sub-objectives, and might transform as the mission progresses. The skill of the game writer and narrative designer lies in their ability to 'wrap' these objectives in ways which fit with the established fiction of the world, reinforcing or extending lore.

As with other media, game storytellers have different approaches to character creation. Game writer Charlie Webb describes his process in these terms: 'Typically, I enjoy defining characters as contrasts to one another. Figuring out types which might offer compelling conflict and chemistry. It's holistic work, understanding how they fit into the overall world of the story and within the boundaries of whatever collection of named characters they'll be encountering.' Narrative lead Rianna Dearden's approach is very much contingent on context: 'Absolutely depends on the project. Sometimes responding to concept

---

11 Stanislavski, Constantin (2019) *An Actor Prepares.* London: Bloomsbury

art, a theme, something missing in the game. It's very rarely a blank page. So, the first thing is always finding what to respond to!'

As we've seen, attempts to apply established approaches to character from films, novels and theatre plays need to be carefully applied to account for the interactive and participatory nature of games. A main point of divergence between games and other media is around replayability, a key aspect of games. It's a point that the journalist Steven Poole makes in *Trigger Happy* (2000), his seminal book about games, which a number of academics have subsequently explored. As Poole says, imagine a story in which the central character keeps coming back to life, as happens all the time in games when a player makes a mistake. Hamlet's death at the end of the story would lose all resonance if you knew he wasn't actually dead, that he might abruptly leap up again and continue soliloquizing about the nature of existence. 'Good night, sweet prince,' suddenly loses its impact. In a similar vein, and while we're spoiling old stories, the same might be said if Anna Karenina picked herself up from the train track, dusted herself down, and fell into the arms of her lover Vronsky.

To underline the point, we can take examples from sequential media where this rule is consciously broken – think of all the times comic book or soap opera characters have come back from the dead, and in the process lessened the impact of their original demise. Amongst this diverse group of characters we might include Wonder Woman's love interest Steve Trevor who magically came back to life in the 2020 sequel *Wonder Woman 1984, Eastenders*' Dirty Den Watts who survived apparent certain death, and Bobby Ewing turning around in the shower and in the process torpedoing the preceding season's worth of *Dallas* storylines. Arguably these genres have special dispensation in this regard, but even then the death in each case is cheapened by the resurrection of the character.

US academic Henry Jenkins once suggested that games will only have come of age once we can cry at the death of a character.[12] Yet for a death in a story to have the necessary emotional resonance, the character in question needs to stay dead. Poole discusses an oft-cited example of the death of a key character in *Final Fantasy VII* (1997), which is frequently used to indicate that games can indeed have just this emotional effect. But as Poole points out, this particular death occurs during a Full Motion Video sequence – a cut scene – over which the player has no influence. Nothing the player does will affect what happens to this character, so the logic is the same as it is in a movie or book. The character in question is dead and will stay dead. This is precisely why it's emotionally affecting.

The same principle applies to avatars that players have created from scratch and whom they play as – a common feature of MMORPGs. If you invest time, effort and – crucially – emotional engagement in a character, then that character's demise will be upsetting, precisely because there's no way of restoring them. It's called 'permadeath' because in this context there's no reset button. But as the game developer Dean Hall argues in relation to the multiplayer zombie survival game *DayZ* (2018-), this is part of the appeal of the game – if you don't get things right your cherished character will be gone forever. Permadeath is very definitely the exception that proves Poole's rule.

Different games have different approaches to this problem. For instance, *Helldivers 2* (2024) leans into the vulnerable nature of player-characters as part of its overall satirical schtick. Though the game isn't an official adaptation or extension of Paul Verhoeven's 1992 movie *Starship Troopers*, the influences are very near the surface. For

---

12 Jenkins, Henry (2007) *The Wow Climax: Tracing the Emotional Impact of Popular Culture.* New York: New York University Press

one thing, the game reprises the approach of the propaganda films from the Verhoeven movie to help wrap a very similar premise, in which humans have to attack and destroy giant bug creatures on various alien planets. As part of this approach, the short-lived, expendable nature of player-characters is highlighted, so that when you're inevitably killed you're replaced with an identical-looking but actually different character. Your avatar's inherent disposability fits the sardonic premise like a glove. Unless you're actually good at the game of course.

Aside from the character controlled by the player, contemporary video games will often include various kinds of Non-Player Character (NPCs). Sometimes these characters are equivalent to the extras we might see in the background of movies, although depending on the kind of game the player might have the ability to interact with them. In *Grand Theft Auto V* (2013), for instance, the player will encounter many civilians on the streets, sometimes walking past, sometimes huddling together in conversation with other NPCs, sometimes standing and considering the world around them. While it's eminently possible to ignore these bystanders, it's also possible to go up to them and get in their way so they grumble and change direction or run away. Because it's *GTA*, it's also possible to start a fight and eventually kill the character, although they might fight back or run away, and others might come to their assistance.

Novelist and essayist EM Forster identified characters which do not develop as 'flat characters', as opposed to 'round characters' which are complex and three-dimensional, and go on emotional journeys. Non-playable characters like the *GTA* bystanders are flat in the same way that minor characters in a film or novel might be considered flat. This doesn't mean they're not memorable, funny or otherwise engaging. Indeed, part of the pleasure of the *GTA* games is the sense of a living world engendered by these characters.

This is just one kind of NPC, though. Others include ones that the player might converse with, such as the quest-givers we might find in *The Witcher 3* or *Baldur's Gate 3*. The satirical *Fallout* games include many artfully written, characterful quest-givers. To this end, game writers and narrative designers will go to a lot of effort to ensure that even minor characters the player encounters don't feel superficial. Game writer David Freeman's concept of 'emotioneering' outlines strategies for imbuing such characters with depth.[13]

Depending on the design philosophy of the particular game, other examples will deliberately stop the player from engaging with civilians. Sometimes this is done by simply omitting civilians from the environment, with some games choosing to provide a fictional framing as to why this is the case. In *Sniper Elite 4*, for instance, we wanted to suggest that areas had been abandoned before the arrival of the player character, as indicated by overturned tables and half-eaten meals, as well as by the many collectible documents detailing the lives of the characters that the player could discover in the environment.

Another approach is to suggest that an environment is busy at the beginning of the game in a cut scene, but that subsequent events mean the location has had to be evacuated. For instance, early in Rocksteady's *Batman: Arkham Knight* (2015), the game gives us a diner crowded with well-realised characters which is then subject to a nightmarish chemical attack by the villain Scarecrow. We subsequently see the city being evacuated, with busloads of civilians being ferried out. This means that the player can enjoy tackling anyone they encounter in the streets without worrying that they're innocent bystanders.

Budgetary and technical considerations play a part in this too, and they are key elements which differentiate screenwriting for games

---

13 Freeman, David (2003) *Creating Emotion in Games*. London: New Riders

from screenwriting for other kinds of visual media like television and film. A game like *Assassin's Creed Syndicate* (2016) utilises 'crowd tech' to allow a player to make their way through an environment in a convincing manner, Ubisoft's 'Bulk System' allowing for the generation of multiple low-resolution characters who react in different ways depending on the player's proximity. This approach is cost effective but also allows for the technical implications of having so many characters on screen at the same time. Similar considerations are true of cut scenes, both in terms of the time and expense involved in building distinct characters but also the impact on frame rate.

Of course, this is nothing new. Historically speaking, the look and behaviour of video game avatars have been determined by creative responses to technical limitations. Pac-Man's distinctive look was supposedly inspired by the craving of its creator, Toru Iwatani, for fast food. The story goes that Iwatani had been struggling with the look of the player's avatar. Having ordered a pizza, he removed the first slice and experienced a moment of epiphany – and so was born the yellow disc with a mouth that would become an instantly recognisable icon of popular culture.[14] Similarly, the plumber Mario (originally called 'Jumpman') was given coloured sleeves to differentiate his arms from the rest of his body as he moved. He wears a hat because they couldn't do hair, and sports a moustache to cover the fact that we can't see his mouth move.[15]

This early history is peppered with all sorts of extraordinary creatures, from the likes of Q-Bert – a short round, orange creature

---

14 The story's almost certainly apocryphal of course – the video game equivalent of Parisian cinema-goers in 1896 fleeing a theatre because they believed a steam train was about to crash through the screen. Almost certainly untrue, but nonetheless an important part of the medium's mythology.
15 According to Iain Lee's beguiling Channel Four documentary about video games from the year 2000, *Thumb Candy* – Thumb Candy - Documentary (youtube.com) – which is still worth a watch.

with a long proboscis but no arms, only legs – to the ostrich-mounted knight in Atari's *Joust* (1982). As the technology changed, game characters became more sophisticated, not only in terms of how they looked but also how they behaved. Characters who'd first appeared in the arcade and eight-bit eras became more nuanced, such as Link from *The Legend of Zelda* (1986). Sequels set in the same universe also helped to extend the range of characters within a franchise, such as the *Mario Bros* games that followed the original *Donkey Kong*. Another colossus appeared in 1991, with the arrival of the first *Sonic the Hedgehog* game for Sega's beloved Genesis/Mega Drive console.

But in other ways diversity has been altogether harder to discern. Like the action movies they sought to imitate, many games featured square-jawed, caucasian, heterosexual men with little in the way of emotional hinterland. The apotheosis of this is the swaggering Duke Nukem, protagonist of multiple games from 1991 onwards, complete with cheesy dialogue. Over time, as the technology evolved and developers' aspiration to create more complex stories also advanced, more nuanced, three-dimensional protagonists emerged. The first *Metal Gear* game, which popularised the stealth genre, appeared in 1987 and featured a character called Solid Snake, inspired by Kurt Russell's Snake Plissen in John Carpenter's 1981 movie *Escape from New York*. Over subsequent instalments, Solid Snake would continue to evolve as an engaging and interesting protagonist. The grizzled, noir hero Max Payne arrived in 2001, complete with *Matrix*-style slow-mo gun play. Max was yet another white male hero but one with flaws and interesting motivations, rooted as he was in the pulp tradition that flows from Marlowe to Tarantino.

The awareness that players might wish to control and engage with other kinds of character was a long time coming. Lara Croft first appeared in 1996's *Tomb Raider*, and though the archaeologist-adventurer schtick was clearly influenced by Indiana Jones and the matinee heroes that influenced him, the character remains an obvious but significant breakthrough. Fascinatingly, the character could have been even more radical – early concept work drew on Swedish rapper Neneh Cherry for inspiration, while she was originally South American, styled as Laura Cruz.[16] With that knowledge it's disappointing that the version that graced those early games featured a Lara with disproportionately oversized breasts and tiny hips, though the character would evolve through later instalments and various reboots into an avatar more rooted in both physical and emotional reality.

For a while Lara seemed to be the only female character in games outside of *Donkey Kong*'s Pauline and the eponymous *Ms. Pac-Man* (1982), a version of Pacman supposedly transformed by the addition of a ribbon.[17] It wasn't perceived that there was a need for any kind of female representation *beyond* Lara. Indeed, early in my game storytelling career I pitched an idea with a female central protagonist and was told by a male exec, with a total absence of irony: 'It's been done, hasn't it?' As academic Helen W Kennedy notes, Lara exists at the nexus point between the idea of games as representation and games as simulation. Lara's simultaneously an objectified sexual figure for heterosexual male players but also a transgressive figure because we get to play as her and experience the events of the game through her eyes.[18] In this way she's another potent example of the ways in which the real and the virtual worlds collide.

---

16 Tomb Raider over the years: How Lara Croft went from schoolboy fantasy to woke action hero | British GQ | British GQ (gq-magazine.co.uk)
17 Fascinatingly, the game actually started life as a modification of *Pac-Man* – a 'mod' – but owing to legal issues ended up as an official entry in the series – How an arcade classic broke all the rules - Polygon
18 Game Studies - Lara Croft: Feminist Icon or Cyberbimbo? On the Limits of Textual Analysis (gamestudies.org)

Intimately connected with issues of diverse representation is the imperative for game storytellers themselves to be more diverse, as well as the industry more widely. To this end, external narrative design consultancies like Montreal-based Sweet Baby provide story development and writing services and can source writers with specific backgrounds to help provide the necessary insights. For instance, Insomniac's *Spider-Man: Miles Morales* (2020) features a central character drawn from the Marvel comics with Puerto Rico heritage, but the existing writing team didn't feel they had the required knowledge to authentically write this character in isolation. Insomniac made the decision to work closely with Sweet Baby on the project. The resulting game was critically lauded for its integrated, dynamic storytelling rooted in genuine experience.[19]

But the need for diverse storytellers is more fundamental still. Beyond issues of diversity and inclusion at the representational level, diverse storytellers mean that the kinds of stories games can tell will be more surprising, more captivating. It's not just in technological terms that innovation is essential for the industry. If the medium is dominated solely by white, heterosexual CIS males like me, the stories we can weave will themselves be limited to specific worldviews and experiences. More than any other medium, games have the capacity to recombine existing elements in new ways. A key part of this reinvention involves new ideas and new perspectives, told through new kinds of character, as well as familiar archetypes.

As with other aspects of storytelling theory drawn from other media, theories about character creation need to be modified not just for the game medium but for the specific project. In some games, it's

---

19 Some gamers fundamentally misunderstand Sweet Baby's role, seeing them as inserting diverse representation unnecessarily into games. On the contrary, they help provide the authenticity that particular kinds of game badly need. They are themselves highly accomplished storytellers and world-builders.

much more the case that you're pulling on a costume and performing as a character who's already been created for you. In other contexts, the player-character might be far less defined, merely a cipher for your actions in the imaginary realm. In some games you have the ability to create a completely fictional persona for yourself, one that's totally distinct from your real world self. Alternatively, you might want to make a version of yourself that's closely aligned to that of the real world. Whether you behave like you do in the real world is another question.

Allowing players the ability to create their own characters enables a feeling of connection and personal involvement but it lessens the authorial control over that character, a decision which has its own profound implications for storytelling. A roster of characters that a player can choose from makes franchise expansion that much easier. The ways in which a player-character is allowed to interact with NPCs is a crucial design consideration, but also an ethical and philosophical choice on the part of the dev team. And just as games change the nature of characters, they also change how we should think about the words that flow from their virtual mouths...

8.
SPEAK EASY

It's 1998. The location is London's South Bank Centre. As I await my hero, I can't help but fidget with nervous excitement. The rest of the auditorium is buzzing with similar, heightened levels of anticipation. The murmuring erupts into rapturous applause as the man we've been waiting for appears. I am delighted to see that he is every bit as tall and gangly as I've come to expect from the numerous televisual and print interviews I've imbibed over the years. Not to mention his own non-fiction writing, in which he talks hilariously about his own life and the creative process. Neither me nor any of his other adoring fans realise that in three years' time the man in question will be dead, at the absurdly young age of forty-nine.

His name is Douglas Adams, famed writer of *The Hitch-Hiker's Guide to the Galaxy* radio series (1978) and its various other manifestations, the comparably surreal Dirk Gently novels and numerous other bits and bobs in various media, including a stint as story editor of *Doctor Who*. He's here to talk about his latest endeavour, the video game *Starship Titanic* (1998), which was first mentioned, albeit fleetingly, in the third *Hitch-Hiker* novel, *Life, the Universe and Everything* (1982). He even shows us some clips of the new game, and we get a flavour of the familiar Adamsian humour, a sort of high-speed collision between Wodehouse and Lewis Carroll by way of Monty Python. Adams is a long-standing early adopter of technology, and is at the forefront of exploring the power and potential of interactive storytelling.

Adams had played the game *Myst* (1993) and this had revived his interest in game design, more particularly what we would now term 'narrative design'. He was struck by how under-populated *Myst* and its sequel *Riven* (1997) were, and wanted to create a game full of interesting characters with which the player could converse using the keyboard. To this end, he worked with developers to create a text-parser dialogue system containing over thirty thousand words. To bring it to life, voice actors such as Monty Python alumni John Cleese and Terry Jones were brought in to record over ten thousand lines of dialogue, amounting to some sixteen hours of material. The script was written by Adams and Michael Bywater, along with Neil Richards.

Starship Titanic is not what you'd call a classic but the approach to dialogue illustrates an important point about games. Historically speaking, to create a sense of an immersive, convincing world populated by engaging characters, video games have required a lot of dialogue. *Hades* (2020), a so-called 'roguelike' featuring a repeating structure in which the player will inevitably keep dying as they try to escape the titular hellish realm, is heavily reliant on its beautifully wrought dialogue to convey a sense of progression. Sprawling open world games like the Western *Red Dead Redemption 2* and science fiction themed *Cyberpunk 2077* also feature vast banks of dialogue.

Video game dialogue takes many distinct forms depending on the context. Most obviously, it's an important facet of cut scenes including dramatic exchanges of the kind we would recognise from more established storytelling media like the theatre, television and film. As I discussed earlier, such scenes are designed to move the plot along while adumbrating character, though they might also be scene-setting, establishing objectives for the player or rewarding the player for a mission successfully completed. The familiar screenwriting rule of 'show don't tell' applies, since ideally the images and action are conveying the bulk of the meaning. Convention suggests that good dialogue is believable and makes the audience engage with characters as well as wanting to find out what happens next.

Exposition is a challenge for writers working in all different kinds of storytelling media. The term refers to the action of rendering important information to the audience to help them understand the setting, plot developments, characterisation or motivation. When dialogue is inelegantly handled or leaden-sounding, it's often described as being 'exposition-heavy'. Video game dialogue is particularly prone to this, since its primary function can often be to describe a task the player must undertake, a set of rules they must abide by or other gameplay conditions that don't lend themselves to naturalistic-sounding dialogue. The genre of game can have a lot of bearing on what's acceptable or not. For instance, the heightened dialogue found in certain high fantasy or science fiction games only works because it is consistent with our expectations of the genre.

Writing for games is different to writing for other media, as Antony Johnston notes: 'First, games as a creative industry is less mature than film or TV, the two other main audio-visual creative media. Cutscene animation has less fidelity than living actors on film, and running dialogue programmatically rarely if ever feels as convincing as in traditional screen media, which can run a simple linear track at 24 frames per second. Second, interactivity rears its head again. Active players are less patient than a passive audience, especially when trying to complete a game task while characters are talking. So brevity, and economy of both dialogue and character, are all paramount. There's little time or appetite for extended soliloquies or even lengthy conversations outside of cutscenes – and often not much within them, depending on the genre and target audience.'

Dialogue in other media is as much about subtext, the undercurrents and motivations powering a character's speech, as it is about text. As in real life, what a character says and what they think aren't necessarily the same thing. Screenwriting theorist Robert McKee talks extensively about the 'gap' between the surface level of the dialogue – what we hear – and the subtextual level. So while exposition-heavy dialogue in which plot points or characterisation is delivered inelegantly can make players wince, believable-sounding dialogue that lacks subtext is similarly problematic because it's only operating on a superficial level. As with other dramatic media, the challenge for game writers is to convey both exposition and subtext in a way which sounds naturalistic, framed by genre expectations and the rules of the established storyworld. But there are other significant factors at play too.

Andy Walsh, a writer who's worked on everything from *Horizon Forbidden West* (2022) to ITV's long running soap opera *Emmerdale*, describes writing dialogue for games in these terms: 'Whilst dialogue in other media is an art of narrative information, in games we often have to work in gameplay information too. The player needs to understand where to go, or how to complete something. They must understand the choice they are making. Good dialogue in games fits into the space the writer has (see narrative design) and manages the difficult art of melding the demands of dialogue in other mediums (comedy, tragedy, connection, plot) with the needs of gameplay (direction, context, gameplay flow).' Making dialogue that's fundamentally functional in nature sound consistent and believable is a chief challenge for the game writer.

Let's look at a couple of examples. For instance, we can see an interesting point of comparison in the *God of War* (2018) and *The*

Last of Us (2013) games. Both were acclaimed for their dialogue and deal with thematically similar issues around parenting. However their approaches to storytelling and the dialogue which emerges are rooted in their distinct fictional worlds. The *God of War* games draw extensively on various world mythologies, most obviously Greek myth but Norse myth too. The language spoken by main character Kratos is necessarily heightened and declamatory in nature, evoking the dramatic traditions of the Greeks. At the same time, Kratos' son Atreus is searching for validation and love from his father, and his uncertain dialogue and impulsive actions in the game support this. We see this early on in the 2018 game when Atreus tries to bring down a wild animal with his bow and is chastised by his father. We feel it all the more because as a player we've been given control of the boy during this sequence. The functional dialogue from both Kratos and Atreus is intended to teach us mechanics, but it's done in a way which is consistent with their characterisation and so feels seamless.

In contrast, *The Last of Us* games – along with the lauded television adaptation produced by HBO – are set in an apocalyptic world in which a particular fungal virus has turned vast swathes of the population into ravening creatures akin to zombies. Because of its near contemporary setting the language employed is believable, but the subtextual level is there to be detected. In the first game the lead character Joel is mourning the loss of his daughter Sarah and his inability to save her, events we see play out at the very beginning of the game. Twenty years later, Joel is tasked with escorting a mysterious young girl called Ellie across the ravaged state to a specific location. Joel's subsequent interactions with Ellie speak to his guilt at the death of Sarah and resistance to commit to a substitute daughter lest events repeat themselves. Joel's terse, abrasive dialogue reflects the necessity of distancing himself emotionally from Ellie. Again, this is as true of the functional in-game dialogue in which the player is cajoled into acting in a certain way or their decisions are reinforced as it is of the cinematic dialogue.[1]

For game writer and narrative director Kim MacAskill, voice is the element that differentiates writing for games from other media. 'I wholly believe that writing dialogue for game characters is different and it has to be,' she says. 'Depending on the game, we risk not being in control of camera angles, character animation and other non-verbal ways (used by TV and film) of showing characterisation. Often, voice is the only thing we have to communicate and nailing voice prints of characters is essential. To clarify, a voice print can both refer to how a character sounds (by voice) and can also mean the blueprint a writer has created to explain how a character will and won't sound. Nailing the voice print isn't just useful for characterisation, it's important for continuity – particularly in cases where a writer may leave and a new writer has to take over. A simple voice print may simply say something along the lines of, 'Kratos will always speak in brief sentences and use powerful word choice but he will never be emotive, jovial or cruel.' In nailing this voice print, not only can a writer consider if their dialogue is true to the character, they can also blind-test it with other devs by handing over a few lines of dialogue and getting devs to "guess who said it".'

As with many other elements of storytelling and worldbuilding, different studios take different approaches to dialogue depending on the nature of the project and the studio in question's culture. Additionally, whether the dialogue is part of a cut scene or in-game audio has a huge impact on how it's captured. Cut scenes often require motion capture to take place, in which the characters' facial and bodily movements are recorded as data (though it's possible to

---

1 Another way in which cinematic and in-game elements are 'sutured' together, recalling Julian Holland-Oliver's point about the avatar being a 'dynamic suture'.

separate facial and body capture, which brings both advantages and challenges). If facial capture is happening then dialogue tends to be recorded at the same time, and for a number of reasons there's little flexibility with this dialogue once the mo-cap session has begun.[2]

This is why it makes sense and is good practice to lock dialogue prior to the motion-capture shoot, given how expensive motion-capture studios and their extremely skilled teams are to hire. Letting performers extemporise around the screenplay can result in more realistic-sounding dialogue but the quid pro quo is that subtext is lost as a new line which sounds better replaces the older line. A way around this is to work with the actors during table reads of the script and through workshopping. This means that dialogue can be shaped around the performer, but that changes can be made which retain the subtextual intent of the original dialogue before locking the script ahead of the shoot.

As game writers Kim MacAskill, Antony Johnston and Andy Walsh attest, writing dialogue for games is different to writing for media like film and television. As with other aspects of storytelling, there are still broader principles we can look to, including around the vexed issue of dialogue creation. For instance, master dramatist David Mamet argues that dialogue arises from what a character wants and stresses the need to emphasize the rhythmic, almost poetic nature of everyday speech.[3] According to Martin Esslin in his book *The Theatre of the Absurd* (1961), playwright Harold Pinter felt that people are in fact terrified of communicating. In its evasiveness and repetition,

---

2 Much more on these processes in Chapter 10.
3 As outlined in Mamet's contributions for *Masterclass*, an online education platform David Mamet Teaches Dramatic Writing | MasterClass | American Buffalo, Glengarry Glen Ross

Pinter's dialogue reflects the horror involved in actually connecting with other human beings.[4]

Beyond cut scenes, in-game dialogue can often sound Pinteresque, precisely because of this need to repeat and reassert objectives or other gameplay-driven imperatives. There are multiple different varieties of in-game dialogue. As a player is moving through an environment, we might hear dialogue that provides information about the world that's being explored, or supplies character development, or indeed both. As I mentioned previously, specific dialogue lines can be activated when a player approaches an object of interest using a 'trigger volume', in other words the player-character's proximity to the specified location. Alternatively, a 'look at' function can be activated when the player encounters a specific object that the narrative design team want called out in the environment.

Within the discipline of game writing, the generation of in-game dialogue can often be viewed as a secondary activity to that of writing cut scenes. Much of it has a functional purpose to serve, helping to guide the player through the environment. For instance, simply hearing enemy guards talking in a stealth game serves to indicate their presence and location. On some projects external screenwriters are used to create cut scene scripts, while the internal team are employed to originate the in-game dialogue that serves to stitch the cut scenes into the wider tapestry of the gameplay.

As well as the narrative team, cut scenes are liable to involve an army of cinematics developers, animators, artists, performers, performance directors, audio developers, producers and motion capture technicians. Cut scenes are high profile, polished and spectacular, and often used in trailers to promote the game. When video game stories are reviewed, these tend to be the elements that

---

4 Esslin, Martin [1961] (2001) *The Theatre of the Absurd.* London: Methuen

critics concentrate upon. In comparison, in-game dialogue is often viewed as forgettable, throwaway material. It's only worthy of critical appraisal or fan comment when it's *bad*.

The irony is that the player will encounter in-game dialogue much more frequently than the kind they experience in cut scenes. Bespoke in-game dialogue will help reinforce the story beats outlined in cut scene elements. This might include reiterating objectives and plot points, but also deepening our relationship with the character we play as. If it's a team or squad of characters, in-game dialogue can help build these relationships in a meaningful way. This also extends to the more systemic kinds of dialogue a player-character and their team might utter in response to situations. Often this latter kind can show character through response to extreme events, as in a battle with a formidable opponent or set of opponents.

This latter category is referred to as 'barks', which can apply to the player-character and their allies but also enemy NPCs the player will encounter. Barks are context-dependent and will be triggered according to specific criteria. In the case of enemy barks, this helps create a sense of dynamism in the world by showing that opposition AI are responding in a way which is logical and immediate. Barks need to be realistic – at least according to the internal logic of the storyworld in question – but their repetitive nature means the game writer will have to take pains to ensure they don't become irritating through over-exposure. Large open world video games will often boast vast 'bark sets' as a means of avoiding repetition but even then it's to some extent unavoidable, since similar events will inevitably occur, triggering the dialogue attached to these events.

For this reason and in a fundamental sense, it's a form of dialogue writing absolutely distinct from most other kinds of dramatic or indeed literary writing, in which as a rule we value memorable lines. Game writers and narrative designers are tasked with thinking up multiple different ways of saying the same thing over and over. In a battle sequence of a war game this might include coming up with multiple different ways of saying 'Grenade!' Systemic dialogue is a challenge to write because it simultaneously needs to convey a specific action the player is undertaking themselves or which is being targeted at the player, but in a way which often needs to be utilised in multiple different locations or scenarios.

Aside from barks, bespoke in-game dialogue can offer up a flexibility for writers distinct from that of cut scenes and cinematics more broadly. In the case of player-character dialogue in a first-person or third-person context, such dialogue is not dependent on the facial capture techniques often found in high end cut scenes, where lip syncing is absolutely vital. Since player-character dialogue in this context – often erroneously described as 'V/O' in game development – is relatively cheap to record, an actor can be brought into the audio studio to record additional or replacement lines. Increasingly 'flappy lip' technology is available to allow in-game characters to match this dialogue, although frequently no visual will be attached. This flexibility is vital because level design inevitably evolves through the course of a project, which in turn can mean that new or different art assets are required.

Placeholder dialogue is often used to ascertain whether a line is working on its own merits, or whether it's being triggered in the correct place. This often takes the form of 'robovoice', computer-generated speech derived from the script. However, since this is frequently as mechanical as it sounds, it doesn't always give a good indication as to whether the line of dialogue is sufficiently naturalistic sounding.

Another approach is to use 'scratch' audio and get members of the dev team to record versions of the lines, though since such performances tend to be highly variable they can also come across as inauthentic and amateurish. To this end, developers are increasingly exploring 'emotional voice synthesisers', Artificial Intelligence systems that can generate more authentic-sounding placeholder speech. At the time of writing, none of these systems are replacements for actual actors. To this end, the only real way of understanding if lines are truly working is to use real performers, though this should only happen once design is locked and unlikely to change.

As with so much of game storytelling, context is king. In some instances, in-game dialogue can battle with the player's attention as they're executing other actions and is often lost. Swinging through the streets of New York City in *Spider-Man* (2018), it's very easy to miss the witty dialogue of the individuals around you. For this reason, trying to convey crucial plot information through in-game dialogue is not always advisable. For this reason, some in-game dialogue is perhaps better understood as a mechanism for *reinforcing* rather than telling the player new information, though it can definitely help create the sense of a wider living world. Objectives can be reaffirmed or clues given as to the locations of specific items, which in tandem with visual clues help guide a player towards their destination. In-game text, diagrams or other graphical information supplied by the User Interface can often be crucial in making sure the player knows exactly where they're headed and what's expected of them.

In-game dialogue such as barks can be finessed during the recording process. One level in *Blood and Truth* involves player-character Ryan Marks having to enter a block of flats that are under demolition to rescue his mother from the hands of Tony Sharp. Along the way Ryan is tasked with dispensing with multiple hoodlums who speak 'Roadman'-style dialogue, a particular dialect common to urban parts of London. As I'm about as far removed from this subculture as it's possible to imagine, I spent a lot of time researching the script. Additionally, since we'd cast performers with specific knowledge of the dialect, we were also able to draw on their knowledge and expertise in enhancing the script and making it sound suitably convincing.[5]

Genre is a key influence on the kinds of in-game dialogue the game requires. In the World War Two stealth game *Sniper Elite 4*, it was useful if the player could locate enemy combatants. To this end, I was tasked with creating multiple in-game NPC conversations, which served both a gameplay role and storytelling purpose. The player could either choose to steer around the enemies unnoticed, sneak up on them and kill them stealthily or attack them noisily, thus eschewing the stealth mechanic and bringing other enemies to the player's location, all guns blazing. These conversations could be used in a variety of ways to help build the storyworld, perhaps mentioning important villains and their plans or giving clues as to the location of a specific weapon. Often they would allude to the wider context of the war. At other times I chose to emphasise the 'bystander' nature of these characters, channelling their inherent triviality to the fictional world and expendable nature.[6]

Beyond genre, game storytellers are often required to work on existing franchises. Often these might have originated in different media like films and television, and arrive with their own mythologies, as well as distinct themes and tones. For licensed games, a template for how particular characters speak might already exist. For instance, while working on the *Splatter Royale* DLC for *Evil Dead – The Game* (2022) I was tasked with writing and polishing dialogue for characters who'd originated in the spinoff television series *Ash Versus the Evil*

---

5 It paid off. The esteemed video game review magazine *Edge* described the dialogue in this sequence as 'note perfect epithets of modern-London' (*Edge* September 2018).

6 Authoring this kind of dialogue often makes me think of Tom Stoppard's *Rosencrantz and Guildenstern Are Dead* (1966), which explores the nature of chance in relation to two minor characters from Shakespeare's *Hamlet*.

Dead (2015-18). To ensure the dialogue was consistent I was able to use the original television script and actors' performances as a guide. In a similar vein, it might be necessary to mimic the cadence of dialogue originated by other writers on the project. It's not unusual for external writers to be brought in to provide a 'tone pass', aligning the approach of the dialogue across the project when multiple writers have been involved.

Other games make branching dialogue an integral aspect of their design. I've already mentioned the cyberpunk-themed *Deus Ex* as an important example of an earlier game which utilised a dialogue system to enable player choice in ways which profoundly affected the path of the story. A more recent game like *Starfield* also uses dialogue options to enable players to develop particular relationships with NPCs. *Detroit: Become Human*, meanwhile, takes a different approach, asking players to make their choice first and then enacting action and corresponding dialogue which flows directly from that particular decision.

In the sword and sorcery game *The Witcher 3*, the player can interact with NPCs using a dialogue tree. In common with these other games, *The Witcher 3* focuses on enabling player choice but the dialogue choices offered to players maintain consistency of character. As YouTuber You the Player notes, the game concentrates on the player-character Geralt's *relationship* with NPCs, rather than seeking to change Geralt himself, or necessarily impact the story later on.[7] The game's Animation Technical Director, Piotr Tomsiński, emphasises the need for players to generate an emotional connection with other characters, in order that they can make meaningful choices later on.[8]

---

7 'The Brilliant Dialogue of Witcher 3' - You the Player (youtube.com)
8 'GDC - Behind the Scenes of the CInematic Dialogues in The Witcher 3: Wild Hunt' (youtube.com)

As this example illustrates and as with so many aspects of game storytelling, different design philosophies can produce markedly different results. Christy Dena, a writer-designer-director, makes the point that dialogue choices can involve a level of moral complexity: 'For instance, in an interactive storytelling class I ran for games, film, animation and multimedia students, I spoke about how a dialogue choice does not have to be limited to how the antagonist sees the world. They've given you a choice between your best friend dying or a town, and that choice is meant to pain you. But what if, unlike your antagonist, you don't see death as an end? What if you don't see your choices as purely your own?'

Sometimes the approach to this kind of branching is much more limited. In the Virtual Reality thriller *Blood and Truth* these moments are constrained and driven by gameplay choices the player makes. Most notably, there's a scene in which the player must chase Keach, the oleaginous brother of the villain Tony Sharp, down multiple hotel corridors before trapping him. The intention is that the player should then interrogate Keach, either by firing their gun at the space around them, or wounding Keach. This was so the player could elicit the key information about Tony's whereabouts, which would be provided by grabbing Keach's mobile phone. Unfortunately the specifics of VR and related constraints meant that the phone had to be dropped from the sequence. Without this element, though, a key plot point about Tony's location had to be spoken aloud by Keach. This was all good and fine, unless the player chose to immediately shoot Keach dead rather than interrogating him.

Since reworking the sequence was impossible for technical, scheduling and financial reasons, we had to rapidly come up with an alternative to plug the plot hole. We'd already established that the player-character Ryan Marks' gifted sister Michelle had hacked into the hotel's radio system, allowing the player to overhear useful chatter. In the sequence immediately following the interrogation of Keach the player is required to crawl along a ventilation shaft a la John McClane in *Die Hard* (1988). We quickly recorded dialogue in which the details of Tony's location were revealed by the radio conversation between Tony's gangster accomplices. For those players who chose to kill Keach rather than interrogate him, this would mean that the plot hole was filled.

In fact, the Keach interrogation problem from *Blood and Truth* is a good example of how audio alone can be used to assist gameplay, reinforce plot points or, as with Keach, fix a potential plot hole. Audio-only dialogue that is not dependent on facial capture is an extremely versatile tool for the game storyteller. Many games will include an unseen guide for the player that's presented as a form of radio communication and assists the player throughout missions. Because audio on its own is so much cheaper to capture, audio-only dialogue provides a flexible storytelling method much more capable of adapting to changes in game design.

The different kinds of dialogue a game project might require again points to the hybridity and complexity of the medium. Dialogue needs to be consistent and convincing to ensure players believe in the characters they're playing as or otherwise encountering, as well as selling the world of the game to the audience. Very often it serves a functional purpose, helping the player understand what's required of them. Again this needs to be consistent with the characterisation of the fictional individual presenting them information, whether it's the player-character offering clues or reinforcing decisions, or an NPC providing hints or worldbuilding colour. Consistent dialogue serves a role in helping stitch together the component parts of the game, from cut scenes to scripted sequences, from in-game exploration and puzzle-solving to combat situations. The creation of such dialogue can be time-consuming and particularly for ongoing games with a constant need for new content, expensive.

Unsurprisingly, then, AI looks like it will increasingly play a role in the creation of dialogue for certain kinds of game experience. With regard to the various emotional voice synthesisers that are under development, it's feasible to imagine a process in which a performer provides a bucket of spoken lines. This would then constitute a dataset from which new dialogue could be derived as required, without bringing that performer back into the recording studio. For ongoing games, this would present a valuable way of generating original, authentic-sounding dialogue to accompany new missions, environments or gameplay. As with so much of AI technology, though, the impact on performers would need to be assessed and a strategy for meaningful remuneration worked out.

Such a development would mean that the approach employed by *Starship Titanic* and so many subsequent games of recording many thousands of lines of dialogue would potentially become redundant. Whether this is artistically or ethically desirable is a matter of urgent debate, not just for the games industry but for other storytelling industries too. From paranoid androids to neurotic elevators, Douglas Adams' work frequently humanises machines to pointed satirical effect. For all his pioneering enthusiasm for new technologies, I doubt he would have wanted people entirely removed from this part of the storytelling process.

9.

ADVENTURES IN TIME AND SPACE

Storytellers play with time and space. We decide when and where things happen and in what order. Maybe the story occurs in a single location or across multiple places, perhaps in different rooms in a house, or different countries, or different galaxies. Equally, the events we're describing might elapse over the course of an hour, a decade or a millennium. Maybe they happened a long time ago in a galaxy far, far away. Maybe they're happening now, or next Tuesday lunchtime, or in some far distant epoch. Maybe they take place in a parallel world or universe to ours. Deciding how to arrange stories in time and space is as integral to the process of storytelling as creating characters or cooking up plots. And as different kinds of media have emerged, so the techniques through which time and space can be manipulated have changed too. Video games are only the latest instance of this.

Many different flavours of storytelling theorist have sought to articulate the role of time and space in the creation and consumption of narratives. Aristotle is often (erroneously)[1] credited with the Three Unities of Action, Place and Time, which suggest that a tragedy should have one principal action, take place in one location, and occur over a period no longer than twenty-four hours. In the 20th century, writer and philosopher Paul Ricoeur focussed on the relationship between narrative and temporality, in terms which – appropriately enough – have proved enduring and influential in the academic study of narrative.[2] Meanwhile, the film scholar Christian Metz talked about 'the time of the telling' and 'the time of the told', highlighting the fact that stories already exist before they're unfolded to us – arguably the antithesis of interactive storytelling, in which the narrative is created in the moment by the participant.[3]

As ever, interactivity is the element that means video games have to think about time and space differently to other media. In most kinds of storytelling we move forwards through time and are propelled through space according to a specific sequence laid down by the author. Novels and short stories use the medium of the written word to manage our navigation along temporal and spatial axes. If the author decides to return to a location it's because the plot determines they should, or there's some emotional beat to be found in that particular spot. There's also the question of speed. Media that utilise words can be much more rapid in how they convey a story compared to visual-led media like television and film, which generally requires establishing

---

1 The Three Unities were conceived by the Italian author and critic Gian Giorgo Trissino in 1514, who claimed he was following Aristotle's precepts as laid out in *Poetics*. In actual fact, Trissino wouldn't have had access to *Poetics* and was basing his understanding on another of Aristotle's books, *Rhetoric*. Mistranslations probably contributed to Trissino's poor understanding.
2 Ricoeur, Paul (1984, 1985, 1988) *Time and Narrative.* Chicago: Chicago University Press
3 Metz, Christian (1974) *Film Language.* New York: Oxford University Press.
This was a point made by video game scholar Jesper Juul when he was wowing academic audiences as a PhD student back in 2001.

shots to help contextualise events for the viewer. For instance, Dylan Thomas' extended radio poem *Under Milk Wood* (1954) begins with a dizzying, whistle stop tour of the fictional Welsh town of Llarregub[4] in which we meet a succession of extraordinary characters.

Other kinds of dramatic media face different challenges. Changing the scenery in a stage play can be an arduous and time-consuming activity, and playwrights plan their stories around such limitations. Television and cinema can exploit editing to move location but must navigate budgetary constraints. The academic Derek Johnson notes the fiscal savings derived from the reuse of sets and props between the various *Star Trek* shows produced by Paramount in the 1990s.[5] None of these factors are necessarily weaknesses. Franchises like *Star Trek* and television soap operas arguably draw their strength from the familiarity associated with limited sets and locations, the backdrop to ongoing and interweaving storylines and consistent fictional worlds and universes.

As we know by now, video games aren't like most other storytelling mediums in a key, fundamental regard. Video games are primarily a *spatial medium*. This isn't to suggest that games don't use temporal mechanisms to deliver story, that's clear from cut scenes and their ilk. It's more that the deceptively simple act of intervening in a fictional world changes things. Whether you choose to take one path over another, discover a secret corridor below the crumbling monastery or an ancient map behind a waterfall, can make all the difference to how you understand the story. This is the case even if the key story beats remain essentially unaltered, as with very many games. Those key narrative moments might be delivered by cinematic sequences which are primarily temporal in nature, but how you unlocked them

---

4 Read it backwards. Given his inherent playfulness, I suspect Dylan Thomas would have excelled in video games.
5 Johnson, Derek (2013) *Media Franchising*. New York: NYU Press.

while travelling through the space of the game world might differ significantly.

Games have limitations, because the technology through which they're created has limitations, and so does the development process. Every new space the player encounters has to be built and stored. Many contemporary games operate on the Z-axis, affording the player the ability to move across the environment, from a haunted house to a Roman colosseum to a dilapidated space station caught in a decaying orbit. Depending on the kind of game, this exploration might be heavily controlled, a kind of 'railroad' approach akin to ghost train fairground rides, or alternatively the player might be afforded varying degrees of agency to roam around the environment. The ultimate expression of the latter are open world games such as Rockstar's later *Grand Theft Auto* games, *Red Dead Redemption II* and CD Projekt's *Cyberpunk 2077*.

The kind of game will dictate the particular smoke-and-mirrors approach that's required. *The Last of Us* begins with a touching cut scene between Joel and his daughter Sarah, as she gives him the watch she had mended for his birthday. Sarah then falls asleep beside her father. When she awakens she's in her bedroom and we're able to control her. As we explore the house we realise there's no sign of Joel, and our unease mounts along with Sarah's. It's only when we enter the dining room that Joel bursts in, in a state of high anxiety. We can explore the house as much or as little as we want, but the dramatic moment of Joel returning won't occur until we've triggered it by going to a specific room. Importantly, although the player's actions move the sequence forward, the game will only progress down one sequential path in time once you've completed your spatial exploration of the house.

None of this is new. From the get-go, video games experimented with space and time. A key way in which this happened was off-screen space, the implied realm beyond the one we explicitly experience on the screen in front of us. In *Space Invaders* we knew that the eponymous spaceships and monsters would keep coming, because there were always more of the blighters just off-screen. *Asteroids* supplied a hyperspace function that would temporarily remove the player's ship from the game space before dropping them back at another location on the screen. *Pac-Man* similarly featured exits and entrances at either side of its neon maze which functioned as a sort of hidden tunnel system and allowed the yellow disc an escape route or a means of surprising the marauding ghosts. In each case, the fictive world of the game matched with the requirements of the gameplay.

The idea of hidden space that the player gradually uncovers was taken further still in side-scrolling games. The most famous example is probably *Sonic the Hedgehog*, though that followed in the wake of many others, made possible by the technology of newer arcade machines and the advent of 8-bit home computers, of which my beloved Atari 800 was an example. Like the static screen platform games that preceded them, side-scrolling games presented increased challenges as the game continued, unfurling continuously as the scenario scrolled behind. Later parallax effects added depth of field to the background, a technique also used by racing games like *Pole Position* (Atari 1983).

The emphasis on the Z-axis for many contemporary games means that game storytellers have to take creative decisions that are sometimes heavily influenced by the nature of the game engine being employed for the project. In contemporary game development, levels and connecting elements are positioned spatially within the game's editor to speed up loading them in. Their relationship to each other can therefore have an effect in terms of how these different elements can be utilised from a story perspective. In *Blood and Truth*, for instance, when the player gets into a lift the game will fade down to allow the next location to be loaded into memory, before fading up again. Again this is another way in which game storytelling is perhaps closer to theatre writing, in which the playwright must consider the spatial implications of having to change scenery, as opposed to film or television in which movement between locations can be accomplished much more readily through the power of editing.

Another obvious way in which games *generally* differ from other storytelling media is in their approach to repetition. Film and television screenwriters, for instance, will work hard to avoid 'double beats', in which a similar action or plot point recurs more than once (unless they're deliberately aiming for some kind of symmetry). In many ways, repetition is hardwired into the DNA of video games. We play a game, we get killed or fail at a task, so we start again.[6] This isn't normally considered an issue, but rather part of the appeal of the experience. If at first you don't succeed, try again, and keep trying until eventually you clear the obstacle course, unlock the clues or defeat a particular boss. In the old days this process could be particularly unforgiving if you'd used up all your 'lives' trying to complete a particular challenge, but the ability to save game progress transformed that.

Where this might potentially become an issue is with regards to story. If a player has failed to overcome the obstacle put in front of them, repeating the same set of gameplay challenges might be frustrating but not as frustrating as having to sit through the same cut scene over again. For this reason, many cut scenes have a 'skip' function so the player can avoid seeing them for a second time. Actively repeating a task or challenge is at least active and engaging, and there's huge satisfaction to be derived from finally completing it.

---

6 If it's a good game. If it's a bad game we just put down the controller and slag the developers off on social media.

There is little to be derived from watching the same cinematic over and over again, telling you the same things. (In fact some games even offer players the ability to skip such scenes straight away, so they don't even have to sit through them once).

As I discussed in Chapter 7, it's also the case that, from a storytelling perspective, most games ignore the fact that the player-character has died either once or repeatedly during gameplay. It's an accepted convention of game storytelling, in the same way that in musical theatre or film characters suddenly bursting into song isn't mentioned, even if the surrounding context is heavily realistic in nature. In this important sense, ludonarrative dissonance is part of the contract between the player and the game, and storytelling doesn't necessarily need to worry about it – with some instructive exceptions. For instance, *Prince of Persia – Sands of Time* (2003), leans into its Arabian Nights influences by framing its fiction as a story that's being told to you. When the player-character dies – as he invariably does, many times, when I'm playing it – the character's narration pipes up to say, 'No, no, that's not what happened', and then the game resets.

Another significant way in which games repeat is in spatial terms. Game development is expensive, both in the sense of the number of skilled craftspeople required to originate, build and promote the game, but also in the very particular computing sense of being 'expensive' in terms of how much memory is used up. As a result, many games reuse locations the player has already visited, perhaps re-dressing them or letting the player enter the environment from a different direction. Increasingly bigger games will utilise maps – the layout of the level – for different gameplay modes.

Very often the need to return to a particular space is driven by cost efficiencies but, if correctly employed, this revisit can be utilised to impressive dramatic effect. For instance, by forcing a player to come into the space from a different entrance point they might gain a new understanding of the space they've been exploring. Alternatively, the player could encounter the familiar location at a different point of day or in a strikingly different context. To this end, the location might be dressed differently, with art assets designed to create a sense of decay, or a battle having taken place in a particular space since the player's original visit.

At an advanced stage of the original science fiction game *Halo*, the player has to hurriedly escape from the Pillar of Autumn, a spaceship that's been self-destructed by the player themselves. As the player rushes through the environments they see the effects wrought by the Flood, a parasitic alien species that mutates organic life forms and transforms settings into grotesque, decayed locations. Seeing these familiar environments recast as scenes of devastation is supremely disconcerting, and helps amp up the terror associated with this particular adversary. Similarly, part way through the first *Devil May Cry* game (2001), the player-character Dante comes into a location he has previously visited but which is now cast in darkness. As the player starts to explore the familiar surroundings, the game's terrifying puppet adversaries drop from the ceiling in an extremely successful jump scare.

Limitations in terms of space can be turned to the advantage of the fiction at a fundamental level, so that it becomes intrinsic to the gameplay. *Deathloop* (2021) uses an aesthetic rooted in 1970s action movies and subsequently mined by Quentin Tarantino in many of his films. The game takes place on a mysterious island. The player assumes the role of Colt who quickly discovers he's trapped in a time loop, in part thanks to enigmatic messages left by himself. Each time Colt dies, he finds himself back at the beginning of the cycle, and he can't escape the island unless he breaks the loop. In its demarcated location and circular structure, *Deathloop* is constrained in terms of both time and space, making it a prime example of a game which turns its inherent limitations into its central premise.

A looping story is an obvious conceit for a medium which is necessarily highly repetitive, and indeed is central to a particular sub-genre of game. Each time a player is killed in a roguelike[7] game – sometimes known as 'roguelite' – they're sent back to the start point and have to begin all over again. The player must play through again and again, using the knowledge and skill they've acquired to advance further. With each new playthrough elements of the level are randomised, creating additional challenges (something *Deathloop* doesn't do, one of the reasons it's not a roguelite, although it shares many other characteristics). Roguelikes are very cost effective to produce because of the re-use of assets.

A prime example of a roguelike is *Hades*, in which the player-character is tasked with trying to escape the titular realm from Greek mythology. Each time the player-character is killed they're thrown back to the beginning and must play through once more. However, thanks to the complex and vast dialogue system I mentioned in Chapter 8, characters respond differently to you each time, advancing the story in the process and making the world feel like it's alive and responsive to your actions. The game's characters are brilliantly conceived and implemented, which helps balance out the inherent frustration of constantly being sent back to play through again.

The science fiction horror and third-person shooter *Returnal* (2021) similarly leans into the inherent repetitiveness of games. Like *Deathloop, Returnal* features a time loop, but this time it's repurposed for roguelike gameplay. The player takes the role of Selene Vassos, a space pilot who has become trapped on the alien world Atropos but

---

7 The 1980 game *Rogue* gives its title to the sub-genre although the form itself arguably has its origins in older 'dungeon-crawlers', notably *Beneath Apple Manor* from 1978.

who is also stuck inside an ever repeating time loop. As with *Hades*, crucial to the success of roguelikes like *Returnal* is a design which encourages players to keep playing despite their continuous defeats. Alongside evolving gameplay, cleverly conceived storytelling plays a critical role in differentiating one run from the next, so the player feels like they are making progress in understanding the alien world they find themselves marooned on.

The same principles of revisiting a space can be applied to wildly different genres of game. A point-and-click adventure like *The Excavation of Hob's Barrow* requires the player to constantly return to areas, talking to characters or applying particular objects from their inventory to particular tasks. This can only really be accomplished by experimentation and exploration, as new information comes to light and new possessions are acquired. Often a problem can only be solved by understanding and applying the correct sequence, and this can only be learnt through repeated visits to different locations to understand which actions have to be carried out where and in what order, often using specific objects the player has acquired.

Conversely, sometimes the structure of the game requires that areas a player previously visited are no longer accessible. There might be a story reason for this or a gameplay reason. The location in question might have served its purpose in terms of the narrative, or it might cause plot problems if the player can return to the area. Alternatively, gameplay, the story or a combination of the two might require that the player is channelled in a specific direction to help progress the game.

For instance, at one point in *The Excavation of Hob's Barrow* the player chases a little girl who has apparently hidden inside a hole. Thomasina, the player-character, needs to go through a series of actions to acquire a lantern so she can follow the little girl down the hole, a la *Alice in Wonderland*. However, upon entering the hole

Thomasina is suddenly confronted by a ferocious badger, a shocking jump scare using one of the developer's trademark unexpected close-ups. The little girl, it turns out, didn't go down the hole at all, despite some misleading, disturbing giggling that suggested she had. When the player later tries to go down the hole, Thomasina's voice declares that she has no desire to encounter the badgers again.

Another narrative technique games borrow from more established storytelling media is that of *ellipsis*, a technique which allows the story to advance through time in a rapid fashion. Ellipsis works on the basis of omission, leaving out elements that are obvious, don't need stating or otherwise slow the story down. This technique relies on the player being able to intuit the off-screen events and fill in the gaps themselves, in a similar way to that of a cinema audience or television viewer. Jumps in time can be effective storytelling techniques but also offer ways around problems like pacing and more prosaic challenges associated with budget. In common with television and cinema, and theatre storytelling before that, a surprising amount can be achieved through carefully curated implication.[8]

For example, in *Blood and Truth* the story is told through the framing device of the CIA Agent Carson interrogating the player-character Ryan Marks. At the mid-point of the story, when a key dramatic event occurs, we needed to converge the flashback storyline with the present day. To do this, we created a scene in which the player-character's sister learns what's happened, just as blue lights appear and the sound of police sirens comes to dominate the soundtrack, before fading to black. The implication that this is the point at which Ryan and his sister were arrested is clear, but it also circumvented the need to build police cars and create police officers.

---

8 Novelist Ernest Hemingway was a big proponent of the so-called 'Iceberg Theory', otherwise known as the 'Theory of Omission', as outlined in his non-fiction book *Death in the Afternoon* (1932).

Sometimes decisions around how to handle time and space emerge organically through the creative process, rather than being planned. On *Blood and Truth* we concluded that an early portion of the game's story continued for too long a period without any gameplay. Our solution was to overlay the dialogue from the preceding interrogation sequence on a scene showing Ryan Marks' family in flashback. To marry the audio and visual elements up, we utilised a slow-motion technique on the flashback scene, only syncing up the flashback scene's audio with the visuals once the framing dialogue was over. The finished scene helps to elide the two time periods, as well as creating more visual interest for the player in a scene which was otherwise dominated by exposition.

Another familiar technique is that of narration, which can summarise events for the player and move the story on as required. On *Sniper Elite 4* we used the player-character's voice to frame the set up of the game and provide the wartime context in which the game is set. The narration was supported by a series of impressionistic animations showing key images, including maps and significant wartime leaders, as well as a stirring soundtrack. The benefits of this approach are numerous, in that it provides important exposition in a dynamic and tonally consistent fashion, but in a way which is much cheaper than full fat FMV sequences. This is especially important for projects in which the storytelling budget is smaller than might be found on much more high profile projects.

As in novels, movies and theatre plays, it's eminently possible for the story to jump around in time, using flashback and flashforward techniques. This is distinct from the non-linearity involved in a player exploring an environment and completing a set of tasks or objectives in the way they choose, as facilitated by level design. Just as with other kinds of storytelling, the success or failure of such an approach is heavily dependent on adequate signposting. Sometimes this can be accomplished in an explicit way through captioning – 'Three Months Earlier' – although subtler techniques can be employed. As ever, the nature of gameplay and the focus it necessarily imposes on the storytelling means that multiple jumps in time and space, let alone jumps in character perspective, have to be handled with the utmost care.

As I said at the beginning of this chapter, the ability of video game stories to remake time and space is far from unique to this medium. The power to concertina or elongate time, to move from location to location at will, is a prerequisite of all storytelling. What makes video games so different from these other media is the combination of interactivity and connectivity. In this key regard, games are the epitome of the digital world which we all now inhabit, in which repetition, elision and non-chronology are increasingly commonplace, in which time and space are constantly disrupted. As with so much else connected to game storytelling and worldbuilding, it's the complex, participatory nature of the medium that means we need to adapt and invent new creative processes to bring them to life.

10.
PROCESSES, PIPELINES AND PERFORMANCES

For everything they share in common with other storytelling media, video games do lots of things very differently. Contemporary games are fantastically complex ecologies, bringing together many different crafts, from coding to multiple kinds of design, from art to sound, and from writing to acting. Just like these other disciplines, storytelling and worldbuilding for games demands clear and unambiguous procedures and protocols. These in turn require clear outcomes, as well as pinch points at which progression can be reviewed and assessed. While there are commonalities across the industry, different studios place different levels of emphasis upon the importance of narrative. As a result, approaches to the implementation of narrative also differ from studio to studio, and even from project to project.

This is not to suggest that the more sophisticated the processes the better the storytelling. Smaller studios with correspondingly smaller budgets can still produce extraordinarily engaging stories and build deeply immersive worlds. As with any artform, fiscal and technical constraints frequently lead to imaginative solutions. As games like

The Return of Obra Dinn (2018), *What Remains of Edith Finch* (2017) and *Everybody's Gone to the Rapture* (2015) amply demonstrate, a clever conceit that's expertly executed can produce arresting, immersive storyworlds that put franchises with enormous budgets to shame.

But it's very much a case of cutting your cloth to suit. A project with a miniscule or even modest narrative budget needs to think innovatively about how best to approach storytelling, rather than aping the approaches of bigger studios and projects with deep pockets and more expertise. More than anything, problems with process can lead to fundamental problems with story and worldbuilding that no amount of subsequent development can overcome.

One of these differences relates to the role of the script in the process. In other dramatic media such as film and theatre, the script sits at the apex of the storytelling process, the top of the hierarchy which will largely dictate the rest of the production. It's certainly true that for some narrative-led games the script plays a central role in determining choices by other crafts in the development process. But on the whole the script and the story are seen as being much more malleable than in film and television. In fact, script and story development frequently take place in parallel with other kinds of development, with these other crafts informing the narrative as much as the narrative informs them. This might take the form of exploration around art style, experimentation with coding and investigation into different design approaches, all of which can help shape and determine the approach taken by the storytelling department.

Rick Porras, co-producer and additional unit director of Peter Jackson's *Lord of the Rings* trilogy and story consultant working across film, television and games, puts it this way: 'With movies you first do pre-production and then production and then post-production. You're doing it in a very specific order and sometimes you have to overlap these processes but it's linear, right? With video games there's more of this conversation going back and forth. It's very exciting to see how technology has evolved our different mediums, it gives you more powerful options and more time to make decisions but if you're not careful in making the right choices at the right time, it can also cause your budget to grow. But maximising that creative punch is exciting.'

In terms of games, at the beginning of the process there is often some idea of the story, as distinct from the script, even if it's purely a concept or scenario. Theme and tone are often key factors that will need to be addressed early, and these conversations are often driven by narrative in concert with art and design teams. These will then inform the creation of 'game pillars', the fundamental parameters that will guide the project throughout its development.

An existing franchise might require a compelling sequel, prequel or to extend the franchise in another direction. Many game franchises reinvent themselves from title to title, such as the *Final Fantasy* games, which means game storytellers must look to tell new stories consistent with the franchise's pillars. Additionally, game storytellers may be asked to revive a dormant franchise if the licence for that franchise has passed to a new developer.

Occasionally the opportunity to originate a completely new idea arises. Sometimes story teams will be approached to do this, pitching ideas for new projects. Alternatively, the wider studio may be asked to come up with game concepts, and even to vote on those ideas to identify a favourite to pitch or develop further. In smaller studios, a studio director may originate a particular idea and instruct a team to work on it. In my experience game studios generally aren't interested in external pitches for games in the way we find in the television and film industries. It's also common for a project to start out as one idea and then evolve into something completely different as the creative team changes, especially if the project is long gestating.

Studios without evolved internal narrative departments might choose to work with outside writers, narrative designers and story consultants, either in a freelance relationship or via a narrative design agency like the California-based Blindlight, Montreal-based Sweet Baby or UK-based Linx Agency. Such external relationships have to be carefully handled to make sure the narrative direction remains consistent. For some projects, specific writers may have been hired because they possess particular experience garnered in the real world, for example those with military training. Alternatively, they may possess experience working on similar types of game or other relevant media. For instance, a game rooted in a specific historical epoch would logically want to utilise writers and narrative designers with knowledge of that particular point in history. Many writers are also fans of existing franchises and bring with them extensive understanding of that franchise's lore. This is particularly useful when the IP in question is long established and the lore is therefore extremely complex.

Writers, narrative designers and other kinds of story consultant can join a project at any point in its development. Some projects might have a well-established idea of what form the individual levels and gameplay will take, and in fact may have gone so far as to build them. They may also have designed and built characters, and even gone so far as to scan actors' likenesses. In instances such as these, the story team is often involved in working the sequencing of the missions into a plot and incorporating existing characters into this plot. Such factors can place severe limitations on the kinds of story that can be told. But creative challenges like these are also part of the appeal for storytellers choosing to work in this medium.

For Rick Porras, our external story consultant on the VR game *Blood and Truth*, there are interesting historical parallels from the early days of cinema in terms of shaping a video game story using existing assets: 'I often wondered when we were working on the story,' he says. 'Were we doing something similar to what others had done before in the early 1900s where they might have made a bunch of sets, props and costumes for a specific movie, and then they were keen to reuse as much as possible. It was fun to think about the similarities even if the tools over that hundred years were far different.'

Despite the differences in terms of how story and script tend to be regarded, game studios increasingly borrow established story creation and development techniques from other media. Notably, contemporary studios with more mature narrative development pipelines increasingly utilise the 'Writers' Room' as a mechanism for originating and progressing game stories. Writers' Rooms are an approach derived from the US television network, in which groups of writers come together to develop the scenario and the story. This might include obvious elements such as plot, character and act structure, and depending on the approach might choose to explore worldbuilding more widely. In my experience, Writers' Rooms need to be carefully steered to ensure their effectiveness. As Zak Garriss, head writer on the acclaimed video game *Life is Strange: Before the Storm* (2017) observes, Writers' Rooms often work best when the individual leading the room arrives with a series of specific questions that need to be answered.[1]

In addition, narrative teams are often tasked with creating character biographies, sometimes working in isolation, sometimes working in concert with colleagues from art teams and design. As a result, representatives are liable to be brought in to lead or assist in the casting process alongside colleagues from other crafts. Other key documents the narrative team is likely to be asked to originate

---

1 Productive Dissension: How a Diverse Writers' Room Created Life is Strange: Before the Storm (youtube.com)

are pitches outlining a story concept and treatments detailing the story. As story development continues, the documents required become more granular. These can include beat sheets explaining the unfolding story in specific dramatic and gameplay sections, and level briefs co-authored with design and art colleagues outlining the narrative flow of a particular mission or level.

The interactive attributes of games call for certain kinds of document unique to the medium. For game developers, it's vital to understand the player's journey in relation to the player-character's journey. Various kinds of document can help map out this relationship against the timeline of the game's story. If there are moments at which the player knows something but the player-character doesn't or vice versa, this will need to be accounted for in this documentation, which may take the form of some kind of map or diagram to help visually convey the various elements. Other crafts in addition to the storytelling team will need to review and input into this documentation.

For many games, these documents provide the foundations for what will eventually become the screenplay. Because game projects can differ markedly, there is no standard script layout as in other storytelling media such as radio, television, film and theatre.[2] The unspoken rule is to use whatever format works best for the project, or the specific component of the project currently being focussed upon. For this reason, some games don't require any screenplay.

Generally speaking, a story-led game is likely to require a script akin to a movie screenplay since it will probably comprise cinematic sequences written according to conventions recognisable from film screenwriting, even if the scene contains elements of branching and other varieties of interactivity. Depending on the kind of project, a

---

2 In the early 2000s I had an extended conversation with MIT's Henry Jenkins about the possibility of creating a standardized screenplay format and touring various game developers in the US to workshop it. Alas, it never came to pass.

script tool might be used which can account for the specifics of the gameplay during in-game sequences. Some studios have a bespoke version of this tool, although 'off-the-shelf' solutions are also available. Other modes of game with more restricted narrative elements, like multiplayer, may require a spreadsheet that the narrative team populates with systemic dialogue and which the audio team subsequently implement.

Many games utilise motion capture techniques, in which live action is translated into data. In their book on the subject *Performing for Motion Capture* (2022),[3] John Dower and Pascal Langdale date motion capture back to the rotoscoping techniques first utilised by the animator Max Fleischer over a century ago, which involved filming live performance and then tracing over it.[4] Dower and Langdale identify three distinct types of digital motion capture: optical or line-of-sight capture in which performers wear Lycra suits covered in reflective markers which are then tracked by infra-red cameras in a studio space known as the 'volume'; inertial capture, which utilises sensors based at key points on the body to send data wirelessly to a computer and which requires a studio; and the cheapest option, markerless capture, in which outline and depth sensors are used to track body shapes.

There are a number of key advantages to using motion capture. Most obviously it means animators don't have to 'hand craft' work. Capturing movement as data means it can be inserted wholesale into cinematic, gameplay or hybrid sequences and then manipulated as required. Crucially, motion capture in the strict sense of the term

---

3 Dower, John and Langdale, Pascal (2022) *Performing for Motion Capture: A Guide for Practitioners.* London: Methuen

4 A version of the technique is employed in Ralph Bakshi's 1978 animated version of *The Lord of the Rings*. The effect is terrifying and definitely one of the high points of the movie.

refers to capturing the movement of the skeleton of a performer rather than any other traits. This means the process doesn't record skin, hair or any clothing, which are added later.

As Dower and Langdale note, motion capture can be seen as returning to a much older embodied form of performance that was displaced by certain kinds of theatre. They suggest that while silent movies reintroduced the necessity for pantomime style performance – as evidenced by the emergence of physical performers like Charlie Chaplin and Harold Lloyd – the arrival of the 'talkies' meant the emphasis moved to the performer's face and away from their whole bodies.

In contrast, performance capture – 'PCap' – refers to the recording of an actor's face. This process can be expensive, depending on the kind of capture. If a well-known actor has been cast, developers might opt to capture an individual, in addition to their body, so that the finished model has an extremely close resemblance to the performer in question. Other approaches aren't necessarily lower quality but might mean the resemblance to the performer is less evident. Undertaking motion capture and facial capture suggest the project is striving for at least some degree of realism, though the extent to which this is disguised by other additional stylistic layers – bespoke character designs, clothing or VFX elements like a magical aura surrounding the character – can differ massively from project to project.

For instance, the apparent realism of the visuals in a contemporary game like *The Last of Us* can mislead writers unused to the medium into thinking they're writing for film or television. Unless the project is an interactive film then this is generally not the case.[5] In actual fact, game writers are fundamentally writing for a medium that is

---

5 Notable exceptions include interactive films like *Her Story* (2015) and *Erica* (2019).

animated, irrespective of whether or not motion and performance capture has been used to underpin those animations. This means that certain approaches a television or film writer may utilise are not necessarily available, and that complexity of action needs to be avoided or treated with care. For instance, having a character remove a handkerchief from their top pocket, mop their brow and replace that handkerchief would be a simple action in television or film. In video games, it's potentially a highly complicated set of movements requiring months of bespoke work on the part of the animation team.

Damien Goodwin, a highly experienced performance director with credits including *Star Wars Outlaws*, *The Casting of Frank Stone* and *Returnal*, identifies both the similarities and differences between directing for games as opposed to other media like television, film and theatre: 'In all mediums you are collaborating with a writer/s, cast, crew, production company or development team to build a vision and bring a story to life. However, the individual processes and means of getting where you need to go differ according to the type of material you are working on, the genre and who you are collaborating with... In some circumstances, you might not receive the script, character bios or outline until a few days or even hours before you are in studio with your cast. The script is also unlikely to be complete and you often only receive a document with a collection of lines in which the precise context isn't immediately apparent.'

Depending on the kind of project, the narrative and cinematic team may choose to cast individuals from a broader template rather than a very specific character biography. They could then choose to build and nuance the character according to the individual they've cast, leaning into the actor's own traits, whether they're physical, temperamental or biographical. Equally, if time allows it may be possible to workshop with the actors to help render the finished script more naturalistic. Sequences which are hybrids between cut scenes

171

and gameplay – and necessarily more active than might be found in a more conventional cut sequence – might be better to workshop and block to make them altogether more dynamic.

The kind of game and the kind of sequence being captured will clearly have a dramatic impact on the approach taken in the motion capture volume. With their inherent sequentiality, more traditional, non-interactive cut scenes are easier to implement and will feel familiar to performers versed in film, television and theatre. Cut scenes are liable to be a key point of drama in the narrative, rewarding the player-character for having successfully completed a mission, or establishing what their objectives are for the next mission. As a result, cut scenes are seldom subdued affairs, rooted as they are in a heightened form of drama derived from the specific genre of game, in which wizards unlock spells or space marines are sent on interstellar missions. This necessarily has an impact on the kind of exposition games engage in, and often leads to criticisms that they're overwritten in comparison to other dramatic media like film and television.

For Goodwin, the lack of context presents additional challenges for directors and performers working in this medium: 'Clearly, imagination is the key ingredient here, and arguably more so than any other medium. The role of imagination is intrinsically important for actors and directors alike. When shooting in the volume you may work with character rigs and have a sense of the environment too – however, sometimes you have nothing, and with none of the usual paraphernalia of a film shoot or theatrical performance, the director and actor have to rely solely on their creative imagination to bring a character and story to life.'

Some sequences will be interactive to a greater or lesser extent, and thus require different outcomes to be captured. For instance, certain interactive sequences may require the player to mash a button repeatedly to force a particular positive outcome, but it may also be necessary to capture the negative outcome, or at least the response to a negative outcome. Alternatively, branching narrative in which the player can initiate different outcomes will require the sequence to be broken up into smaller segments. Some actors can struggle with this as it means refocusing their understanding of the character's arc and is liable to be very different to their prior experience, unless they have performed in games before or have comparable expertise, perhaps in improvisational techniques.

More obviously different are gameplay sequences in which the player can move their avatar in any direction and possibly also the camera. From a directorial viewpoint, this means that the composition of a shot cannot be framed in the same way it would be for an edited sequence as you would find in a cut scene or scene from a television or film production. This can also be the case in VR productions, since even in more linear sequences the player might be given the opportunity to look around themselves. From a performance viewpoint, in both instances the storytelling is much closer to a theatre play, in which the audience has the agency to look where they choose.

This is particularly important for those sequences in which the player is an active participant, as Damien Goodwin notes: 'Everything revolves around the Player and the choices they make. It's therefore all about encouraging the Player to have agency in the story and to take ownership of it. As a director, it's important to develop a deep knowledge and appreciation of how stories work in games as well as what the mechanics of the story design are. What are the kinds of choices a character makes? How do they branch and what effect do those choices have on the character and their environment etc? It is the desire to motivate and influence the choices of the Player that drives the creative decisions and the way a character reacts.'

Some projects may choose to shoot sequences purely as motion capture without employing PCap to capture facial performance.

There is often a budgetary or logistical imperative to capturing body and face separately, though splitting the various elements of the performance can cause a variety of challenges (for experienced teams these are far from insurmountable, however). For action sequences, in which performers with stunt skills are required, it makes a lot of sense. This is particularly the case if the player is in the midst of action gameplay – most obviously a combat sequence – in which they may not necessarily be able to see the facial responses of fellow characters up close.

As Damien Goodwin says, maintaining a coherent performance in these situations is essential. 'Consistency must also be conserved when one, two, three, or even four actors play one role,' he suggests. 'For example, one actor might be scanned for likeness, while another actor may perform the physicality, another may voice the character, and, sometimes, there is also a stunt performer performing the character's action and fight sequences. Multi-actors playing one role is another challenging part of the process and almost entirely unique to games. When this is the case, it is important for each actor to develop a clear understanding of their role and become fully connected with the character they are playing. For this to happen the director needs to ensure each actor is embedded in the story and that they have ownership of the essence of the character and share the same energy, attitude and tone as their counterparts.'

In addition, particular types of game can bring their own distinct challenges, as Rick Porras argues. 'I think we had a unique situation on *Blood and Truth* because it was VR, so everything was POV. So you know that also changed the shooting process… It was like theatre but where the audience could look anywhere with a stage that was everywhere and easily ignore the characters before them. And of course it was just one long shot without an edit.'

Fascinatingly, Porras talks about how he tried to engineer the equivalent of edits to change the rhythm and meaning of a scene: 'I was trying to think about how to put it in. A percussive moment, so to speak. You know, someone entering the frame. Someone coming into the room, someone getting up and walking over to someone, someone grabbing a cup. Someone doing something that would draw the eye or ear on where an edit might occur. Obviously the priority was telling the story of what the game design team wanted the player to learn or do about character or plot but I didn't want to lose out on these other elements so the player could feel more, experience more, and not be in some static environment.'

As with other media, writers aren't necessarily invited to the set or involved in the shoot. This might well depend on the location of the capture stage – for instance, flying a British team to a far flung location in LA or Vancouver is an expensive undertaking, and the writer may not necessarily be considered an essential member of the team. In some instances, though, it may be useful for the performers, director or animation lead to be able to consult with writers or other members of the narrative team. The writer might take the role of 'riding' the script during the shoot to make sure the dialogue and actions are being implemented correctly, since they're liable to be the most familiar with it. In this case the writer will become equivalent to the script supervisor role found on television and film sets. Additionally, narrative designers can help ensure that cinematic elements are properly aligned with gameplay moments, ensuring that the transition between these elements makes sense and is appropriately blocked in terms of movements.

To a large extent game storytelling and worldbuilding is driven by voice. Generally, once cut sequences are recorded, the dialogue is considered locked since reworking facial capture is expensive and time consuming. It is possible to employ Automated Dialogue

Replacement (ADR), another technique borrowed from film and television, in which an actor may be brought in to re-record lines that weren't hitting the quality bar in the first instance, or to change lines, perhaps because a plot point or other elements have changed. The challenge when changing lines is to ensure that the replacement line matches with the lip movements of the original. On *Blood and Truth*, we used ADR in a limited fashion to enhance some lines and add dialogue where the character in question was facing away from the 'camera'.

In contrast, in-game dialogue tends to be much more flexible, depending on its purpose and how it's being implemented. As I explored in Chapter 8, in-game dialogue is frequently as much about gameplay and objective-setting or reinforcing existing objectives as it is about characterisation, moving the plot along or establishing the world of the game. If performers who appear in cut scenes also appear in gameplay then we would either bring them into an audio studio on-site or use an external audio provider to record these lines. This is another way in which cut scenes and gameplay can be 'sutured' or stitched together to help make the game feel like a continuous, immersive experience. Typically, voice direction can be carried out by the same individual who conducted motion-capture direction with these actors, since this is a good way of ensuring consistency of performance. Alternatively, other members of the narrative team, or audio team, may be required to direct these sessions.

The involvement of the audio team can be particularly important when it comes to recording other kinds of in-game dialogue, particularly bark sets, the systemic dialogue that triggers according to certain gameplay conditions. Sound design teams will understand the kind of performance needed for certain kinds of bark, for instance when a patrolling security guard is suddenly aware of the player's presence, or when a gunfight is in full flow. The kinds of barks required can affect the flow of the recording session, since it makes sense to ask the performer to deliver quieter barks towards the beginning of the session, leaving shouting to the end so the individual's voice isn't unduly stressed.[6] Since the Covid-19 pandemic an increasing number of actors have their own home set-ups allowing them to deliver dialogue down the line. It's also increasingly common to direct sessions virtually from a completely different physical location to that of the performer or sound engineers.[7]

Recording sessions are expensive and the time available is limited, so there's generally a necessity to get through the required material as quickly as possible. For this reason, while some varieties of in-game dialogue may originate in screenplay format, by the time they're being utilised in voice recording sessions they're liable to be in some kind of spreadsheet format. Barks and other kinds of in-game dialogue will probably be written into a spreadsheet in the first place. Some studios have their own bespoke software systems into which material can be directly entered. More sophisticated dialogue systems may be able to 'ingest' screenplay format and convert it into spreadsheet format for recording purposes. Each line of dialogue is treated as an audio 'asset' that will have its own unique identifying code to help manage its place in the database and provide a straightforward way of playing it in the game engine.

Once dialogue is recorded, it will need to be translated into different languages, a process known as localisation. For many years this was understood in terms of FIGS, the acronym referring to French, Italian, German and Spanish, but increasingly games are

---

6 This can also be a consideration if the actor is appearing in a theatre play that evening and is understandably nervous about wearing their voice out through lots of shouting or other kinds of projection.

7 I've been involved in voice recording sessions in which the actor is in Los Angeles, my colleague has been in Madrid and I've been in London.

released in many more territories, requiring many more languages and dialects. For each of these languages, an actor with the requisite language skills will be required, and the dialogue will need to be re-recorded as needed. On occasion, the writer of the original dialogue will be queried about the exact meaning of a phrase, either in terms of its gameplay context, or in terms of what a particular piece of slang might actually refer to. Localisation will also apply to on-screen text. For languages which are more wordy like German, this may mean that the original 'string' – the piece of text including spaces and alphanumeric symbols – has to be rewritten since the translation will be too long and can't fit into the allocated number of spaces.

The implementation of systemic dialogue like barks tends to be the province of the studio's sound design team, since it's driven by the game's audio system. For other kinds of dialogue, it may be possible – or indeed required – that a narrative designer goes into the game's editor and places the 'hook' that corresponds to the piece of dialogue, meaning that the speech in question is triggered at the appropriate point in gameplay. In my experience the placement of these dialogue strings can be a highly creative aspect of the role, allowing the narrative designer to experiment and shape the flow of the story in-game.

The complexity of games means that problems are inevitable. These 'bugs' are often associated with technical issues, and developers go to huge efforts to prevent them from occurring. Large scale or recurrent bugs which stop a game from properly functioning can be lethal or at least highly damaging to a new game, such as the problems experienced by *Cyberpunk 2077* when it first launched. This is why studios employ armies of Quality Assurance testers to identify errors and inconsistencies like this, and why bug-testing and bug-fixing is so essential to the game creation process.

Story is not exempt from this quality testing process. As with other crafts, problems can be large or small. Hopefully, fundamental issues of plot, structure and character have been attended to as part of the pre-production process, and the implementation of these elements has happened as intended.[8] Nevertheless, contradictions can emerge, perhaps between dialogue and environmental storytelling, resulting from mis-communication between the narrative, design and art crafts. More minor issues might involve spelling mistakes or 'legacy' names or terms that were changed early in the development process but weren't fixed in every instance. Issues associated with on-screen text problems can be remedied fairly easily by simply attending to the string in the spreadsheet the game is pulling its information from.

Outside the realm of bugs, external pressures can cause difficulties for games ahead of release. One game I worked on had a piece of dialogue intended to herald an explosive combat sequence. Just ahead of release, however, a terror attack occurred in real life in which the perpetrator was reported as saying the exact same phrase as the one we were using in the game just ahead of initiating the atrocity. As the dialogue in question was uttered by the player-character in gameplay and the character's lips weren't visible, it was a relatively straightforward task to remove the line in question and replace it with another piece of dialogue that performed the same functional role.

As a relatively new medium, and one which is dependent on ever changing technology, the processes involved in creating games are themselves constantly evolving. As with other elements, processes and approaches are taken from other storytelling media but they cannot normally be applied wholesale without some level of adaptation. This extends from documentation to the ways in which actors are cast, through the various components of performance to

---

8 Fundamental issues like this are really hard to fix late into the process.

the implementation, synthesis and appraisal of the game's various storytelling elements, and the ways in which these interact with other parts of the game's ecosystem. Changes in technology, coupled to the particular needs of the project, mean that none of these processes are necessarily cast in stone – as with many other aspects of this dynamic medium, everything is subject to change and nuance.

11.
ETHICAL DIMENSIONS

Leicestershire in the East Midlands of the UK, 2004. Seventeen-year-old Warren LeBlanc persuades a friend to go with him to a local park called Stoke Woods, known locally as The Dump. The friend in question is fourteen-year-old Stefan Pakeerah. Warren tells Stefan they're going to meet some girls, but this isn't true. What in fact follows is a frenzied, horrific attack in which LeBlanc bludgeons and stabs Pakeerah to death using a knife and a claw hammer. LeBlanc is subsequently convicted and awarded a minimum of thirteen years for the crime. He's released in 2020, despite concerted attempts by Pakeerah's family to appeal the decision to free him.

Initial reporting of the events suggested that LeBlanc had been obsessed by a notoriously violent video game called *Manhunt* (2003), and that a copy of the game was discovered in his bedroom. *Manhunt* is a stealth game made by Rockstar, developers of the *GTA* series. The player is tasked with controlling James Earl Cash, a Death Row prisoner who must earn his freedom by participating in a series of snuff films and killing various criminal gang members. The game is extremely violent and its use of dark and disturbing imagery a tour de force in grubbiness and unease. The instructions for the game suggest pulling the curtains for maximum atmospheric effect. The game knows the genre it's mining intimately, and exploits the tropes and techniques adroitly.

Though the case was covered in a number of newspapers, the *Daily Mail* in the UK used the horrific events to attack video games and the culture surrounding them. To this end the *Mail* launched a campaign with a front page headline demanding: 'Ban These Evil Games'. This was a carefully calculated echo of a previous campaign the paper had undertaken in the 1980s to get so-called 'video nasties' banned. In that case the *Mail* had campaigned successfully to ban the first two *Evil Dead* movies, *The Texas Chainsaw Massacre* (1974) and *I Spit On Your Grave* (1978), from video rental shops. As well as *Manhunt*, this time around the *Mail* went after *Grand Theft Auto III* (2001) and the little remembered *State of Emergency* (2002), all created by Rockstar, as well as some other titles.

Except this time it didn't work. As more details of the case became apparent, it emerged that the *Daily Mail* and a number of other media outlets had reached the wrong conclusions. In actual fact the *Manhunt* game had been found not in the perpetrator's bedroom at all, but in that of the *victim*, Stefan Pakeerah. The police would subsequently conclude that the game had no connection to what happened and that the motive for the attack was 'drug-related crime'. The court concurred and stated that LeBlanc, and LeBlanc alone, was culpable of the murder.

The alarmist reporting of the initial crime by sections of the media was what we would term a 'moral panic'. The phenomenon was first identified and outlined by the British academic Stanley Cohen to describe attitudes to the Mods and Rockers in his hugely influential study from 1972.[1] Rocker culture of the time concentrated on

---

1 Cohen, Stanley [1972] (2011) *Folk Devils and Moral Panics*. Abingdon: Routledge

motorcycles while mod culture focussed on fashion and music, with many mods riding scooters as opposed to motorbikes. From May 1964 onwards, the press began reporting conflicts between the two tribes at various seaside locations on Britain's south coast. Cohen argued that the media over-exaggerated aspects of sub-cultural activity when it was perceived as a potential threat to existing societal norms, and that the reportage led to further socially unacceptable behaviour.

These days news stories about video games and their apparent deleterious effects are a reliable source of clickbait for digital citizens eager to reinforce their prejudices. What connects earlier moral panics – whether it's video nasties in the '80s, Mods and Rockers in the '60s, horror comics in the '50s or jazz music in the '20s – is that the cultural phenomenon in question hadn't happened before. To an inherently conservative mass media and large swathes of today's social media landscape anything new is strange and foreboding, and therefore a threat to the established order. It's the Shock of the New, and because gaming technology keeps evolving, it's always new.

Often this menace is framed not as a hazard to the person or organisation voicing the opinion but rather vulnerable individuals or groups they're seeking to protect for their own good. Part of the problem is that games have their own rituals and customs, which become more byzantine depending on the platform, genre and particular game or franchise. As with other subcultural activities this is part of the appeal, but such codes and conventions can be difficult for outsiders to fathom. Players moan about having to 'grind', or talk about their favourite 'ARPG', while complaining about 'loot boxes' or their preference for 'PVP' over 'PVE'. Such opinions are often passionately held and forcefully expressed via online forums, which can be startling and worrisome to behold if you don't understand the lingo.

To the outsider, video games can be intimidating, wrapped as they are in this lexicon of exclusive terminology, black, grey and white boxes that unexpectedly give rise to pulsating, interactive audiovisual imagery that seem intent on hypnotising our loved ones. What's worse is that these are games, and as we know games are played exclusively by young people, unless it's chess or crown green bowling. Of course this is a peculiarly Western perspective – other cultures like the Japanese have long understood that games aren't just for children. But despite ratings systems intended to identify when adult themes and imagery are present, the perception of the medium as inherently juvenile persists. So that when sex and violence do arise, we're upset because they don't match our expectations of what the medium is.

The problem is further complicated by a resistance on the part of much of the wider culture to understand that games are increasingly a storytelling medium. Inevitably, as with other kinds of storytelling, conflict is often expressed through violence. Many of the original fairy stories we grow up with have dark, often gothic origins, far removed from the more familiar Disney versions. Early in our lives we hear stories of heroes and heroines wielding swords or spells, vanquishing dragons or armies. World mythologies are replete with such tales, from Perseus and the sword he uses to decapitate the fearsome Medusa, through to Thor's hammer and the war god Kibuki of the Baganda people. Shakespeare's tragedies, most obviously *Macbeth, Romeo and Juliet* and *Hamlet*, feature violent acts that are intrinsic to the plot. The most violent of Shakespeare's plays, *Titus Andronicus*, is seldom staged, because of the ethical (not to mention logistical) challenges involved in representing mutilation and cannibalism on the stage.

In terms of violence, the view that video games are ethically suspect and morally corrosive finds its most pervasive expression in the Columbine High School Massacre. On 20 April 1999, two twelfth grade students, Eric Harris and Dylan Klebold, rampaged through the school with automatic weapons, killing twelve students and one teacher. A further twenty-one people were injured by gunfire and three more people were hurt as they tried to evacuate. The perpetrators killed themselves in the school library, where most of the students they'd murdered had also died. Until the Parkland High School shooting in 2018, the Columbine massacre was the deadliest mass shooting at a US high school.

In the months, years and decades that followed the attack, America sought to identify reasons for an inexplicable atrocity. Many factors were highlighted, including bullying, depression and violent films, as well as violent video games.[2] It is certainly the case that Harris and Klebold played a number of violent shooter video games, including *Doom* (1993), *Quake* (1996), *Duke Nukem 3D* (1996) and *Postal* (1997). Writing in 2007, a psychiatrist, Jerald Block, argued that the games had become a sanctuary for the duo and a means of releasing their pent-up aggression. Block went on to suggest that the decision by the parents to stop the duo from playing the games may have been a significant contributory element in their decision to enact the violence. A fellow psychiatrist, Brooks Brown, argued for the challenges of making any definitive judgement, but did suggest that the virtual worlds of the games helped Harris and Klebold plan their actions.

Whatever the complex truth, the response to the Columbine Massacre and attempt to identify violent games as the primary catalyst has maintained a purchase on the wider culture's view of video games ever since. The ubiquitous academic Henry Jenkins once again found himself at the forefront of the debate, becoming the industry's unofficial mouthpiece in the subsequent Senate

---

2 Gus Van Sant's movie *Elephant* (2003) was based on the attacks, and posits violent video games as one of the key reasons for the killers' actions.

investigation.[3] As Jenkins would later recount, the Committee clearly expected him to link media consumption to violent actions and were disappointed when he instead suggested ready access to guns ought to be a far bigger consideration for policy-makers.

The debates around game violence are amplified further precisely because games are not a purely representational medium, unlike the films and television shows that influence them and with which they're often compared. They don't just depict versions of the real world or fantasy realms and the horrors they contain but offer interactivity chiefly through gameplay. As we saw in Chapter 4, a player performs an action that will have a consequence, and from this they gain a sense of agency. But in certain contexts, this can be highly problematic. For instance, a game like *Custer's Revenge* (1982) not only depicts the rape of a Native American Indian woman but focuses its gameplay progression *around* the act. In other words, unless the player engages in the act of sexual violence, they won't advance and therefore succeed in the game.

Similarly, Rockstar's *Grand Theft Auto: Vice City* (2002) infamously offered players the ability to have intercourse with a sex worker, kill the sex worker and then steal back their money. More recently, another Rockstar game, the Western themed *Red Dead Redemption 2* (2018), featured a suffragette character that the player could choose to murder by, among other things, feeding to an alligator. These days social media allows players who participate in these activities the ability to show them online, effectively bragging about their actions and inviting other people to condone them – or perhaps getting a perverse satisfaction from the outrage it provokes in some quarters.

Writer-designer-director Christy Dena is a long-standing practitioner and theorist. She cautions against singling out the games

---

3 Tying Columbine to Video Games - The New York Times (nytimes.com)

medium in discussions of ethics, suggesting that non-interactive media have their own responsibilities in this regard. As Dena suggests, there are ethical considerations involved in artforms driven by thinking and observation, as we see in films, novels, plays and poetry. Nevertheless, she argues that, 'With interactive forms, there is the potential addition of learning by doing. It is important, therefore, to pay attention to what we're training (or reinforcing) people to do. I think about what mental models, decisions, and actions about their relations with themselves, other humans, and the rest of nature am I facilitating? I feel a moral obligation to, and delight in, giving players opportunities to practise ways of co-flourishing.'

Dena's point about games being a 'doing' medium is crucial for understanding issues around representation. Interactivity complicates how we portray people and cultures in a way that's very different to other traditionally non-interactive storytelling media. As in *Vice City* and *Red Dead Redemption 2*, affording players the ability to treat diverse NPC characters in an abusive fashion mitigates against the desire to portray traditionally neglected groups in a positive light. A common response from developers is that they are purely providing a framework for players to make a decision and that in fact this is the key power of the medium. Through being confronted with difficult choices, the argument goes, players can explore moral dilemmas through the outcomes of the decisions they make and the ramifications that flow from them. In this we see an echo of a pervasive libertarian streak which has long characterised Silicon Valley, and arguably contributed to the current Wild West state of particular connected digital technologies, most obviously social media platforms.[4]

---

4 I've argued elsewhere that the *Grand Theft Auto* series is basically a virtual version of Antonin Artaud's 'Theatre of Cruelty'.

The issue of agency is a key one to consider in relation to ethical considerations around games. Game writer and narrative director Kim MacAskill frames it in these terms: 'Players are creative, they like to break things and not every player will use a feature/decision for the reasons intended by a studio. For example, if I give a player a LEGENDARY MACHINE GUN with the intended purpose to shoot down a wave of brutal enemies, have I considered what else they might use that gun for? Are there innocent characters around? Animals and children? Can they be harmed? Do I need this gun to be limited in how often it can be used to stop-kill? As soon as you consider the agency a player has, the sooner you have to creatively think of ways of stopping going too far or too silly.'

Games are not alone in being sites of culture war conflict. The phenomenon is visible across the pop culture firmament, from movies to comics to music and, of course, politics. Though the battle between progressive and reactive forces has existed for as long as popular culture in the meaningful modern sense can be said to have existed, digital connectivity has served to render such discourses visible.[5] In cinema we can see this in relation to the casting of Kelly Ann Tran in *Star Wars: The Last Jedi* (2017) and Leslie Jones in Paul Feig's 2016 reboot of *Ghostbusters*, which resulted in both actors receiving sustained racist online abuse. Nor is the phenomenon limited to popular culture. At the time of writing, the casting of a black female Juliet in a West End production of the Shakespeare play has attracted enormous racist abuse.[6]

Games, though, can make the dubious claim of having been at the nexus of such debates from the earliest point in the current

---

5 To adapt a point about fandom's use of the Internet originated by Henry Jenkins.
6 Tom Holland's 'Romeo & Juliet' costar Francesca Amewudah-Rivers receives support after her casting sparks racist remarks | CNN

culture wars. In August 2014, the disgruntled ex-boyfriend of game developer Zoe Quinn went online and suggested that Quinn received a favourable review of a game she'd worked on because she'd slept with the journalist in question. The allegation was wholly untrue but nevertheless spread to 4chan, a website where users can post anonymously and which had a history of denigrating Quinn's work. A vitriolic campaign was targeted against Quinn and others who sought to defend Quinn and her work, notably fellow game developer Brianna Wu and the feminist media scholar Anita Sarkeesian. This became known as 'Gamergate'.

The Gamergate campaign was the most organised example of online misogyny in relation to games, and its use of doxing – in which private individuals' personal details are publicized online – along with rape and death threats shows how terrifying its more extreme advocates can become. There are many other examples of this kind of toxic behaviour, ranging from responses to the creative decisions of game studios and the wider ecology of story consultancies. Recent examples include Playground Studio's revelation of the lead female character in their new *Fable* game who didn't match with some online commentators' required standards of beauty, to an extraordinary attack on the narrative consultancy firm Sweet Baby and its supposed Wokist agenda. While some studios and publishers choose to ignore such attacks, others are clearly influenced by the perceived commercial implications of upsetting a portion of the consumer base, even if that element is relatively small.[7]

From the early days of the medium, the game's scenario or story served to contextualise the actions of the player, which necessarily implies an ethical stance. That said, particular genres can be harder to frame than others. I would argue that if a war game claims to be

---

7 But highly vocal.

realistic then it has a moral duty to represent the result of warfare. Suffice to say, this hasn't always been the case, though there are some notable and sometimes surprising exceptions. For instance, *Spec Ops: The Line* (2012) shows the unintended consequences of using white phosphorus on a group of civilians, an action the player is implicated in. For the most part, though, war games based on real world scenarios are often reluctant to show the impact of modern weaponry on civilian populations. Indeed, some games are developed in concert with the military, such as *Full Spectrum Warrior* (2005) and *America's Army* (2002 onwards), and are even used to train service personnel.

In contrast, games which take a particular anti-war position do exist but are often removed from the mainstream. The extent to which this happens depends hugely on the kind of game and the particular nature of the agency the player is awarded. Gonzalo Frasca's *September 12th: A Toy World* appeared in response to the War on Terror, itself provoked by the terrorist attacks on America on 11th September 2001. The Flash-based game was released in 2003 and presents an isometric perspective on an unnamed Middle Eastern city. Mingling with the civilian population are stereotypical-looking terrorists, complete with bandoliers and machine guns.

The player can launch a missile strike on these terrorists, but when the smoke clears it becomes apparent that all they've succeeded in doing is creating more terrorists. The game has no win condition, which is very much the point. Since firing the weapon is the only kind of interactivity on offer, the player has only one choice – either play or don't play. For this reason *September 12th* highlights the distinction between what constitutes a 'game' which in most designations must have a definitive outcome, and a 'simulation', which recreates a scenario but doesn't necessarily have a conclusive end point the user must work towards. The Flash game aesthetic of *September 12th* – the antithesis of those war games featuring photorealistic audiovisual imagery – might seem a peculiar candidate for such a definition, but it's perhaps best understood as a simulation of a philosophical conceit.

This War of Mine is a more mainstream example of an anti-war game. Created in 2014 by Polish-based 11 Bit Studios, *This War of Mine* is a survival game in which the player controls civilians making their way through extremely hazardous war settings. In common with other games I've mentioned, it's inspired by real world scenarios, notably the Siege of Sarajevo (1992-1996) and by multiple other historical events. The player must make decisions on behalf of civilians with no military experience in an effort to ensure their survival until a ceasefire is declared. The game has been critically lauded but has also proven commercially successful, resulting in multiple new DLCs with additional scenarios.

Putting players in scenarios based on events of real world trauma is challenging for the video game medium in a way which doesn't necessarily apply to sequential media. Scottish studio Traffic's *JFK Reloaded* (2004) presents a simulation of the events that resulted in the assassination of President John F Kennedy in Dallas, November 1963. Specifically, the player is tasked with assassinating JFK according to the findings of the Warren Commission, the real world committee that investigated the death of the President and concluded that he was killed by a lone gunman, namely Lee Harvey Oswald.

When *JFK Reloaded* was released it provoked predictable outrage from a variety of places, especially since the game offered a £100,000 reward for anyone who could assassinate JFK in the way outlined by the Warren Commission's report. This, clearly, could be seen as the purpose of the game – to illustrate the implausibility of the official view on the killing.[8] Oliver Stone's 1992 film *JFK*, meanwhile,

---

8 For what it's worth, I don't personally think it was a conspiracy – read Norman Mailer's *Oswald's Tale – An American Mystery* (1995) for the definitive take on Kennedy's death.

provoked a different kind of controversy, primarily in the way in which it combined simulated footage with actual footage. Stone's film, though, is remembered as a formidable critique of the official government position, while *JFK Reloaded* remains far from the public consciousness beyond the initial outrage it provoked.

It's not a stretch to describe game writers and narrative designers as the moral core of many projects, identifying problematic representation when other disciplines might be intent on the gameplay possibilities of a particular scenario or the aesthetic qualities of a specific art asset or environmental setting. In my interview with her, Christy Dena suggests why: 'This is only sometimes the case, but this does happen largely because the writer/narrative designer needs to glue the creative elements together and facilitate player motivation and meaning. Since bigger projects often recycle the same conflict mechanics and extractive relations with characters and environments, it is up to storytellers to make this interesting and fulfilling. Because when repeated the way they are, they're not wholly fulfilling in themselves.'

This isn't to suggest game storytellers are necessarily more ethical than other developers, but speaks more to the fact that part of the role often involves researching elements of the story and game world, and having an implicit understanding of the fictional world that's being constructed. The necessity of understanding the game's overarching narrative structure often means that game writers and narrative designers have an overview of the game which other crafts might not be privy to. I've worked on multiple projects where myself or the wider narrative team have had to push for a more ethical, considered stance in terms of how the game's world, story and characters are portrayed. Sometimes we succeed, very often we don't.

In common with other storytelling media, games exist at a crossroads between art and commerce, and many creative decisions are made in respect to this ongoing, pervasive tension. But from both an artistic and commercial standpoint, it feels important that video games are allowed to engage with contemporary issues and concerns in a meaningful way. Most studios have decisively moved from a position where only certain demographics are portrayed and allowed to play an active, integral role in the unfolding story or wider fictional world. Most understand that curbing the ability of storytellers to depict diverse worlds limits the kinds of stories we can tell. This, by extension, suggests the need for ever more diverse game storytellers.

Ethically this is the right course of action but also makes sense commercially and culturally. It doesn't mean that games stop being fun. Just like TV, cinema and novels, some stories are fun, some are serious. But the more games can do to present themselves as a medium capable of exploring complex issues in a meaningful and sensitive way, the more seriously this supposedly trivial medium will be treated by the wider commentariat. We just need to remember that when the real world collides with the virtual world, it isn't without impact.

12.
DEAD AUTHORS AND EMERGENT STORIES

In 1967, the French literary theorist and philosopher Roland Barthes radically changed how we think about the creation of stories. Barthes formulated the concept of the 'Death of the Author', arguing that how a story is interpreted cannot be guaranteed by the storyteller.[1] This makes a lot of sense. Readers, viewers and players all possess their own subjective understanding, perceived through a prism of personal background, experience and myriad other factors. Someone who is schooled in the study of literature might therefore have a very specific comprehension of Thomas Hardy's *Jude the Obscure* rooted in their knowledge of Hardy and late 19th Century English novels. But someone heralding from a working class background who never went to university might see themselves in Jude's struggle and interpret Hardy's story quite differently. Both perspectives are, of course, valid.

That said, lots of authors aren't prepared to lie in their coffins and concentrate on developing rigour mortis. For instance, the novelist

---

1 Barthes, Roland [1967] (1977) 'The Death of the Author' in Barthes, Roland (1977) *Image Music Text*. London: Fontana Press

Philip Pullman talks about how he's '...a strong believer in the tyranny, the dictatorship, the absolute authority of the writer.'[2] Many writers will recognise this assertion of authorial intent and creative control, the power involved in originating and shaping a particular artistic vision. Since the writer thought it up and put all the hard time and effort into executing it, this position seems eminently reasonable. In fact, for reasons that are cultural, societal and commercial, public discourse is absolutely rooted in this concept of authorial supremacy. Whether it's the latest Amitav Ghosh novel, the new Lucy Prebble play or the photography of Cindy Sherman, we routinely discuss works of art in terms of a single creator. We even do this when the medium in question is heavily collaborative, as is the case with many kinds of mass media storytelling, cinema being the obvious one.[3]

In a sense, of course, all storytelling is to some extent collaborative and emergent. When we create a story in a traditional medium, we're doing so in expectation that the audience will activate the meaning in that narrative. In its most fundamental terms this might mean simply understanding what happens in the story, the order of events, who does what to whom, that kind of thing. The extent to which the audience has to work at understanding the story's deeper meaning obviously differs from example to example. Roland Barthes even differentiates 'readerly' texts which don't require much effort to be understood and 'writerly' texts which demand much more active engagement on the part of the reader.[4]

The interactive nature of games muddies the waters even more, leading Espen Aarseth to develop the concept of ergodic literature I

---

2 philip-pullman.com
3 Famed film critic Roger Ebert even cited the lack of authorship guiding video games as the reason why the medium would never be considered 'Art'. Clearly he hadn't heard of French post-structuralism - or if he had, he decided to ignore it.
4 Barthes, Roland [1974] (2000) *S/Z*. Oxford: Blackwell

discussed in Chapter 2. As we have seen in many different examples, games present stories for players to activate and engage with using multiple inventive techniques. While many games feature a story spine that's surprisingly linear, some offer branching possibilities where the player gets to choose which path they take. Environmental storytelling encourages players to explore and read the world around them to understand it. A discarded meal or an overturned table might suggest to us that a building was rapidly evacuated. A ruined colosseum might speak to a lost civilization. More didactic techniques exist too, like graffiti on a wall or written documents left in an environment or on a person's body. A letter or diary entry might describe the character of a person we killed or might meet later or might never meet. Actively exploring and finding such story fragments, guessing what happened in a location or choosing a path are all part of the fun. Games are, by definition, a collaboration between player and game-maker.

Author-led storytelling is at odds with a much older, oral tradition in which a storyteller might have sat around the fire and incorporated suggestions from the audience, shaping the story according to their preferences. At this stage in the evolution of storytelling, Pullman's tyrannical author with their singular vision, brooking no input, hadn't been born. Stories were a collaborative exercise, in which a tribe or other social grouping would contribute and participate. We can see in this tradition the roots of other kinds of participatory storytelling like fan fiction, in which enthusiasts of a particular franchise or storyworld create their own, often unlicensed tales using familiar characters, locations and events.

Game storytelling, particularly of the multiplayer variety, hearkens back to this older, oral tradition. In a key sense it is collaborative and improvisational, more akin to children playing together with toys or props. *World of Warcraft* (2004-) or *Elder Scrolls* (1994-) in which players band together to complete a quest are prime examples of such collaborative storytelling, in which the framework for an adventure is supplied to the players but their own interactions render the story a unique creation of their own devising. As well as the improvisational techniques we may find in some varieties of theatre, there is an obvious trajectory here from the *Dungeons and Dragons* roleplaying game that emerged in the 1970s and continues to prove hugely influential on wider popular culture.[5]

Arguably, though, the need for an audience renders all storytelling collaborative. A theatre play, a feature film and a television drama need spectators and a novel needs a reader. As I explored all the way back in Chapter 2, none of these media are truly passive, but for some examples the audience is required to be much more explicitly involved in proceedings. This is true of experimental theatre or film, *avant garde* literature and even some more popular forms like Choose Your Own Adventure books and improvisational comedy. This is even more the case with video games, which won't do anything unless the player interacts with them.

Cooperative play, in which two or more users play together, has been a mainstay from early in the medium's commercial history. In 1978 Atari released *Fire Truck*, an arcade game in which two players need to cooperate to drive the titular, articulated vehicle, with one person steering the front and activating the acceleration and brakes, and a second player at the rear controlling the back of the truck. More recently, games like *A Way Out* (2018) and *It Takes Two* (2021) offer cooperative play across split-screens, in which each player must assist the other to achieve gameplay goals. Strictly speaking, though, many early video game experiences were more combative

---

5 Netflix's 1980s-set supernatural series *Stranger Things* being an obvious example.

than collaborative. Some of my earliest, most enjoyable video game memories involve racing against friends in the Formula One themed *Pit Stop 2* (1984), battling my opponent's army in *Beach Head II: The Dictator Strikes Back* (1985) or round-housing them in *The Way of the Exploding Fist* (1985).

Online games have similarly been around for a long time, evolving as networked technology itself has evolved. The internet gave rise to new genres, most notably the MMORPG,[6] which exploded in popularity towards the end of the 1990s. With these came new and very different storytelling opportunities, the result of players being given a world or even universe to explore. There were also rulesets to exploit or subvert, items and artefacts to discover and, most crucially, other players to fight against or team up with, creating clans, guilds or other collectives. Such games have existed in one form or another for a long time, developing their own intricate narrative ecologies and becoming iconic: *Elder Scrolls, Ultima Online* and, of course, *World of Warcraft*.

WoW began in 2004, though the original game, *Warcraft: Orcs and Humans*, dates back to 1994. Created by Blizzard, *WoW* is an MMORPG set in the high fantasy world of Azeroth. The player can create their own avatar and then explore the environment, fighting monsters, finding treasure and interacting with other characters, including both AI-driven NPCs and fellow players. Although it is perfectly possible to play the game solo and not interact with other players, this is explicitly a game that encourages collaboration. To this end, the world of the game is enormous and complex, offering up different regions to explore and a variety of races with their own distinct characteristics and cultures. Since its inception, ten major

---

6 Massively Multiplayer Online Role-Playing Game, in case you've forgotten.

expansions have been released, adding additional story elements for players to engage with.

The long history of the game means that many players tell stories related to their unique experiences within the world. The influential video game website and blog Kotaku collected together some of these accounts, all of them anonymous.[7] One respondent talks about the community's increasingly desperate attempts to try and destroy the fearsome Lich King, only succeeding when a dead shaman rose from the grave and tipped the scales in their favour. At other times the stories are specific to a particular player's experience, like the respondent who talks about their sheer excitement at seeing a naked gnome, their first encounter with another species in the game. Even a singular encounter like this speaks to the collective experience of joining the community, of becoming part of a distinctive imaginary realm but also a member of an exclusive-feeling club.

WoW has collided with the real world in other, more notorious ways too. In May 2011, *The Guardian* carried an extraordinary story.[8] The article explained how, after a day's hard labour breaking rocks and digging trenches, prisoners in the Jixi labour camp in north-east China were forced to toil inside *WoW*. The *virtual* jewels and treasures the inmates acquired, either through mining, fighting mythical creatures or overcoming fellow adventurers, were then sold online by prison warders for real money. None of this was intended by the game's developers of course – it's as though the fiction of the virtual realm somehow leaked into our universe.

Sometimes developers will choose to create a major event in the game world without necessarily knowing the nature of the response from the player base. In the case of the vast science fiction game *Eve*

---

7 25 World of Warcraft Players Tell Their Best Stories (kotaku.com)
8 China used prisoners in lucrative internet gaming work | China | The Guardian

Online (2003-), developers CCP decided to initiate a full-scale attack on the game's New Eden galaxy by a mysterious alien force known as the Drifters. At that point in the game's history *Eve Online* had been running for sixteen years, and the decision to shake things up wasn't without controversy. While NPC factions had historically caused challenges for human players, an attack on this scale was unprecedented. As a result, human players were forced into forming alliances with other players they would have previously fought against, abandoning their own ongoing wars with each other and between different human-led empires.[9]

Other momentous events aren't necessarily planned and can even be the result of a minor oversight or decision. In January 2014, also in *Eve Online*, a player accidentally forgot to make an in-game payment on their space station, meaning that it was suddenly open to capture by opposing forces. Because it was positioned at a crucial strategic location, a colossal battle erupted as forces tried to take control of the space station. Elsewhere in the game's universe, other skirmishes erupted as competing navies and ships attempted to prevent the resupply of vessels to the area. The resulting clash became known as the Battle of B-R5RB and involved over seven and a half thousand players, at that stage potentially the biggest such battle to ever occur in a video game. The game's developers subsequently memorialised the event by erecting a monument to the fallen, a perfect example of the ongoing collaboration between the game's creators and its participants. It's also a prime example of another way in which real worlds and virtual worlds can collide – the mundane reality of a missed payment leading to a mammoth conflagration in an imaginary realm.

In addition to multiplayer and cooperative play of the kinds I've just described, video games offer another, distinctive kind of

9 EVE Online is in chaos after an unprecedented alien invasion | PC Gamer

emergent storytelling in the form of 'procedural narrative'. Though multiple competing definitions exist, loosely speaking this is a design technique in which a framework for a story, scenario or world is created dynamically through the interaction of algorithms and player behaviour. The concept can be slippery because it can manifest in different ways depending on the intentions of the creatives behind the particular project. Fundamentally, the computer or console is working from a set of defined criteria which in concert with player input can lead to unique narrative experiences.

For instance, procedural *generation* is a technique that can be used to create unique elements in a fictional world or universe and is arguably better understood in terms of worldbuilding, a topic I'll explore in more depth in the subsequent chapter. The roguelike *Hades* – which I looked at in Chapter 9 – uses procedural techniques to generate different levels each time the player is killed and chooses to replay. Similarly the science fiction game *No Man's Sky* (2016) presents a procedurally generated universe for the player to discover, constantly creating new planets and biomes to explore and new creatures to encounter. This is achieved by using algorithmic techniques, in which the basis of the art asset in question is already established and the game is able to riff off these parameters to create new and convincing elements for the fictional universe.

Other approaches involve the generation of actual storylines. In Latitude's text-based *AI Dungeon* (2019), Artificial Intelligence is used to create storylines in response to input from the player. Akin to a piece of improvisational performance, the game begins by offering a choice of settings such as fantasy, zombie and apocalyptic, and then elicits more input from the player as required. As the game continues, the player is able to input 'Do', 'See' and 'Say' followed by instructions, as well as a broader category called 'Story' in which the player determines the unfolding events. The player is very much in a position of co-creation with the game, and can share their work with others in a number of different ways.

As I touched upon in Chapter 4, one of the key things that differentiates games as a medium from other kinds of storytelling is the ability to remember. This is especially vital when it comes to procedural storytelling of the kind employed by the 'Nemesis System' featured in Monolith Productions' *Middle-earth: Shadow of Mordor* (2014). Set in Tolkien's enduringly popular fantasy realm – more of which later – the *Shadow of Mordor* takes place between the events of *The Hobbit* and *The Lord of the Rings*, as portrayed in the film trilogies directed by Peter Jackson.[10] The player controls Talion, an original character created for the game, on a mission to avenge the death of their loved ones. The Nemesis System allows Uruk non-playable characters – a more evolved, much more fearsome version of orcs – to remember their interactions with Talion and respond accordingly.

Smaller narratives occur driven by the rivalries these interactions create, enhancing the main narrative and helping to deepen the player's sense of immersion in the fictional milieu. For instance, an orc you killed is liable to remember the exact circumstances and manner of its death. When it returns, it will bear a grudge and constantly express its intention to take its revenge on you. These techniques make your experience of Tolkien's realm feel unique, and in turn give the sense of a world that's dynamic, alive and unpredictable, just like the real world.

In fact, an emphasis on characters of the kind we see in the Nemesis System is often at the root of a lot of procedural storytelling approaches. Others include the Charisma.ai storytelling engine, which facilitates the creation of characters for use in interactive

---

10 Meaning that the game shares a design aesthetic with these movies, something I'll discuss in more depth in subsequent chapters.

experiences, including but not limited to games. The approach is driven by Artificial Intelligence but doesn't require any coding expertise on the part of the creator. Instead, storytellers are able to assign variables to their characters like memory and emotional responses so they can respond dynamically to a variety of inputs from the user. The voices of the characters are themselves generated by AI and as this technology advances, so the quality of these voices is liable to improve.

For Charisma.ai's CEO Guy Gadney, a focus on character was a no-brainer. 'So the way that we looked at story was through three lenses', he says, 'which are that a story can be made up of… the story world, which is where it all happens; the narrative, which is what happens in the story world; and then the characters… And what we found was that for the purposes of what we wanted to do it was the characters that we should focus on. This meant designing characters in a way that could evolve based on what the player said and would evolve consistently within the narrative.' Gadney goes on to suggest that the storyworld is not critical to emotional engagement in the way that characters are.

This makes a lot of sense, since characters are often the element that make the experience feel unique and alive. In the tactical role-playing game *Wildermyth* (2021), the player is offered a choice of randomised characters to control through the fantasy-themed adventure. Each character is assigned both a trait such as 'compassionate hothead' and one of three classes – mystic, warrior and hunter – which can be further fine-tuned depending on the player's proclivities. Crucially, the story beats remain the same, with the procedural nature of the game focussing on the way these characters develop. As well as ageing, making friendships and forming rivalries, the characters acquire new skillsets which in turn can lead to new kinds of storytelling. This results in unique playthroughs each time.

The more responsive the characters are, the better. Video game storytellers and developers have long aspired to create convincing interactive characters, an aspiration that extends well beyond games and into related fields of technology. In fact, bringing to life a dynamic, computer-created and controlled character goes to the very core of discussions around Artificial Intelligence. The ultimate expression of this can most famously be found in the Turing Test, created by Alan Turing, the computer scientist and mathematician. Originally called the 'imitation game', the test tasks a computer with exhibiting sufficient intelligent behaviour so as to fool a human user into thinking it's actually a real person and not a machine. Turing originated the idea of the test in a paper in 1950. In late March 2025, OpenAI's GPT-4.5 officially passed the Turing Test, being identified as human 73% of the time, significantly more than the actual humans who participated.

An early entrant in the Turing Test was ELIZA. Named for Eliza Doolittle from George Bernard Shaw's 1913 play *Pygmalion*, ELIZA is a 'chatterbot' created in the mid-1960s by MIT computer scientist Joseph Weizenbaum. More prosaically, she's a natural language computer program designed to emulate conversation in a way which makes it seem that she understands your replies and is therefore able to further the interaction in a meaningful way. ELIZA is presented as a psychiatrist, an important fictional framing device which helps explain the nature of her responses. For instance, she'll begin a session by asking how you are. Even if you respond with an answer that includes specific elements related to how you feel, she will then answer with another generalist question. At points, however, ELIZA will incorporate elements of your responses into her questions, to make it feel as though she is genuinely listening. Though she didn't win the Turing Test, at the time of ELIZA's creation some commentators were convinced she was real, much to Weizenbaum's puzzlement.[11]

As with many such interactions with contemporary chatbots, there is a strong element of smoke and mirrors involved to make the user feel as though ELIZA is a real person. These are techniques we see again and again in the history of video game characters. In *Dead Meat* (2023), for instance, the player is tasked with interrogating a murder suspect. Asking the character direct questions will only elicit denials. To really find out if the suspect did it, the player needs to get to know the character. The developers' aim is that the story should progress no matter what the player inputs into the system. As the developer Thomas Keane told *Edge* magazine: 'We are setting the framework, creating the lore, the characters, the dynamics, and then it's up to the player to bring their free, open creativity and their own ideas to that experience.'[12]

As the veteran game storyteller Emily Short observes, some players might actively be put off by the ability to say anything to a character knowing that the NPC can say anything in response.[13] Storytelling is by definition a curated experience, reliant on boundaries drawn by the storyteller.[14] Part of the pleasure of engaging with ELIZA is that we understand the codes and conventions involved in talking to a psychiatrist, even if we've never encountered one in real life. If characters are given some parameters – they're an elf, a suspected murderer or indeed a psychiatrist – then that provides the framing for how that character can interact with a user or player.

---

11 Over his career Weizenbaum became increasingly convinced we shouldn't confuse AI for humans - Weizenbaum's nightmares: how the inventor of the first chatbot turned against AI | Artificial intelligence (AI) | The Guardian
12 *Edge* magazine #395 April 2024 – 'Artificial interaction'
13 Ibid.
14 Much more on this later, when we discuss transmedia storytelling.

The multiplicity of approaches to machine-authored storytelling means that there are, inevitably, different perspectives on its strengths and weaknesses, possibilities and limitations. Games with vast worlds or universes that are constantly created afresh, or NPCs that can say anything, sound at face value dazzling and enticing. But part of the pleasure of exploring fictional worlds is surely the familiarity involved, the ability to recognise and navigate around an imaginary realm, to encounter characters we've met before.

Part of the appeal of games like *World of Warcraft* and *Star Wars Galaxies* obtains in players being able to traverse a familiar space with recognisable characters, including fellow player-characters. This means that when fresh elements are added – new locations, new enemies to defeat, new quests to fulfil – they stand out precisely because they're different. In such contexts, emergent storytelling occurs because of the endless possibilities afforded by interactions with other players. These might be competitive or cooperative, and all the variations in-between. Many gamers find huge emotional meaning in such interactions, which can lead to enduring friendships and even romance.

Collaborative storytelling of this kind is of course very different to AI and procedural storytelling. It is, however, another way in which game storytelling refreshes debates around Barthes' Death of the Author. Many storytelling practitioners working in this sphere make similar points. While AI might give us characters who appear convincing within the context of a particular fictional realm, what such interaction lacks is subtext, the meaning behind a line of dialogue or action. Yet Guy Gadney, CEO of Charisma.ai, argues that these elements of a script have always been subject to change thanks to the input of actors and directors. Gadney doesn't believe that the role of the writer or storyteller will vanish with the advent of AI-driven engines like Charisma.ai, and in fact such developments are heavily embedded in much older dramatic arts like immersive theatre and street theatre. Engines like Charisma.ai provide the framework, but it still takes a human, creative intelligence to shape the story, much like a choreographer or director does.

13.
HOW TO MAKE A WORLD

Tallinn, Estonia, 2019. My partner Anna is an academic and writer. She's here for a conference with me and the kids tagging along, cleverly transforming the expedition into a family holiday. It's sunny. We've taken the opportunity to explore the town and our meanderings have brought us to the front door of Alexander Nevsky Cathedral at the summit of Toompea Hill. It's an extraordinary building – designed by Mikhail Preobrazhensky in the Russian Revival style, begun in 1894 and completed in 1900. The cathedral is majestic, and with its ornate, storybook domes, inherently fantastical.

The interior of the orthodox cathedral is, if anything, more sublime than the exterior. Vast reaching stained glass windows provide much of the light, depicting storied images from the Christian faith. Elsewhere there are numerous candles, illuminating pockets of the church but simultaneously creating huge shadows of unknowability.

In the cathedral, occasional, whispered comments emerge and gradually dissipate. Every movement causes an echoing noise that seems to reverberate through me. I can feel it in my stomach and in my bones. It's strangely cold too, given the warmth outside. I can smell incense. In fact, every sense is stimulated. The builders of this extraordinary place knew how to exploit my bodily sensations in all manner of clever ways. It's an approach to design and storytelling that feels oddly familiar.

Afterwards, in Tallinn's midday sunshine, I think about the experience. In its carefully curated manipulation of the senses, the cathedral is designed to give a glimpse and a sensation of the most powerful of beings, an unknowable deity that created an entire world, perhaps even a universe. Because more than anything, churches and other sites of worship are about anticipation. You think this is spectacular and awe-inspiring? Wait till you see what comes next. Heaven, Nirvana, the After Life. Maybe you'll get to see His, Her or Their face. The cathedral builders, with their creation of a shared experience that knows how to expertly shape embodied responses, would have made great game developers.

It's for this reason that the space this most reminds me of isn't the gameplay space itself, but rather the *lobby* area of an online video game. That's the space where you wait until the match starts, just like you'd find in the pirate game *Sea of Thieves* (2018), the comic science fiction adventure *Deep Rock Galactic* (2020) or the grim satire of the *Warhammer* game *Vermintide 2* (2018). Lobbies give clues as to the world you're able to enter, pointers as to the universe you're about to explore. It's here you can meet like-minded individuals – fellow worshippers – and swap insights. Perhaps you'll join up with friends you know or make some new friends. Crucially – and the parallels with religion keep coming – it's also where you can buy things to enhance your experience and show your devotion.

Just as religion and mythology gives us multiple variations on a theme, so do video games. Some game worlds are vibrant and colourful, like the adrenalin-soaked race courses of *Mario Kart* or the witty, endlessly malleable gameplay of Lego's licensed *Star Wars* and Marvel games. Others are far more serious, such as the shadowy environments of the long-running fantasy epic *Diablo* (1997-) or the austere surroundings of the science fiction franchise *Destiny*. And just like the worlds conjured by religion and the mythological, even the darkest of games are capable of engendering pleasure and sometimes even euphoria.

This urge to create virtual universes or imagine other realms expresses an ancient human desire. Many religions – both the ones that are actively practised and the ones that have evolved into mythology – have mechanisms for conveying them, whether they're buildings to worship in, sacred texts to study or songs to be sung. From Paradise to Mount Olympus, from the Egyptian Land of the Dead to the Celtic Tir-na-nog, world culture fairly bristles with alternate realities. Just like video games, these realms are depicted and experienced through a mixture of ritualised behaviour, and conveyed through storytelling that is both temporal and spatial.

Changing technology has always transformed the kinds of worlds we can explore. The arrival of the printing press in the mid-1400s gave religion the power to disseminate detailed explanations of the realms that awaited those who were good and those that weren't, at least according to the strictures laid down. But in time mass publication and widening literacy brought competing virtual worlds to the populace too. Political imaginings and revolutionary tracts of how a world of poverty and suffering could be transformed into something better. Books advancing utopias built on radically different philosophical principles. Most were forgotten. Some changed the real world in dramatic and lasting ways.

The emergence of the novel in particular brought other kinds of intricately realised realm. Margaret Cavendish's *The Blazing World* (1666) was a significant early example of science fantasy storytelling, one which would exert a powerful influence on subsequent works. The sub-genre of 'Travellers' Tales' took us to Jonathan Swift's

Lilliput and Robert Louis Stevenson's *Treasure Island* (1881-82), as well as many other locales that today we don't remember quite so well. Sometimes these worlds were very close to our own, like the London of Charles Dickens and Arthur Conan-Doyle's Sherlock Holmes stories. Sometimes they were worlds set in the far-flung future, in the deepest parts of the sea or distant space like that of HG Wells and Jules Verne. Other times they were extraordinary fantasy realms like Lewis Carroll's Wonderland and L Frank Baum's Oz. Through the course of the twentieth century they would continue to evolve through the works of Isaac Asimov, Robert Heinlein and Leigh Brackett, to name just three luminaries of the so-called pulp era.[1]

But it's impossible to talk about worldbuilding without reference to JRR Tolkien. From literature through cinema, from television to radio and games, his influence is pervasive and enduring.[2] There are the adaptations of his most notable works of course, most obviously Peter Jackson's *The Lord of the Rings* (2001, 2002 and 2003) and *The Hobbit* (2012, 2013 and 2014) trilogies, but also highly successful BBC Radio dramatisations in the 1980s. More recently Amazon's *Rings of Power* transformed some of Tolkien's ancillary material into a big budget television series. And there are the games. From Melbourne House's versions of *The Hobbit* and *The Lord of the Rings* to tie-ins to the Jackson movies to Games Workshop's miniatures range, Tolkien's stories have been adapted and dramatised into ludic form, but also frequently expanded upon.

---

1 Wolf, Mark (2012) *Building Imaginary Worlds: The Theory and History of Subcreation*. Abingdon: Routledge
2 The pervasiveness of Tolkien's worldbuilding isn't to everyone's taste, though. In his brilliant, under-appreciated book *Wizardry and Wild Romance* (2004), science fiction and fantasy author Michael Moorcock is highly critical of Tolkien's middle class cosiness, deriding it as 'Epic Pooh'.

Arguably a key element in the enduring appeal of Tolkien's world is a sense of playfulness. According to the academic Michael Saler, Tolkien always wanted his world to be a collaborative undertaking, and Saler notes that for fans it was considered 'a playful site, one that permitted participants to challenge normative narratives of the Primary World, including those of the nation, religion, and identity.'[3] This might go some way to explaining the enduring power of Tolkien's creation, as well as identifying a subversive streak that feels at odds with Tolkien's inherently conservative politics, as evidenced in his love of the bucolic over the urban.

The Hobbit and *The Lord of the Rings* take place in Middle-earth, but this is itself situated in Arda, a densely conceived world in which Tolkien could explore his own creative impulses. In *The Silmarillion* (1977) Tolkien recounts the myths and stories of the universe of Eä and the world of Arda, which corresponds to our planet Earth. Middle-earth is just one of the continents of Arda – the others comprise the Blessed Realm of Valinor, the region of Beleriand and island of Númenor, heavily influenced by the story of Atlantis. Since it's telling the vast story of these lands, *The Silmarillion* necessarily contains condensed versions of *The Hobbit* and *The Lord of the Rings*, as though we're viewing them from fifty thousand feet.

But Tolkien's position as the grand master of worldbuilding arguably owes as much to his scholarly activities as his fiction. He was an esteemed academic and folklorist, as well as an expert practitioner. In 1939, while giving the prestigious Andrew Lang Lecture, he coined the idea of 'subcreation'. Some eight years later the lecture would form the basis for his essay 'On Fairy-Stories', and the term would become integral to describing and analysing the process of worldbuilding,

---

3 Saler, Michael (2012) *As If: Modern Enchantment and the Literary Prehistory of Virtual Reality.* Oxford: Oxford University Press

otherwise known as the creation of a secondary world – or indeed universe.[4] Tolkien was an expert in linguistics, and in fact constructed the world of Middle-earth because he wanted a place to explore and experiment with his invented languages. Unsurprisingly, he saw language as a critical part of the subcreative process.

Language was a critical component of the first digital worlds that started to emerge in the 1970s. Multi-User Dungeons (MUDs) are multiplayer virtual worlds that operate in real time, typically bringing together role-player elements, combat mechanics and some kind of framing story with social elements like online chat. In this way they anticipated the complex immersive worlds and universes of games like *World of Warcraft* and *Destiny* by several decades. The key difference is that MUDs are text-based, creating their shared worlds through the word alone, akin to the standalone text adventures of the 1970s and 1980s produced by Infocom and others.

The first MUD was created by Richard Bartle and Roy Trubshaw at Essex University in 1978. Using a system known as a Local Area Network (LAN), participants could connect to a server and interact with each other and with aspects of the environment. The world of the game would continue for some time before periodically resetting itself. A key point of difference with the games that came before was that it was a dynamic world, in that player actions could influence how the world developed in a lasting way. This mutability made MUDs immersive and thrilling, and laid the groundwork for larger scale games like the MMORPGs that came later.[5]

The journalist Matthew Ball suggests that MUDs are effectively a computer-mediated version of *Dungeons and Dragons*, which is a

---

4 Tolkien, JRR (1938) 'On Fairy-Stories' in Tolkien, JRR (2006) *The Monsters and the Critics and Other Essays*. London: HarperCollins
5 Bartle, Richard (2003) *Designing Virtual Worlds*. London: New Riders

helpful way of understanding them.[6] That said, Bartle makes the point that the 'Dungeon' component of the MUD acronym derives from the fact that his co-creator Trubshaw had been playing a version of the text-based adventure *Zork* called *DUNGEN* and simply wanted the word 'Dungeon' to complete the acronym. Despite the acronym, MUDs don't have to be set in dungeons – although, of course, many did indeed borrow the sword and sorcery theming from *D&D*, which itself is arguably influenced by Tolkien's subcreation from years earlier.[7]

MUDs come in all different flavours. For instance, a MUSH is a Multi-User Shared Hallucination, which is notable for allowing users to add and embellish the virtual world as they see fit, perhaps adding new rooms or objects. Historically MUSHes tended to favour the more social aspects of online interaction, though they subsequently became used for role-playing games. A MOO, meanwhile, was a MUD, Object-Oriented, and featured a fully functional object-oriented programming language, giving players even more flexibility to alter the world.

Bartle and Trubshaw's impulse for creating virtual worlds are fascinating and instructive when thinking about contemporary games, particularly in terms of an industry which has historically been conservative in its attitudes to diverse representation. Bartle and Trubshaw joined Essex University in the late 1970s. Both were working class, northern students, and subject to petty prejudice. Bartle is on record as saying that in creating MUD they wanted to

---

6 Ball, Matthew (2022) *The Metaverse: And How It Will Revolutionize Everything.* London: WW Norton and Co

7 'Arguably' because the extent of the influence – if any – of Tolkien on *Dungeons and Dragons* is a subject of ongoing controversy.

make a 'world... better than the real world' in which participants could experiment with their identity and find themselves.[8]

As we saw in Chapter 7 in relation to Robbie Cooper's *Alter Ego* exhibition, digitally-created virtual worlds have long been a site of what we might now call identity politics. Bartle is very clear that the creation of that first MUD was a 'political act', and indeed his sustained interest in the ethics of digital subcreation extends into his book *Designing Virtual Worlds*, published in 2004. Of course it's true that all acts of creation are in some way political. Games and virtual worlds which try to posit themselves as apolitical are simply re-presenting the status quo and often reinforcing various stereotypes and the dominant worldview that comes with it. But Bartle and Trubshaw's work was a first radical step in constructing virtual worlds that challenged norms and enabled players to explore alternate versions of themselves unfettered by society's preconceptions.

This subversive urge continued through other games and virtual worlds as the medium evolved. Originally created in 1985 and released for the Commodore 64's Quantum Link online service the following year, *Habitat* was devised by Janet Hunter, Randy Farmer, Chip Morningstar and Aric Wilmunder. It's considered to be the first attempt at a large scale, commercial virtual community, an early example of a MMORPG.

Habitat stands out because unlike most of its MUD predecessors, it was really the first concerted attempt to make a graphically-led virtual world. Players were able to dial into the game using their modem and control their avatar, offering a third-person perspective on their character. They could see and interact with other players and objects within their particular locale. In fact, the creators of *Habitat* stressed the importance of community interaction above any other

---

8 Richard Bartle, from *The Origins of the Metaverse* (BBC Radio Four 2022)

factor, believing this would be key to the success of cyberspace, far more than the technology itself or the system's use of information.[9]

In *Habitat* it's possible to see the continuing significance of identity in virtual worlds which was so crucial to Bartle and Trubshaw in their work but also another important instance of collaborative storytelling. Writing in 1993, ground-breaking American game designer Brenda Laurel notes the element of 'co-design' inherent in allowing users to collaborate with *Habitat*'s system to create the look of their 'agent' or avatar. As she says, this might extend to gender and age as well as 'general attractiveness' which the player chooses to present to other players in the virtual world of the game.[10]

At the same time, *Habitat* is also useful to think about because of the ways in which it recreates and reinforces established ways of doing things, particularly around how society operates and communal rule-making. The citizens of the game were responsible for creating its rules and enforcing them. Since avatars could be robbed and even murdered by fellow players, the early stages of the game were evidently chaotic and anarchic. In time, however, the community was able to develop the rules and regulations necessary to maintain order, including a kind of police force. This remains an ongoing tension for game worldbuilders – the extent to which virtual worlds recreate societal norms and conventions versus the extent to which they challenge and subvert them.

Another important tension exists around the point at which storytelling and worldbuilding intersect. The virtual worlds of Margaret Cavendish, Lewis Carroll and Tolkien were conveyed through sequential and non-interactive novels. Later inheritors of the tradition like novelists Susanna Clarke, NK Jemisin and

9 The Lessons of Lucasfilm's Habitat (stanford.edu)
10 Laurel, Brenda (1993) *Computers as Theatre*. Essex: Addison-Wesley

Ursula Le Guin, along with film directors like Steven Spielberg, George Lucas, Tim Burton and Bong Joon-ho similarly work in non-interactive media.[11] By comparison, digital worlds are often dynamic and responsive, spatial and exploratory. We've seen that they can contain sequential stories but very often such stories are activated by the actions of the player. Equally the spatial world of the game can be presented in a sequenced way – many games force you along particular routes. Open world games often do this as a means of progressing you through the game's story or indeed stories plural.

Understanding where storytelling ends and worldbuilding begins is big business. Insights and approaches can originate from any number of places with varying degrees of validity, manifesting as guidebooks, articles in journals, online tutorials, in-person masterclasses, creative writing weekends, you name it. Beyond the professional storytellers with experience conceiving and building fictional worlds for a variety of media, many academics have analysed case studies and drawn their own conclusions regarding the techniques of different world-builders.

For the narrative director Karen Hunt, worldbuilding is very much a facet of storytelling: 'Storytelling for me, is "the what"? What are you doing? We are telling a story. How are we telling it?' Narrative lead Rianna Dearden's view of storytelling is similarly all-encompassing: 'Storytelling is the giant umbrella (sorry, love a metaphor!) It's the method you choose to tell the plot, explore the characters, chronicle the history. It's everything from how a weapon is taught to how you communicate that that button will take you to the main menu, and then everything in between.'

Narrative designer Anjali Shibu, meanwhile, breaks the two into discrete camps: 'If I was to keep it simple, I'd say Storytelling is the

---

11 The obvious exception being George Lucas, who has long been interested in the power of interactivity, and to some extent Spielberg too.

What? Why? Where? When and How? for your characters. What's their motivation? Why does it drive them? Where is it driving them to or where do they intend to go? When did (will or can) it affect them? How does (or did) it change them or their worldview? And, how do you show this to players without telling?' For Shibu, worldbuilding refers to, '...the literal building blocks of the world. Anything related to the environment from billboards and advertisements to language, clothing, setting, slang, and how it affects the NPCs and therefore our character. This is where lore about cool swords or little voice recordings come in too!'

Yasmeen Ayyashi is similarly clear on the distinctions but also the overlaps: 'In relation to narrative design (in experiential contexts), storytelling is the act of narration space, over time, through various "tellers". The definition of "tellers" in this context expands through characters, objects and environments, to consider the dynamic relationships between all the elements that make up the diegetic world... Worldbuilding on the other hand is the creation of the consistent logic of the world within which the story takes place. It is the process of articulating diegetic worlds.' For Ayyashi, worldbuilding is where the act of collaborative storytelling finds its focus: 'The practice of worldbuilding for experiential narrative formats involves a voluntary relinquishing of control – on the part of the narrative designer – to allow narrative threads to emerge within the frameworks that they've created for participants to engage with, in the active co-creation of the storyworld. They design the subjectivity into the narrative experience.'

Social media commentators often have strong opinions on the subject of worldbuilding too, though they can lack the insight, rigour and experience of professional world-builders and analysts. In one particular example that began on Reddit and subsequently spread to the X platform – still referred to by most people as Twitter – a poster criticised the latest animated film from acclaimed director Hayao Miyaki, *The Boy and the Heron* (2023). The poster bemoaned the lack of logic behind the film's worldbuilding as evidenced in its magic system and the ways in which its characters 'scale' against each other. For this individual, not explaining these crucial aspects made it impossible to be invested in Miyaki's story.

For context, Miyazaki's films are renowned for their impressionistic, dreamlike quality. Films like *Laputa: Castle in the Sky* (1986), *Spirited Away* (2001) and *Howl's Moving Castle* (2004) are widely considered masterpieces of animated storytelling. The 'rules' of the world are never explained because it's not necessary and one suspects Miyazaki would be baffled if he was asked to start rationalising his creations in this way. We travel with Miyazaki's characters through their stories in worlds which defy explanation, and that's fine, because that's the nature of his stories.

What's fascinating is that the author of the post was trying to port across an understanding of fantasy derived from the gaming sphere to a particular kind of storytelling which is poetic and discursive. From a gaming perspective it's perfectly valid to talk about the importance of rule systems, since the scale of many games means that the world and its mechanics have to be built in a systemic way. Bespoke elements are certainly impactful but they're also time-consuming and expensive to create, and so are often used sparingly. Of course movies engage in reuse but to nowhere the extent required by many contemporary video games.

In a similar vein, some commentators have advanced 'soft' worldbuilding to describe an approach in which most elements of a fictional world are not explained, as opposed to 'hard' worldbuilding where the logic behind every aspect is worked out in minute detail. At face value the term 'soft' worldbuilding might seem fine, but it's not a term that stands up to scrutiny. Worldbuilding is by definition 'hard', otherwise what's being described is simply storytelling. As I talked about in Chapter 9, storytelling is as much about what you don't say as what you do say – explaining everything to your audience will inevitably slow the momentum of the story.[12] Worldbuilding, by contrast, requires these details to have been thought about in depth, even though they aren't necessarily made explicit.

Arguably games are much better suited to intricate worldbuilding than most other media, precisely because of their exploratory nature. Uncovering a world is part of the pleasure of many kinds of game. The extraordinary, unforgiving dark fantasy epic *Elden Ring* exemplifies this approach, in which stories are to be unearthed by the player, definitely not handed to them. Sequential media must necessarily balance worldbuilding with the need to maintain the impetus of a plot. Tolkien, for instance, spends a lot of time describing Middle-earth to us in *The Lord of the Rings*, but is careful to return to the action as required. When George Lucas made his *Star Wars* prequel trilogy he arguably concentrated on worldbuilding at the expense of the kind of storytelling that made the original movies so successful.

This chimes with the views of writer, artist and designer Tom Abba: 'Worldbuilding should be invisible, I think. If it's laboured then it becomes the point of the experience, and you'd be better off being a mapmaker. Storytelling assumes a world, and brings it into being without overstressing the world in which it takes place. It's also, arguably, a matter of textuality and (sorry) a postmodern approach.

---

12 Back to Hemingway's 'Iceberg Theory'. Interestingly, game designer Neil Young posited the idea of 'additive comprehension' – a sort of anti-Iceberg Theory – to describe the way in which new story elements can be added to deepen or enlarge our understanding of a story, using the addition of the origami unicorn to later releases of the movie *Blade Runner* as a prime example. Henry Jenkins uses the term in relation to transmedia storytelling – more of that particular subject later.

Readers know a lot of other things, and can be trusted to infer a lot too.'

Despite the differences between interactive and non-interactive media, the worldbuilding we see in today's video games nevertheless owes much to what came before, including religion and mythology, novels and films. The collaborative nature of some kinds of digital worldbuilding allows for subversive storytelling, as we saw in relation to Richard Bartle's intention for the first MUDs through *Habitat* and into contemporary video game spheres. At the same time, virtual worlds can reinforce narratives of subjugation and control we recognise all too well from the real world, whether it's rules of patriarchy, class or gender. Equally, subverting the roles of the virtual world doesn't necessarily mean being progressive – in fact a lot of supposed subversion is toxic and reactionary, often reinforcing power relations from the real world.

Beyond this, the digital worlds of games are increasingly part of interconnected fictional universes spanning different kinds of media, in ways markedly different from the licensed games that have been the mainstay of the industry for many years. Once again, these vast imaginary realms offer as many opportunities as they do challenges. Suddenly TV shows, films, books and other kinds of sequential storytelling media find themselves part of much larger fictional ecologies in which video games carry equal weight. It's time for the Mega-Narrative to raise its head.

14.
RISE OF THE MEGA NARRATIVE

By this point it might not come as too much of a surprise to find out I was kind of a nerdy kid. In the pre-Internet era I got my fixes wherever I could. *Doctor Who* and *Blake's 7* on TV. *Star Wars, Battlestar Galactica* and *Indiana Jones* in the cinema. My dad's collection of pulpy sci-fi novels and short story collections with their lurid covers. Comics, too, like my brothers' copies of *The Tomb of Dracula* and *Planet of the Apes*, and later *Spider-Man* and *The Incredible Hulk*. And, of course, the flashing lights and discordant beeps of the devices that would come to shape my life in so many ways, from early encounters with arcade machines like *Gorf* through handhelds like Grandstand's *Munchman* all the way to my first Atari computer. We didn't know it at the time, but this moment in history was the hinge between the analogue and the digital worlds.

It was also the era of licensed properties. In fact, tie-ins had existed long before I was born. There were the toys based on the Gerry Anderson shows like *Thunderbirds and Captain Scarlet*, not to mention James Bond spinoffs. The *Doctor Who Annual* published by World Distributors first appeared in 1965, only two years after the show started. And before that there were spinoffs from the *Eagle* comic, all the way back through the radio shows that dominated the airwaves in the 1940s and 30s. In fact, you can keep going back – the long running British chocolate range *Quality Street* is derived from a little remembered theatre play of the same name by Peter Pan creator JM Barrie. By my time we were all reading the novel and comic adaptations of big tent movies like *Star Wars* and *Star Trek*, especially as they often came out before the movies in question. Before the Internet, DVDs and VHS tapes, if you wanted to experience an old *Doctor Who* story, the only way of doing it was to get hold of a Target novelisation.

In those days, though, licensed media were utterly disposable. We can see the TV shows and movies from which they sprang as the *ur-texts*, the definitive, canonical version of events.[1] As far as the Intellectual Property (IP) owners were concerned, tie-in comics, novels and other kinds of merchandising were lesser things, easily contradicted and overwritten by the parent show or film. These days, it's very different. Shared storyworlds reaching across multiple different kinds of media are all the rage. Cinemas, television streaming services, bookshops, comic stores and various gaming platforms are packed with stories spun from collective worlds and universes. IP holders struggle to make sure everything is integrated and that everything matters. Whether they succeed or not is another question.

As with the preceding discussion of worldbuilding, the precedents go back a long way. Greek mythology is full of immortal beings, heroes, heroines and monsters who move between tales and are otherwise connected through familial and romantic relationships. In Chinese mythology, the figure of Judge Bao Zheng, a wise and benevolent

---

1 'Canon' is key to this discussion – what fans think is 'real' isn't necessarily the same as what the people in charge of the franchise think is canon.

figure, recurs in multiple tales.[2] Religious tales, too, feature recurring characters across stories, and in the case of the Gospels depict the same events from varying perspectives. There are literary precedents too. Characters from Anthony Trollope's *Chronicles of Barsetshire* (1855-1867) appear in each other's stories, a technique other authors have emulated. Stephen King has carefully built links between his novels, an approach reflected in the television adaptation *Castle Rock* (2018-2020). Even Agatha Christie, who took pains that Hercule Poirot and Miss Marple never met, created other characters that encountered both detectives, suggestive of a shared fictional universe.

The walls of video game universes have been similarly porous since the earliest days of the medium. Mario, for instance, proved such a hit in the original arcade game *Donkey Kong* (1981) that he was soon awarded his own game, *Mario Bros* (1983). As well as further instalments in the *Donkey Kong* and *Mario Bros.* franchise, supporting characters were given their own outings too, such as Mario's brother Luigi, Yoshi and the villainous Wario. Over subsequent decades the expansion of the franchise saw the characters move between genres of game, including the perennial favourite *Mario Kart*, which brings together many different characters in a multiplayer and online environment, and the hectic *Super Smash Bros Melee* (2001). The universe also spilled into other media such as cartoons and films, with varying degrees of critical and commercial success.[3]

The current highly integrated version of shared world storytelling – often described in both commercial and academic contexts as

---

2 As described in Jess Nevin's 2006 book *Heroes and Monsters: The Unofficial Companion to The League of Extraordinary Gentlemen.* London: Titan Books
3 These days different game titles are increasingly set in established fictional universes, echoing the approaches taken by other media. For instance, the Remedy Connected Universe currently contains *Control* (2019) and the two entries in the *Alan Wake* saga. *Deathloop* takes place in the same universe as the *Dishonored* games, albeit centuries in the far future.

'transmedia storytelling' – evolved from the licensed fiction and merchandising that came to dominate the mass media age of the twentieth century. As the term suggests, beyond telling stories set in the same world or universe using the same medium, transmedia storytelling refers to an approach in which all sorts of different media are used to convey stories set in a consistent fictional universe. These can include movies, television shows, novels, comics and video games, as well multiple techniques exploiting social media. The most high-profile version is the one we see in the MCU and *Star Wars*, in which television shows tell stories set in particular eras alluded to in other media, or introduce characters we haven't met before, and characters move between movies and other media. Connective digital technologies make accessing such material easier than ever before.

Video games have long been an essential part of crossmedia franchises. For a risk averse industry, it makes sense to work on licensed properties that benefit from brand recognition, as is the case with big budget movies. Most obviously this 'worldshaping' as opposed to 'worldbuilding' takes the form of adaptation, in which an existing story in a different medium like a film or novel is turned into a game.[4] As with any form of adaptation, the process involves multiple techniques in which the existing storytelling approach of the original work is reimagined for the 'destination' medium. As ever, interactivity can make this task challenging, but when executed correctly it's also extremely rewarding for creators and consumers alike.

Video game adaptations based on hit movies began to appear early in the history of commercially available games. These would often

---

4 I'm using 'adaptation' as a catchall definition here to include dramatization, although strictly speaking we can understand the transformation of a non-dramatic story like a novel or short story into a dramatic form like a video game as dramatization. Adaptation refers to other techniques like adding or removing scenes, cutting characters or introducing new characters.

take iconic scenes from their source material and focus the product around them. For instance, Parker Brothers' adaptation of the second *Star Wars* movie *The Empire Strikes Back* (1980) took the AT-AT battle from the beginning of the film and transformed this into gameplay. In a similar vein, the original 1982 *Tron* movie spawned *Tron: Deadly Discs* (Mattel 1982) and Bally Midway's *Tron* arcade game, which included a version of the light cycle race and tank battle from the film. For films that featured quest-solving aspects as key parts of the plot like *Raiders of the Lost Ark* (1981) and *The Goonies* (1985), the adaptations took these elements and focussed the game around them.

Because video games are by definition active, it makes sense that the action or puzzle elements of films become the basis for the video game adaptation. Beyond the aforementioned brand familiarity, this is the reason that these kinds of stories are chosen for adaptation. In turn, and recalling my discussion from Chapter 5, this explains why certain genres like action and adventure films, science fiction, horror and thrillers lend themselves much more readily to adaptation than some other genres. It's hard to imagine turning a social-realist drama into a commercial video game, though an adaptation of a Ken Loach film might make for an intriguing experimental exercise for an *avant garde* game developer.

For game scholar Jesper Juul writing back in 2001,[5] this was a key aspect in explaining why games aren't really stories at all. Juul discusses the arcade adaptation of *Star Wars*, which focussed on the famous 'trench run' from the original *Star Wars* movie, in which Luke Skywalker pilots his X-Wing space fighter over the surface of the Death Star and delivers the torpedoes into the exhaust port, thus destroying the Empire's space station and saving the day. As Juul observes, while the game emulates the audiovisual look of Luke's attack it doesn't

5 Games Studies 0101: Games telling Stories? by Jesper Juul (gamestudies.org)

translate the exact events of the film, and so isn't really a retelling. In subsequent years Juul shifted his position significantly in regards to an understanding of story and representation in games,[6] but what this position misses is that adaptation is by definition a fairly free form activity anyway. Film adaptations of famous novels frequently change elements, annoying existing fan-bases in the process. Arguably the important point is to convey the spirit of the original work more than anything else.

Both inside and outside the industry, game adaptations are often perceived as cash-ins with little inherent value of their own. Such a view is not without justification, given the history of licensed tie-ins. In 1982, Atari rushed out a version of *ET – The Extra Terrestrial*, an adaptation of Steven Spielberg's all-conquering family science fiction movie from that same year. The game's Christmas release date meant that veteran designer Howard Scott Warshaw only had five weeks to develop it. Hardly surprising that the result wasn't exactly stellar. In fact the game was so terrible it's often cited as one of the major reasons for the great video game crash of 1983, though it was only one of a number of poor quality games churned out by third party producers during that period. For years urban myth suggested that vast quantities of unsold copies of the game had been buried by Atari in a landfill site, a sort of horror story game developers tell each other about the dangers of a truncated development process.[7]

Similar challenges have dogged attempts to translate successful games into other media. Feature film adaptations of video games like *Mario Bros* (1993) and *Wing Commander* (1999) are notoriously bad. Even (arguably) more successful efforts like *Resident Evil* (2002-2016)

---

6 Juul, Jesper (2005) *half-real: Video Games Between Real Rules and Fictional Worlds.* London: The MIT Press
7 In 2014 the site was eventually discovered in New Mexico, though it turned out it contained very few copies of the notorious *ET* cartridge.

and the various *Tomb Raider* movies (2001-2018) were greeted with responses that were decidedly mixed. Of course, the irony is that many of these video game franchises were themselves inspired by genres or specific films in the first place, from the survival horror of *Resident Evil* and *Silent Hill* to the obvious influence of the *Indiana Jones* movies on the *Tomb Raider* games.

The reasons film studios and television production companies seek to exploit existing IP aren't difficult to discern. Simon Pulman, an entertainment lawyer with a focus on complex rights transactions at the intersection of film, TV and gaming, frames it this way: 'Superficially it's commercially driven. *The Last of Us, Fallout* and the *Super Mario Bros.* movie were all colossal hits, which has led to many producers, streamers and studios seeking their own hits derived from games. In success, there's the potential for developing an audiovisual franchise based on games IP, which can be a major driver for media company value.'

But Pulman suggests it's something more too, identifying the emotional pull of game franchises for certain demographics: 'Many of us in our 30s and 40s have grown up playing games all our lives. We have a deep affinity for these characters and worlds, and in some instances we've spent dozens or even hundreds of hours within them. That leads to a strong desire to see those worlds on screen in a different medium, to explore different stories within those worlds, and – in the case of something like *Super Mario*[8] – to share those stories with our friends and families, who may not be gamers themselves. Simply put, games have the richest story worlds and most loyal and passionate fanbases of virtually any IP.'

---

8 Pullman is here talking about *The Super Mario Bros.* movie from 2023, a much more highly regarded outing than its chronic predecessor.

This last point feels really important. As I've discussed, contemporary game worlds are often highly exploratory and therefore need to be dense and richly conceived. HBO's *The Last of Us* television adaptation arguably benefits as much from the worldbuilding undertaken by the game developers as it does from its deft implementation as a TV show. The same could be said of the acclaimed *Fallout* series based on the long running game franchise and the lesser known *Twisted Metal* adaptation, which fandom has similarly greeted with approval. Not that worldbuilding is everything – the *Borderlands* games are famed for a particular kind of storytelling and quirky, immersive worldbuilding, but the recent feature film struggled to be anything less than annoying.

Not that the challenges of adapting between media are limited to games, television and cinema. Narrative lead Rianna Dearden adapted John Wyndham's classic science fiction novel *The Kraken Wakes* (1953) into a video game for Charisma.ai: 'When adapting a novel into a game, there's just too much to tell,' she explains. 'When asking your audience to make intelligent decisions about how to progress, as you do in games, there is less capacity for cognitive load. So, game storytelling often requires a distilling that novels don't. It's especially hard if you love the novel! All these details you adore that you suddenly have to cut!'

The emphasis on adaptation, the translation of an existing story from one medium to another, makes a lot of sense. Depending on the creative decisions of the professionals doing the adaptation, elements like plot, characters and even scenes can be ported across from one medium to another and reimagined accordingly. But adaptation is a very different beast to transmedia storytelling, which involves creating new stories for the medium in question. Not that the distinction is always clear. In Chapter 4, I talked about the opening sequence of *Indiana Jones and the Great Circle*, which reinterprets the beginning of the movie *Raiders of the Lost Ark* in gameplay terms before shifting to tell a wholly new story. The chance to re-enact a famous sequence from a movie is a particularly enticing fantasy, and in the case of *Indiana Jones and the Great Circle* means that the game is both adaptation and transmedia storytelling. *Ghostbusters: The Video Game* (2009) meanwhile takes a different approach by including a sequence that is very similar to the famous scene in which Bill Murray's character Venkman is 'slimed' in the original movie, though technically the game's sequence is a part of the new plot created for the game.[9]

Indeed, some commentators like the late, great film theorist David Bordwell have argued that transmedia storytelling is really just another version of adaptation and needs to be understood in those terms. In a fascinating debate with Henry Jenkins, Bordwell makes the point that a work of art needs to be bounded, in the way that a painting has a frame. Bordwell also argues that the process of adaptation can include invention of new elements, just as transmedia storytelling does. The counter argument, as articulated by Jenkins, is that transmedia storytelling is wholly concerned with creating new material rather than retelling.[10]

As I said at the beginning of this chapter, the roots of transmedia storytelling are traceable back through the 20th century and certainly into the 19th.[11] But the contemporary manifestation finds its origins in the work of academic Marsha Kinder in the early 1990s. She was

---

9 Both Dan Aykroyd and Harold Ramis, who wrote the first two films, contributed to the story for the 2009 game.
10 The Aesthetics of Transmedia: In Response to David Bordwell (henryjenkins.org)
11 I'm really talking here about the emergence of a commercially-driven version of transmedia storytelling of the kind we might recognise from contemporary examples – but as we saw in the preceding chapter, there are many other much older examples of crossmedia storytelling.

the first person to identify the term 'transmedia' in her analysis of children's consumption of media in the early 1990s. Kinder's work explored the ways in which children moved seamlessly between different media types, including television and video games, with an emphasis on *Teenage Mutant Ninja Turtles*.

Henry Jenkins would later take the term, add the 'storytelling' element and expand it to describe the phenomenon of integrated cross-media storytelling. In his book *Convergence Culture* (2008), Jenkins analysed *The Matrix* franchise, exploring the ways in which the Wachowskis, the siblings behind the original 1999 movie, sought to utilise different methods of telling a connected story, set in the same fictional universe, across multiple interrelated media. In addition to the two sequels to the first film, *The Matrix Reloaded* (2003) and *The Matrix Revolutions* (2003), the universe included the PlayStation game *Enter the Matrix* (2003) and *The Animatrix* (2003), an anime series.

In talking about *The Matrix* Jenkins is really referring to a single story that's spread across multiple media. In other words, you wouldn't fully understand the story unless you'd consumed all the constituent elements, including the movie, games, anime and comics. While this is certainly a key way of undertaking transmedia storytelling and something we often see in the indie sphere, in terms of the mainstream it's not that common. When we discuss transmedia storytelling today most people are talking about multiple different stories set in the same universe but told using different kinds of media. A movie tells one self-contained story, a television show another, a video game another, but they all exist in the same fictional universe and may include all kinds of content that links them together. This is important, because it means you don't necessarily need to have consumed all the different elements to understand other stories set within the same universe.[12]

These early debates about what did and did not constitute transmedia storytelling weren't simply an abstract academic exercise. The Producers' Guild of America (PGA) sought to define transmedia storytelling exclusively in relation to what writer and narrative designer Andrea Phillips has termed 'big pieces of media', in other words films and television shows, excluding other approaches from the definition. Phillips, an industry veteran, was one of the leading figures to challenge the PGA's position and has created many innovative works which utilise social media.[13] Writer-designer-director Christy Dena similarly argued that transmedia storytelling is far wider than simply just legacy media. These days, in an age in which digitality and connectivity have democratised methods of production, distribution and engagement, the idea that transmedia storytelling should be limited to legacy media feels absurd.

The *Star Wars* franchise has always been at the forefront of these explorations, utilising multiple different techniques to bring its galaxy to its vast fanbase. Right from the get-go, the original 1977 movie constituted a break with what had happened previously. Creator George Lucas took the decision to receive a large proportion of his payment as residuals from merchandising. Although the success of the first film famously took toy suppliers by surprise, it quickly established itself as a colossus, spawning all kinds of merchandise including an exceptionally popular action figure range produced by

---

12 This has arguably been one of the problems with the Marvel shows streaming on Disney+ – that you needed to have engaged with them to understand the later movie releases.

13 Phillips, Andrea (2012) *A Creator's Guide to Transmedia Storytelling.* London: McGraw-Hill

Kenner,[14] comics from Marvel and of course multiple video games. In the years following the release of the final film of the original trilogy, *Return of the Jedi* in 1983, the franchise evolved in a variety of ways, including an early example of a more integrated transmedia project in 1996.[15] The prequel trilogy led to attempts to emulate the licensing success of the original trilogy, but the contentious quality of these films arguably contributed to some elements of this falling flat.

In 2012, Disney purchased the entire *Star Wars* brand and created a Story Group containing key writers and narrative representatives. Its intention from the outset was to clarify the franchise's complex mythology, identifying those elements which should be considered canon ahead of the creation of new 'official' elements such as the sequel films beginning with *The Force Awakens* (2015) and various television series. At the time of writing, the streaming service Disney+ offers multiple feature films and television series, including many animated shows, which are considered canon, as well as other shows and films from the franchise's history which are framed as 'Legacy', i.e. outside of the official canon.[16] The wider integrated transmedia network includes multiple video games, including the recent Ubisoft game *Star Wars Outlaws* (2024).

The other contemporary colossus is the Marvel Cinematic Universe. Unlike *Star Wars*, the MCU has an eighty-five year history to draw upon and a pre-existing shared universe of characters and events originally outlined in comics to utilise. What began with 2008's *Iron Man* movie has grown into a behemoth that extends

---

14 Palitoy in the UK.
15 *Shadows of the Empire* was a multimedia collaboration between Lucasfilm, LucasArts (alongside Nintendo) and Bantam Books. Among other things it featured a novel, a comic book series, various action figures and a video game.
16 Increasingly elements of the Legacy strand of *Star Wars* have been reintroduced into the 'main' canon.

beyond the feature films and into multiple television series and other media, including comics set within the specific timeline of the MCU, as opposed to those original comics. Subsequent purchases by parent company Disney have brought licensed characters like the X-Men back into the fold, while arrangements with rival company Sony have allowed Marvel Studios to use Spider-Man, another key character that was licensed out at a point when Marvel was starved of cash.

Tellingly, many of these 'Mega Narratives', i.e. successful, highly integrated transmedia franchises, are science fiction or fantasy themed.[17] There are a number of possible explanations as to why this is the case. An obvious one is that the kind of fans who like science fiction and fantasy are also the kinds of fans likely to engage enthusiastically with the object of their fascination in multiple different kinds of ways, including purchasing tie-in material such as comics, novels and games. This is in addition to being involved with the fan community more widely through online forums and real-life events such as comic conventions.

Fundamentally, new additions to a franchise must link the new story to the existing world or universe. Most obviously this takes the form of using imagery we recognise from pre-existing entries in the franchise. This can take the form of familiar characters, locations and events. In *Star Wars Outlaws*, for instance, it's very clear that this game is set in a milieu we recognise from multiple feature films and television series, as well as other media. Vast franchises like *Star Wars* and Marvel feature sub-franchises like the Lego games and toys, which portray a more stylised, humorous version of characters and events we know from the existing canon.

Transmedia extensions can help extend and deepen a franchise's lore. Netflix's beautifully animated steampunk-themed *Arcane*

---

17 Fantasy including horror such as *The Conjuring* shared universe.

(2021-) expands the world of *League of Legends* and its characters so successfully that it's helped to nail down the franchise's contradictory canon.[18] Another animated Netflix series, *Cyberpunk: Edgerunners* (2022) caused players to return to the game to explore elements from the TV show, and played its part in helping restore the game's credibility following a bumpy beginning.[19] This kind of reinvigoration of a fanbase through transmedia is by no means unusual, and can take many different guises.

Sometimes the influence of other franchise instalments produced in other media is less explicit than either adaptation or transmedia storytelling. The recent *Alien: Romulus* (2024) movie, for instance, included multiple references to the well-regarded video game *Alien: Isolation* (2014). In the game, telephones are a recurring mechanic and motif that both serve as a save point for the player, but also herald an intense set piece in which the player is liable to die before they've figured out how to beat it. *Romulus'* director Fede Álvarez is on record as being a huge fan of *Alien: Isolation*, and amongst the wider fandom the game is generally regarded more favourably than the later filmic entries in the series.[20]

But there are other more story-focussed reasons as to why science fiction and fantasy franchises dominate the transmedia sphere. These genres are often better able to deal with the inevitable contradictions that arise from multiple creators working across different media. Time travel, magic and parallel universes are obvious mechanisms these genres can use to help fix problems but also to integrate different branches of continuity. More recent developments in the MCU have

---

18 Arcane is officially canon... (pcgamer.com)
19 Cyberpunk 2077 players are returning in droves thanks to Edgerunners (pcgamesn.com)
20 Playing Alien: Isolation Inspired Fede Alvarez to Make Alien: Romulus' (cbr. com)

led it towards the Multiverse, emulating the approach of the original comics. It was this storytelling technique which allowed the MCU to bring in actors from different eras in *Spider-Man: No Way Home* (2021), which integrated the two preceding Spider-Men played by Tobey MacGuire and Andrew Garfield into the MCU alongside current Spider-Man Tom Holland.

Other science fiction and fantasy franchises utilise other diegetic techniques to stitch together the different elements of the franchise as a way of overcoming contradictions. When JJ Abrahms took over the *Star Trek* franchise he used a time travelling villain to create a separate timeline from that of the original series and subsequent films, known to fandom as the 'Kelvin timeline'. The long-running BBC TV series *Doctor Who* similarly uses time travel and parallel universes to offer up explanations for contradictions that fandom and spinoff writers can then exploit. Even *Star Wars*, which has traditionally shied away from parallel universes and time travel, has created the World Between Worlds, a mystical realm connecting all of time and space, to enable encounters between characters from different eras.

Simon Pulman agrees that real world concerns might influence some creative decisions but by and large thinks it's worldbuilding that's driving these franchise choices: 'It's hard to ascertain sometimes if certain story arcs are creatively driven, or whether there is some business or contractual reason behind them – the tail wagging the dog, so to speak. The MCU has had several challenges in the past four or five years, and one of them is designing an organic-feeling story mechanic to bring the newly acquired Fox characters (*X-Men, Fantastic Four*) into the MCU. The multiverse might have been part of that strategy, and it also theoretically provides a mechanism to recast certain characters (or, in the case of Robert Downey Jr, bring an actor back). With that said, I think the prevalence of sci-fi and fantasy in transmedia is generally because of the richness of those worlds, their expansiveness (temporally and geographically), and their ability to generate lots of stories that may be suitable for exploration across media.'

In transmedia storytelling in its broadest sense, we arguably see the biggest influence of video game narrative and worldbuilding on other kinds of storytelling. As stories that are often spatial as well as temporal, video games bring together traditional, sequential approaches with participatory and non-linear modes of storytelling. Just like games, contemporary franchises are networks of connected stories that require oversight and direction, just on a much greater scale. For this reason it's possible to see the narrative designer role that first emerged in the gaming sphere evolving into something much grander and crossmedial in nature, a sort of Franchise Narrative Director role tasked with managing the dynamics between traditional temporal storytelling techniques and spatial approaches. In fact, this is already happening.

But transmedia storytelling is just the beginning. Digital technology and connectivity have transformed the analogue networks that characterised the licensed tie-in material I devoured as a kid into something much more integrated and easy to access. What happens next is going to be even more seismic – and once again, games are at the root of it.

15.

TALES FROM THE METAVERSE

In many ways, *Animal Talking with Gary Whitta* was just like any other American talk show, the kind we associate with the likes of Jay Leno and David Letterman. The many guests included the singer and actor Michelle Gomez, and other high-profile performers like Elijah Woods, Danny Trejo and Shannon Woodward. It had an opening monologue with jokes and a band led by Adam Nickerson. Admittedly, the eponymous host was a game writer and screenwriter, best known for co-creating the story for the *Star Wars* movie *Rogue One* (2016). But that wasn't what was different about it. It was that *Animal Talking* was live-streamed entirely from a virtual set built inside of a video game, and that all the participants were represented by cute animal avatars.

It was a clever, fun idea, emerging from the extraordinary popularity of the hit video game *Animal Crossing: New Horizons* (2020), which with lucky timing released just as the first Covid-19 Pandemic lockdowns were hitting various territories across the world. The game itself allows players to create and tend their own islands populated by small, anthropomorphic animal creatures, and to invite other players to visit. As a 'life simulator' with a fantasy setting it combines realism and escapism in ways which are simultaneously immediate, cute and creative. The challenges of having your freedom abruptly curtailed meant many people – including my own 14-year-old daughter – found *Animal Crossing* an invaluable coping mechanism, a fun way of staying in contact with her friendship group at a moment of seismic uncertainty.

Of course, the real and the virtual worlds collided in lots of unexpected ways during the Pandemic. Lockdowns around the globe meant that many of us were unexpectedly working, studying and socialising from home using various video software packages like Zoom, Microsoft Teams and lesser known ones such as House Party. Connecting this way, at least in the early period, was often clunky and disconcerting, and contributed enormously to the bizarreness of the whole Pandemic experience. But *Animal Crossing* and Whitta's spinoff talk show are interesting because they seem to prefigure something else, something much slicker and more immersive than staring at work colleagues in a virtual room or attempting to sing Christmas carols with far flung relatives.

In the Fall of 2021 Mark Zuckerberg, CEO of Facebook, announced the impending arrival of something called the 'Metaverse'.[1] According to Zuckerberg, the Metaverse will be a sort of vast virtual universe connecting together different computer-generated worlds and environments. As users we'll be able to move seamlessly between these different realms, working, playing and, crucially, shopping.[2] In fact, Zuckerberg's approach is rooted in this idea of the 'creative economy', in which we're all making virtual things, personalising things or purchasing stuff other people have made. You can see the

---

1 Everything Facebook revealed about the Metaverse in 11 minutes - YouTube
2 Shopping for virtual objects to be used inside the Metaverse, rather than ordering objects to arrive in the real world as currently happens with the likes of Amazon.

logic in the thinking – it's building on what already happens in the social media sphere, across the Internet more widely, and of course, in many video game contexts.

While there was enthusiasm from some quarters, lots of commentators were decidedly cool or just plain hostile about the idea of a vast virtual universe. This was true of both everyday punters on social media platforms like Twitter and technology experts paid to think jolly hard about this kind of thing. While the latter group's scepticism was rooted in the sheer audacity and scale of the task outlined by Zuckerberg, the wider public's hostility felt much more world-weary, indicative of a wider cynicism regarding technology's seemingly endless list of promises to improve our lives. Given that lots of people's direct experience of the virtual throughout the course of the Pandemic were the aforementioned computer-mediated meetings with dead-eyed colleagues, friends and relatives, it's perhaps not surprising.

Certainly the presentation itself didn't help. In a video announcement which would soon become infamous, an awkward Zuckerberg presents a 3D social environment in which different digital avatars interact with each other but also with the real world. The mix of approaches, the jarring aesthetics of cartoonish animation styles with the feed from the real world, make this version of the Metaverse feel as dystopic as anything imagined by science fiction. Fittingly, because the original conception of the 'Metaverse' imagined by Neal Stephenson in his 1992 novel *Snow Crash* is anything but cosy. But managing the myriad modes and stylistic approaches of the Metaverse is liable to be a key early problem for developers to overcome. The pink elephant you use in a video game context might not fit quite so well in a virtual business meeting. It's the very opposite of Julian Oliver-Holland's 'dynamic suture' stitching different experiences together.

Zuckerberg's vision is just one example. There are multiple conflicting ideas as to what exactly the Metaverse is, or should be. Some of these disputes are philosophical in nature, many technological, and lots come from a commercial desire to dominate an emergent new market, which will probably be global in scale – or maybe *universal* is a better description – forever expanding and reinventing itself. What we can say with some degree of certainty is that games, the stories they tell and the worlds they create, will be a fundamental part of the Metaverse. We can say this with some degree of certainty because they already are.

Epic Games, creator of the world-conquering *Fortnite* online game, has been exploring the potential of a vast, interconnected communal space for some time, where users can drift between different kinds of experience including but not limited to games.[3] Tencent, the Chinese megacorporation and world's biggest video game vendor, has seen the potential too,[4] and so has its chief Chinese competitors Alibaba[5] and ByteDance.[6] Nvidia, the US technology giant, has similarly thrown its hat in the ring.[7] And, of course, that's before we even get to talking about Microsoft.[8] The Seattle-based company's interest in the Metaverse is long-standing and as ambitious as anything proposed by its many competitors in the sphere.

The augurs have been there for some time, stretching from the MUDs created by Richard Bartle and Roy Trubshaw in the late

---

3 Fortnite's Epic Games Makes A Metaverse Investment To Scale Up Even Further (forbes.com)
4 Tencent shares its metaverse vision for the first time | TechCrunch
5 Alibaba to test gaming potential of metaverse as Big Tech firms stampede into virtual world | South China Morning Post (scmp.com)
6 ByteDance Debuts in the Metaverse With New Social App | (chinafilminsider. com)
7 What Is the Metaverse? | NVIDIA Blog
8 What Is Microsoft's Metaverse Strategy? (pcmag.com)

1970s all the way into the modern gaming environment and genres like that of GaaS – Games as a Service. As the acronym suggests, these are ongoing games, intended either to provide more revenue for a game a player has already purchased or to provide revenue for a game that was free-to-buy in the first place. An early example is *World of Warcraft*, the Massively Multiplayer Online game created by Blizzard in 2004. *WoW* utilised a subscription model, meaning that players would continue to pay beyond their initial purchase of the base game in order to maintain an ongoing presence in the virtual world. In return, Blizzard would constantly supply additional game elements. *WoW* continues to evolve, and at the time of writing attracts somewhere between 700,000 and 1,650,000 players on a daily basis.[9]

Even that, though, is strictly small fry compared to the four million people each day who play Epic Games' *Fortnite*. With its ongoing content updates, ever evolving lore and broader impact on culture, *Fortnite* has led some commentators to suggest that it's already an established, working version of the Metaverse. Epic Games began development in 2011, eventually releasing *Fortnite – Save the World* in 2017. At this stage the game was a modest success without necessarily setting the world alight. Its fortunes were transformed by the decision to introduce a 'Battle Royale' mode, an increasingly popular kind of game at this point, thanks in no small part to the likes of modded versions of *Minecraft* (which I'll talk about shortly) and the military simulation game *ARMA 2 (2009)*. With the introduction of the Battle Royale version, *Fortnite* attracted ten million players in the space of a month.[10]

As the name suggests, Battle Royale is a particular genre of online multiplayer game in which hundreds of players compete with one

---

9 Latest World of Warcraft Player Count & Subscription Numbers (2023) (headphonesaddict.com)
10 The ENTIRE History of Fortnite: Animated! - YouTube

another until only one is left standing. The name is derived from the controversial Japanese dystopian novel *Battle Royale* (1999) by Koushun Takami and the film version of the same name directed by Kinji Fukasaku. Both the film and the game depict a 'last man standing' competition between junior high-school students, forced to fight to the death by a totalitarian Japanese government.[11] As well as the dog-eat-dog survival aspect, the Battle Royale genre of game typically features an ever-shrinking play zone. In the case of *Fortnite*, one hundred players are dropped onto an island and must fight for survival while the area around them gradually reduces in size.

Despite the ruthless-sounding premise, the game itself is colourful and frenetic, extremely imaginative and often beautifully surreal. There is a lot of humour in evidence, particularly in terms of the costumes players can wear, from chicken outfits to knights of armour and the Marvel character Deadpool. In fact, over its history *Fortnite* has crossed over with many other existing Intellectual Properties, from DC to *Star Wars* to *Indiana Jones, John Wick* and *Stranger Things*, and including elements from many other video game franchises such as *League of Legends, Tomb Raider* and *Alan Wake*.

To accommodate all of these vastly different IP into a coherent whole, *Fortnite* has developed a complex lore with an inbuilt flexibility. The fictional framing device is that the world of *Fortnite* is caught in a loop, and that a group of mysterious characters are tasked with ensuring that the loop continues. This overarching narrative is built around chapters and seasons, which provide coherency and consistency, as well as foreshadowing and cliffhangers. For instance, from August to October 2019, there was a massive build up to the end of Chapter One, in which players gathered live to watch as a black hole

---

11 From Mod To Phenomenon – A Short History Of Battle Royale - Game Informer

consumed the entire game. Following this, the game was unplayable for a full thirty-six hours, as players avidly waited to see what would happen (a mini game was available to help pass the time lest anyone wander off and read a book or something). Amongst the *Fortnite* fanbase this event was, unsurprisingly, a *big* thing.[12]

But it's *Fortnite*'s intersection with worlds outside of the game itself – including but not limited to the real world – that may prove most instructive in terms of thinking about the Metaverse. Twitch is a US-created live streaming video service. Much of the content consists of people live streaming themselves playing games. Advanced players like ImTheMyth and Ninja proved critical in the early days of *Fortnite*, using Twitch to live stream their play sessions to vast audiences. Ninja – real name Richard Tyler Blevins – live streamed play sessions with the rappers Drake and Travis Scott, as well as American Football star JuJu Smith-Schuster.[13]

In the wider public discourse, games are rarely portrayed as being creative, particularly ones which focus around a violent and destructive central mechanic like *Fortnite*. In fact, as both gamers and game designers will tell you, even the most aggressive games are built to engender creative play. Surprisingly enough, as well as hiding, hunting and shooting, another key element of *Fortnite* is constructing. Players are able to build extensively and elaborately, sometimes as a defensive technique but even as a tool of attack, as demonstrated in an extraordinary 'build fight' undertaken by ImtheMyth and live streamed via Twitch.[14] The manifold ways in which players use the mechanics offered to them are startling.

It's really apparent when you watch others play the game. There's all manner of creativity and lateral thought involved in hiding within

12 The ENTIRE History of Fortnite: Animated! - YouTube
13 Ibid.
14 Ibid.

the environment, in finding different ways of travelling across the island and, of course, thinking up new ways of annihilating fellow players. Importantly, improvised approaches sometimes end up being incorporated into the game itself, such as the 'Rocket Riding' glitch which enables players to travel vast distances by jumping on a Rocket Propelled Grenade. Increasingly, developers seek to co-opt this creativity to expand and deepen the gameplay experience. In 2018 Epic Games released *Fortnite Creative*, which leans more fully into this idea of creativity to allow players to conjure their own environments and then invite others to play inside them.

So while Zuckerberg's version of the Metaverse seems creepy and off-putting in many regards, its emphasis on building a 'creative economy' finds a useful template in video games like *Fortnite*. As well as utilising skins from other recognisable storyworlds like *Star Wars* or the character of John Wick, the DIY nature of video games means that players often mod their own unauthorised characters to appear in their favourite games. The approach feels redolent of the OASIS virtual world of Ernest Cline's 2011 novel *Ready Player One* – filmed by Steven Spielberg in 2018 – and often cited as a more appealing model for the Metaverse than Neal Stephenson's original conception from *Snow Crash*.

In contrast with *Fortnite*, *Minecraft* is much better known as a constructivist game, which is ironic since it also features a wildly popular battle mode. *Minecraft* offers a sandbox, procedurally-generated world in which players can create and manipulate blocks to build anything they like. Part of its appeal to younger players and adults alike – including parents – is that it looks and feels a lot like the physical building block toys many people are familiar with from their childhood, most obviously Lego. Created in 2009 by Swedish programmer Markus Persson, it was partly inspired by another game called *Infiniminer* (2009) – with which it shares a very similar blocky aesthetic.[15]

The early version of the game would come to be known as *Classic Minecraft*, and gave players the ability to construct a very basic environment. As with most of these kinds of game, these days a variety of different modes exist. In Creative mode the player has access to unlimited resources so they can build whatever they choose, from a castle to an entire country. Importantly this mode doesn't feature explicit objectives, except those which the player might choose to formulate for themselves in terms of what they want to build. Again, the similarities with physical building toys like Lego, MegaBloks and Meccano are marked.

In contrast, in Survival mode the player is in the position of building a shelter and taking other measures to make sure they're defended against the various hostile creatures inhabiting the world. It's this adaptability that makes it such a good model for the Metaverse. Players can create their own maps – that is to say, carefully constructed environments – for other players to easily explore. It's equally the case, however, that players can come along and destroy other players' constructions. When my children were younger they built their own *Minecraft* environments independently of each other and took great relish in decimating each other's creations, like the kid who spitefully stamps on someone else's elaborately constructed sandcastle.[16]

The constructive aesthetic of *Minecraft* is also a feature of *Roblox*, though the latter dwarfs both *Minecraft* and *Fortnite* in terms of its user base. At the time of writing, the number of active daily users is

---

15 Infiniminer – Minecraft Wiki (fandom.com)
16 Years ago academic Mizuko Ito noted how young players of the constructivist game *SimCity* would destroy their work at the end of a play session by triggering a flying saucer, invoking a sort of *Space Invaders* mentality.

listed as 66.1 million.[17] Significantly, *Roblox* defines itself not as a game but as a 'game creation tool.' To this end it currently hosts 50 million 'experiences', which include games but also lots of other activities, the most popular of which is *Adopt Me!*, a pet simulator. In terms of its sheer scale and the extent to which the creativity of participants is foregrounded, *Roblox* might very well provide the best model for the Metaverse that currently exists.

Though it was originally released in 2004 for Windows in 2006, the history of *Roblox* goes back much further to 1989, when entrepreneur, engineer and software developer David Baszucki and his colleague Erik Cassel created a 2D interactive physics lab called Interactive Physics. Baszucki and Cassel were so impressed with the skill and ingenuity of those who experimented with the tool that they decided to develop it further, on a much larger scale. The Beta version of this new, much more sophisticated tool – what Baszucki calls 'an imagination platform' – was released in 2004 as *DynaBlocks*.[18]

Just like Zuckerberg's statement regarding the Metaverse, the marketing materials for *Roblox* emphasise the ways in which the platform enables people to create together, on a global scale. Imagination and self-expression are also key components of the marketing spiel, but crucially – and unsurprisingly – *Roblox* differs markedly from Zuckerberg's approach in the huge emphasis it places on 'the power of play' in enabling this creativity to come about.[19] In common with other games like *Minecraft* and *Fortnite*, *Roblox* engages in collaborative exercises with other Intellectual Properties. At the time of writing, one of these collaborations includes Cirque du Soleil, the Canadian entertainment company and contemporary circus

---

17 Roblox Statistics 2023 — (Demographics & Financials) (demandsage.com)
18 The Story of Roblox - YouTube
19 Ibid.

producer. By accessing the game, participants are invited to create and manage their own Big Top performance in *Cirque de Soleil: Tycoon*.[20]

The reason that games are so vital to understanding what the Metaverse could be is as much technological as it is aesthetic. From *Call of Duty* to *Fortnite*, online games require immediacy to function properly. When we perform an action like shooting someone, we need the consequences of that action to play out in real-time. Even the tiniest of technical delays destroys the experience, as we know from the lags many of us experienced when using virtual environments during the Pandemic. This is why streaming services like Netflix and Amazon Prime use all sorts of clever techniques to make the experience of watching a movie or TV show as seamless as possible. The Metaverse, for it to be the immersive, continuous experience anticipated by its proponents, will therefore need an Internet infrastructure that can cope with these demands.

Assuming these technical challenges are overcome, what's exciting about the Metaverse as a conceit is that it affords opportunities to experience but also create diverse kinds of story and world. The need for professional storytellers and world-builders will still exist of course, but games like *Roblox, Minecraft, Fortnite* and *Animal Crossing* illustrate the desire on the part of players to invent their own scenarios and riff off what's given to them. In this sense, the Metaverse can be seen as a vast democratic space. But as we've seen in other contexts, creative freedom on this scale comes with its own problems.

As we see with social media and the Internet, there are tensions between unfettered creativity and the need to protect vulnerable participants in online spaces. A 2022 investigation by the BBC revealed that adults were using *Roblox* to create sexual content and experiences that most would consider inappropriate for younger

---

20 Cirque du Soleil Tycoon - Roblox Experience | Cirque du Soleil

people. According to the article, spaces known as 'condos' were created where users could talk about and perform virtual sex. Given that players' avatars can wander around environments at will and that two thirds of *Roblox* users are children, this is a major issue.[21] Just as in the real world, game and Metaverse spaces need to be controlled, demarcated and regulated.

In other words the Metaverse needs rules. This extends from how we engage with it to the experiences that get built, the stories that get told and who gets to tell them. Contemporary games like the ones I've discussed provide very different frameworks in which varieties of creative expression can operate. One way of guaranteeing a consistent rule system that everyone adheres to would be to award control of the Metaverse to a single entity. But such an overarching framework would be extraordinarily powerful, no matter how well-intentioned those behind it might claim to be. As Tim Sweeney, CEO and founder of Epic Games pointed out some time before Zuckerberg's big announcement, if one single force dominates the Metaverse then that force will effectively be a 'god on Earth.'[22]

History shows us that powerful forces have always sought to control the stories that can be told, whether it's the Church, the State, corporate entities or specific demographics. As a society, we'll need to balance the need for control and structure with the importance of being able to tell stories that subvert and question the status quo. The Metaverse could be the most extraordinary democratic site for storytelling ever conceived – or it could just as easily be a free-for-all of bigotry and misinformation. With their mix of storytelling approaches, games are already grappling with these possibilities and challenges.

---

21 Roblox: The children's game with a sex problem (bbc.co.uk/news/technology)
22 Part 4: Tim Sweeney's metaverse quest, and the shaping of Epic Games' soul through Fortnite (msn.com/news/technology)

16.
THE SHAPE OF THINGS TO COME

When American poet Vachel Lindsay wrote *The Art of the Moving Picture* over a century ago, he was trying to reconcile a new medium with the dominant dramatic storytelling mode that preceded it – that of the theatre. The purchase by the older medium on the newer one would prove pervasive, at least until the pioneers of early cinema began to understand the potential in their hands. As cinema evolved from the Lumière brothers' documentarist recordings of workers leaving factories and Georges Méliès' fantastical voyage to the moon, creators began experimenting with composition and editing. They used this new medium to explore the possibilities of bending time and space in ways quite different to that of theatre. They gave us close ups and long shots, continuous editing and montage. The new medium began to shrug off the old.

Other modes of mass media storytelling have similarly evolved from the legacy approaches that inspired and informed them, but it took time. Early BBC radio dramas typically sound exactly like stage plays that were recorded and broadcast, primarily because this is exactly what they were. Television plays, limited by the need to shoot in a studio using cumbersome cameras, were similarly theatrical in their design, implementation and approach to performance.[1] But advances in technology and a broader cultural impetus to experiment with these newer narrative forms meant that mass media storytelling was able to more fully explore the possibilities and potential of the medium in question.

Nevertheless, some storytelling verities remained the same. Ancient notions of structure, the ways in which genre is manifested, the careful striptease of a plot, bear sufficient commonalities we can view them as agnostic of medium. It's not for nothing that noted film and television screenwriter Aaron Sorkin swears by Aristotle's insights. What does differ are the ways in which different media tell stories. Novels can provide psychological insight into characters whereas dramatic media need to show this insight unless they resort to inherently non-realist techniques like the monologue. Stage dialogue is often declamatory in a way which wouldn't work in a realist film. Location changes on stage might involve the removal of scenery, whereas a radio drama can move rapidly between locales.

Take Mary Shelley's *Frankenstein*; or, the *Modern Prometheus*. Coming to read the original 1818 novel is a shock not just because the content is so very different from many of the filmic versions and popular culture constructions of the story and characters. It's a surprise because we're used to cinema and television which jumps around in time and space thanks to editing techniques. Shelley's novel stays in one location for long periods of the narrative. The velocity of storytelling we associate with the modern era – in which we constantly move in time and space – is absent. Conversely, novels written in the age of mechanical reproduction have borrowed the techniques of newer media like cinema and television. From TS

---

[1] Radio with pictures, according to famed screenwriter Nigel Kneale, the genius who created the ground-breaking *Quatermass* serials in the 1950s and so much more besides.

Eliot's *The Wasteland* (1922) to James Joyce's *Ulysses* (1922), at the core of Modernism is an eclectic desire to fragment and juxtapose, to create a tapestry of ideas and imagery.[2]

Now it's the turn of video games to change how we tell stories. They take many of the existing techniques we recognise from other storytelling media like novels, theatre, cinema and television. Many games have beginnings, middles and ends, just as Aristotle tells us all stories must, though they don't necessarily give them to us in that order.[3] Lots of video games have characters, whether they're square-jawed soldiers, an anthropomorphic hedgehog or a yellow disc with a slice missing and a single eye. Many of these characters expound dialogue that tells us how they think or feel, or whether a grenade is incoming. Games use cinematic and televisual techniques when it suits them, shaping these borrowed approaches to their will, discarding them as they see fit.

For writer Andy Walsh, games are very much part of an evolving tradition: 'It's easy to get excited and say we're changing everything! In truth we are an evolution. Theatre has involved immersive and interactive elements throughout its history (even if that industry regularly forgets this). Carnivals, fairs and theme parks have long offered players choice and patterns of play. And woebetide the gameswriter who doesn't read books like *Story*[4] from the filmworld to better understand the needs of scenes, dialogue, plot, pacing and character (such books aren't a roadmap, they're a toolset).'

---

2 Consider, too, the role of the machine in the creation of stories – imagine if Shelley had had access to a typewriter or, better still, a word processor. Although if she'd had the Internet we might not have got one of our best metaphors for the machine age.
3 Older British readers might remember Eric Morecambe playing a tuneless piano in front of famed composer André Previn with the assertion that 'I'm playing all the right notes – but not necessarily in the right order.'
4 Screenwriting theorist Robert McKee's best known book about screenwriting.

Story consultant and film producer Rick Porras makes a similar important point about the precedents provided by early cinema: 'It started off as an experience, right? You know, a train coming toward the camera and people going "Holy shit!" That was an experience, really. And then as they learned how to work in this new medium they realised how much could be done with this new technology in telling stories. And you have people coming from theatre and the literary world and they started to evolve, you can feel that energy in the work.' This recalls the ludology-narratology debate I discussed in Chapter 1, with one group of academics claiming games are best understood as experiences and another group saying they're primarily stories. Except, as narratologist Monika Flundernik has argued, *all* stories are experiences, irrespective of medium.[5]

It's certainly true that video game stories can have inciting incidents, turning points, rising points, mid-points, conflicts, crises, climaxes and resolutions, just like other kinds of story. They can have moments of intimacy and moments of spectacle, action and intrigue, reveals and reversals. Most have text and some even have subtext. Many look like movies or television shows, whereas others are more akin to books and comics that have come to life. Some combine all or many of these techniques into one story or world. They can take us to wholly imaginary realms or show us the world outside our window. They can thrill us, make us sad, make us laugh or terrify us. They do all the things stories do because they are stories, except when they aren't.

But in other ways video games are revolutionary, a break with all that came before, and need to be understood in this light. Never before has a storytelling medium existed in which individuals can

---

5 Fludernik, Monika [1996] (2005) *Towards a 'Natural' Narratology*. Abingdon: Routledge

create their own stories together or explore each other's unfolding worlds in real-time, all from different places on the planet, elsewhere in the country or in the same room. They are the most collaborative, far reaching and adaptive storytelling medium yet invented. To this end, video games twist storytelling tropes and techniques into new shapes and formations. They give us agency to control a character and help them discover things alongside us. They offer up opportunities to take decisions, some trivial, others hugely meaningful. They let us choose what the main character is going to say or do. They make us complicit in characters' actions, helping to unfurl or activate the story.

Dr Alison Norrington, Founder and Creative Director at Storycentral Ltd. expresses just this sentiment: 'By combining emergent narratives, player choice, and deeply integrated gameplay, games are creating stories that evolve, adapt, and feel personal in ways that films or books can't replicate. As game developers continue to innovate, storytelling in games will become even more transformative, redefining what it means to "tell a story" and offering experiences that are emotional, interactive, and immersive.' The performance director Damien Goodwin takes a similar view: 'The barriers between game/story/interface are continuing to be broken down, as are the ways a Player interacts with a game – no longer just pressing buttons, but providing the conversation and genuinely engaging with the world they are in. This could lead us to a place where the Player's own unique experiences, their gender, their demographic and their attitudes are a fundamental part of how a story plays out. If a system can be found to deliver this without diluting the quality of the emotional engagement in a story, it could be a significant and intriguing development giving creators endless storytelling possibilities in the future.'

In an important sense, then, video games represent the coming together of two very distinct strands of storytelling. One is the classically structured story, the approach we're all taught from kindergarten onwards in which the tale we tell must have a beginning, middle and end. This is the stuff of most mainstream storytelling, from the Hollywood movies we consume to the West End and Broadway theatre plays we go to see, to television dramas, novels, situation comedies, sketches and advertisements. The story finishes, and (hopefully) we are satisfied, until the next story comes along, whether it's a completely different tale, a sequel, a prequel, or another kind of continuation. Even soap opera supplies a version of this, in which one plot thread might finish while others are still in progress or just beginning. This is the storytelling of certainties that we're all familiar with and, very often, reassured by.

The other is a Western tradition that arose in the middle of the 20th Century, though its roots are older. The Theatre of the Absurd is famously typified by Samuel Beckett's *Waiting for Godot* (1953), Eugène Ionesco's *The Bald Prima Donna* (1950) and the works of Harold Pinter. In this tradition there are no clear-cut answers, no obvious trajectories for characters' arcs, no neat happy endings that serve to reinforce the status quo – in fact, it's more likely they question or subvert it. Motivations are difficult to discern, scenarios ridiculous and plot points sometimes non-existent or contradictory. As a result, they can seem haphazard, frustrating and impossible to fathom but at their core is a profound philosophical enquiry.[6]

Video games routinely combine both approaches. Many give us certainties and concrete outcomes, just like the ones we're familiar with from a million Hollywood movies and popular fiction more generally. At the same time, the very nature of gameplay often leads

---

6 French existential thinker Albert Camus' essay 'The Myth of Sisyphus' identified the philosophy of the 'Absurd' in 1942. Though the Absurdists didn't always agree with the existentialists they were heavily influenced by existential ideas that were themselves given fresh impetus by the unfathomable horrors of World War Two.

to illogicality, most explicitly manifested in the inherently repetitious nature of games. We might try a puzzle over and over again until we've solved it. Our character might die then spring back to life. Fellow players don't always behave logically and can very often behave with great cruelty. Games can give us the certainty of outcomes achieved, but more often than not they offer frustration and joyous absurdity. Yet we keep coming back for more.

For narrative and experience designer Yasmeen Ayyashi, structure is one of the key ways in which game storytelling is transforming storytelling more broadly. 'Game storytelling is challenging traditional narrative structures,' she suggests, 'and creating a space for writers/narrative designers to question traditional formats of the story. This can be seen through open world games where the player engages with the storyworld and perhaps the framing narrative, without engaging in any story arcs or conflicts. It is also challenging story structures with more spatial formats (hubs and spokes, for instance, in games where there is a literal central hub that serves to present the framing narrative, from which players engage with missions and seasonal content) – which opens up opportunities to narrate from different narrative spheres.' Following Ayyashi's logic, the subversion of structure in this way is actually a radical act, something the Absurdists understood all too well. In this way, games can disrupt the status quo as much as reinforce it.

Game storytelling can be seen as part of the wider impact of digitality on the culture. For creators of all kinds, the digital enables flexibility, the chance to be playful and experimental which we recognise from the gaming sphere. For consumers, too, the ability to flow between different kinds of media has become absolutely natural. We can watch movies on video game consoles and play games on television sets. Home computers have long been the nexus point for different kinds of narrative, from newspapers to video streaming to email to social media to music and, of course, games.

Smartphones allow us to engage with multiple storytelling modes, from games to television to movies to novels, all on the go. Streaming services offer the ability to time-shift, to choose when and how we watch something, to stop and rewind or fast forward at will. Social media and messaging apps allow us to editorialise our experiences with other kinds of media in real-time. These are all very playful activities, evocative of a video game aesthetic, a reimagining of our relationship to the screen in the corner, far removed from the reverence with which live television used to be treated.[7]

Sometimes the influence of video game storytelling on other media is absolutely explicit. Critically well-regarded shows like *The Last of Us, Fallout* and *Twisted Metal* demonstrate that television makers have learnt how to realise game worlds in televisual contexts, often by working very closely with the originators of the source material, i.e. game developers. The more recent *Super Mario Bros* movie and *Sonic the Hedgehog* film demonstrates that cinema has improved in this task, too, though the mixed responses to the *Uncharted, Gran Turismo* and *Borderlands* movies indicates there's still some way to go. The more successful examples show that games with arresting stories and well-thought through worldbuilding can provide fertile well-springs for other media, just as novels and comic books have done for a long time. As with any form of adaptation from one media to another, the process is accomplished by converting game storytelling techniques into the techniques required by the destination media.

---

7 I realise there's a tension here between the idea of television in particular as an inherently trivial medium but for many fans of particular shows, whether it's soap opera, serial drama, sitcoms or science fiction and fantasy series, television has always been an inherently serious preoccupation.

Beyond adaptations of video game properties, there are multiple other ways in which games have influenced other media. The German thriller *Run Lola Run* (Tom Tykwer 1998) uses a repeating structure to tell the story of a young woman trying to acquire a large amount of money in twenty minutes to save the life of her boyfriend. Just like a video game she fails twice and succeeds on her final attempt. The influence of games is never stated but clearly hard to avoid. Alternatively, a film like the science fiction thriller *Edge of Tomorrow* (2014) uses a looping structure and explicitly gives Tom Cruise's main character a respawn mechanic.

Good as these films are, the influence of games on them is primarily structural and stylistic. The participatory playfulness that's inherent to games can affect cinema and other media in much more profound ways too. As narrative designer Anjali Shibu points out, 'Other forms of media too have picked up on the kinds of unique experiences storytelling through games can bring, with movies turning to tech like AR/VR/XR to create a space that you can walk through and experience movie moments among the characters as opposed to on-screen.'

Despite the appetite for playfulness and participation I've explored throughout this book, older traditions survive and thrive. For reasons creative, commercial and cultural, there remains an appetite for stories to be told in certain ways. For the most part movies remain stubbornly like movies and television shows stay linear and defiantly non-interactive – *Bandersnatch* and the occasional phone-in poll notwithstanding. Irrespective of the method used to read them, whether it's bound paper or on a Kindle, novels remain novels. Sure, storytelling forms might acknowledge each other's existence to a far greater degree, as with the Mega-Narratives I discussed in Chapter 14. But part of the appeal of transmedia storytelling as practised by these colossal franchises lies in the pleasure of exploring common imaginary worlds using different storytelling methods.

Rick Porras believes older storytelling media will continue to be resilient but also to benefit from the arrival of newer forms: 'We often talk about these things like, oh, this is going to replace this. Film was going to replace theatre or novels, television was going to replace film, video games are going to replace television and film. You know, there's more competition of course for people's time so maybe fewer people are maybe watching one medium over another, but that doesn't mean these mediums are replacing each other. It doesn't mean any of them are less relevant to the human experience. And it's great to see creators being inspired by games while they're working in film or TV and vice versa, while enjoying what makes each of them special. I'm excited for what's coming next because it's another way for people to tell stories and share and interconnect. I think that's a wondrous place to be.'

What Porras is talking about is another key way in which worlds collide – the worlds of television, film, theatre and the novel with that of the video game. Indeed, the influence of video game storytelling on the wider culture might have been going on for much longer than we think, or is at least part of a natural turn towards playfulness. It may not be a coincidence that the emergence of a certain kind of film-making, alongside a reimagined relationship to extra-diegetic elements like merchandising, occurred in tandem with the boom in arcade games and the first wave of home consoles. The film director Peter Bogdanovich famously lamented the 'juvenilization' of movie making heralded by the arrival of directors like Steven Spielberg and George Lucas in the 1970s and the subsequent dominance of 'big tent' movies like *Star Wars* and *Close Encounters of the Third Kind* that were full of spectacle but little else.[8]

The advent of digital technology has inarguably transformed film production, just as it's transformed so many other aspects of our personal and professional lives. In an interview to promote *Furiosa: A Mad Max Saga* (2024), the latest instalment in the *Mad Max* film series, the director George Miller was asked to compare his experiences making the original 1979 movie with the process of creating this latest addition to the mythology. As well as broadly suggesting that the ways in which audiences interpret cinema and storytelling has evolved, Miller identifies the fact that he can now leave the camera running and not worry about expensive film stock running out. Miller also alludes to the portability of the technology and 'the ability to play with sound'. Even at a more prosaic level, Miller suggests the ability to plan around the weather – presumably afforded by connective technology like mobile phones – transforms how they plan shoots.[9]

Beyond the fundamental ways in which the digital has transformed storytelling creation for many industries, game technology is increasingly being used in production, particularly big budget television shows. Industrial Light & Magic, the long-running subsidiary of Lucasfilm, created on-set virtual production technology called StageCraft to assist in the production of *The Mandalorian* (2019-), a *Star Wars* spinoff television show starring Pedro Pascal as the eponymous bounty hunter. StageCraft utilises Epic Games' Unreal Engine to process images in real-time on a vast, all-encompassing

---

8 As cited in film critic Barry Norman's book on the subject, *Talking Pictures* (1987). Bogdanovich's criticism is unfounded in my opinion – these are two directors embedded in the history of cinema capable of both spectacle and intimacy, much like the directors John Ford and Akira Kurosawa who influenced them.
9 George Miller On Mel Gibson Returning to MAD MAX Series | FURIOSA Interview (youtube.com)

video wall, helping to create a more convincing, immersive environment. First broadcast in 2022, Netflix's mysterious drama *1899* similarly used a virtual production stage called *Volume* and operated by a company called Dark Bay based at Studio Babelsberg outside Berlin.

Creative playfulness is evident in other film-making contexts too. Christopher MacQuarrie, the writer-director of the more recent *Mission Impossible* movies, shapes the story according to the spectacular locations and breath-taking stunts the franchise's star Tom Cruise wants to perform. Since these are action movies, it makes a lot of sense that these elements should drive the film in terms of what we see and experience. As a result, the screenplay is often modified to accommodate these action scenes and their settings.[10] The approach is similar to game development, in which story components – as the 'softest', most malleable of the crafts involved – have to change to accommodate changes in design.

For Rick Porras, the influence of games on cinema is only the latest in a long list. 'If a large group of humanity is playing video games as their primary source of entertainment and experience... then of course that affects how other mediums keep evolving,' he says. 'MTV and the style of that editing surely affected the way people told stories in the eighties. We often have first acts in action films with a cold open now which is what was used in television. Our first acts also now feel shorter than they used to be... Where's that coming from?' As Porras observes, this is far from a new phenomenon: 'The way stories are told are affected by the world we're living in, how we're living in it, and how we've evolved with new technology. That's always been the way.'

----

10 6 Screenwriting Lessons from MISSION: IMPOSSIBLE – FALLOUT Writer/ Director Christopher McQuarrie - ScreenCraft (screencraft.org)

As I've explored throughout this book, game storytelling and worldbuilding is combinatory, collective and connected. It's also fundamentally spatial but it needs to marshal temporality to make sense of this spatiality. Game stories can be as heavily curated, didactic and directed as any other narrative medium. We see this in the beautifully realised games of recent history, from *Ghost of Tsushima* to *The Last of Us* and *God of War*, in which a clear authorial vision is realised through an intimate understanding of the medium's strengths. For the screenwriters and narrative designers involved, games like these are as authorial as any other medium, with all the caveats around Barthes' deceased author that might apply.

Elsewhere, players are able to explore dense worlds together, undertaking quests or creating their own collective adventures as they desire. Games like *Elder Scrolls Online* and *World of Warcraft* offer role-playing opportunities that can be fulfilling but are also subversive and exploratory in more ways than simply venturing across a particular fantastical world. Other collective worlds are less subtle in their gameplay but no less immersive, like the kinds offered by *Overwatch* and *Fortnite*. Though they're often derided as colourful baubles aimed primarily at children, the storytelling and worldbuilding of these games are amongst the most artfully realised in the medium.

Going forwards, the challenge lies in how we fuse together the fundamentals of good storytelling with technology that increasingly allows for emergence and dynamism. When I spoke to Guy Gadney, CEO of the AI-powered storytelling engine Charisma.ai, he recalled the insights of Jesse Schell, who suggests in his book *The Art of Game Design* (2019) that games are the language of 'below-the-shoulder' actions such as running, jumping and punching, whereas the language of Hollywood is 'above-the-shoulder', including emotional responses such as laughing and crying. For both Schell and Gadney, bringing these two elements together will lay the groundwork for a revolution in storytelling.

Performance director Damien Goodwin is similarly enthusiastic about the possibilities: 'With the marriage between art and technology continually improving, it's going to be fascinating to see how this encourages creative people to experiment and explore new ideas and collaborations in future. New tools are being created all the time and although AI does provide a potential threat, if used properly, it's also something that could benefit interactive storytelling exponentially. So, as narrative designers and storywriters continue to leverage AI more freely and game developers unearth innovative ways for gamers and non-gamers to enjoy interactive stories to their fullest, the upshot of these advancements is that players will have greater choice leading to a higher level of immersion.'

As we've seen, the implications of such developments are likely to be far reaching for how we define storytelling and storytellers. Like many others in the field, seasoned game writer Kim MacAskill is cautious about the potential impact of AI: 'With a means to have Chat GTP generate entire cinematics, NPC relationships and so on, it does make me wonder how fast narrative designers will step away from the pen and learn how to create Python commands for an AI if they want to remain relevant. It's my hope that the market and playerbase will find an ethical way to see AI built storytelling as not storytelling at all. It can champion the concept of 'evergreen content' but a purely human authored story will hopefully be valued as actual storytelling. *Westworld*[11] is a place I'd visit in a heartbeat but I wouldn't compare it to a theatre show with a penned story.'

---

11 In Lee Sizemore, the science fiction series *Westworld* (2016-2022) gives us one of the few fictional examples of a narrative designer. Addicted to confrontation, he's an oleaginous prima donna and should probably be used as a template of how not to behave in the role.

Game worlds don't just collide with the real world. Increasingly they intersect with other fictional worlds. Despite some recent commercial and creative bumps, the complex transmedia networks represented by the arrival of Mega-Narratives like *Star Wars* and the MCU are unlikely to dissipate any time soon. It's ironic that as these imaginary worlds and universes become ever more integrated, the walls between them are liable to become more porous. The Metaverse will likely offer ever more opportunities for crossover and creative acts between otherwise discrete fictional realms, as well as chances for creators to build their own worlds in which to tell original stories.

This will necessitate a much more sophisticated understanding of Intellectual Property, one in which gaming culture and creativity has spilled over into audience engagement, in which fans are encouraged to be active and playful with existing properties to a greater extent than has previously happened. The era when corporate IP was jealously guarded feels increasingly a thing of the past, when the licence-holders of *Star Trek* would take cease and desist action against perfectly harmless fan films. Lucasfilm understood this early on with their Fan Film Challenge, in which they offered audiovisual assets to enable fans to create their own short films set in the *Star Wars* universe.

This DIY culture has always been an integral component of gamer creativity, manifesting in multiple different ways, from modding – in which players create new play spaces, adapt existing ones or transform characters and other elements – to Machinima, in which amateur creators build their own stories from game worlds and characters, like the long-running *Red Versus Blue* (2003-2024) series based on the *Halo* universe. In fact, for some practitioners and commentators, it's the broader impact of playfulness on the culture that's of interest rather than games' effect on storytelling per se. 'I think they've changed reading more than storytelling, and readers too,' says writer and designer Tom Abba. 'The ubiquity of games, and play as a properly understood form has changed the way readers approach story, and that, for me, is more provocative than games as an arbiter of change on story itself.'

This perspective is liable to be tested to destruction in the context of the Metaverse. After all, it's likely to comprise virtual worlds which jealously guard their fictional integrity, but which also offer pockets for creative experimentation. This has been happening in the gaming sphere for some time. For instance, a number of franchises that are ostensibly realist in nature have given rise to spinoffs that are fantastical or horror-themed. A good example is *Call of Duty*'s introduction of zombies to its otherwise military-realist milieu. Often, though, creative experimentation is laid at the feet of players. For a long time, games have provided toolkits enabling gamers to build their own levels and share them with fellow players. Additionally, a game like *Fortnite* benefits from a particularly flexible narrative framing device which allows crossovers to occur and is able to diegetically integrate them without breaking anything. *Roblox*, as we saw, lets us build our own worlds, games and stories.

My thesis, as I said at the very beginning, is that game storytelling is fundamentally reconfiguring how we tell stories and build worlds. In many ways it will provide a template for how storytelling continues to evolve through the age of digital connectivity, and whatever version of the Metaverse eventually emerges. History teaches us that for the most part older, more established forms of storytelling don't disappear with the arrival of new forms. People will still read novels, go to the theatre, watch television and cinema. That said, we should expect that we can access these older forms *through* the Metaverse, perhaps traversing a virtual space to a theatre performance[12] or going to a library and choosing a book off the shelf to read. The aesthetics of games – their speed, terminology and approaches to temporality and spatiality – will continue to inform these other media in multiple ways, some obvious, some less so. For their part games, as per Vachel Lindsay's thesis, have made an accommodation with those storytelling forms that preceded it. Just like cinema did with theatre, games have created their own techniques unique to the medium.

Importantly, though, hybrid examples and forms will continue to emerge, bringing together linear storytelling techniques with the potential afforded by interactivity. Streaming and Metaverse technology seems likely to afford possibilities for interactive experimentation that have historically proven challenging and clumsy for media like television, film and theatre. The appetite for curated narrative experiences driven by writers, narrative designers and other kinds of storytellers seems unlikely to diminish. At the same time, worldbuilding architects will provide spaces for audiences to explore and create their own stories, on their own or in collaboration with other participants. As I've discussed, there are precedents for all these approaches in the long history of storytelling, from the oral tradition onwards.

Some of the influences of game storytelling on other media aren't necessarily desirable. Charlie Webb contrasts the tension between the 'light touch' approaches of games like *Helldivers 2* and the emergent stories of *Eve Online* with the more conservative approaches of many mainstream games. Christy Dena makes a similar point: 'The problem is, games are limited by the imagination of creatives. And most creatives are assimilated to a status quo thinking that precludes

---

12 Like the staging of *Hamlet* inside of *Grand Theft Auto Online*, as detailed in the documentary film *Grand Theft Hamlet* (2024)

so much. Storytelling is stifled by earnest but erroneous beliefs about games, business, and life. "Only X and Y people buy games." "All games must include X and Y no matter the subject or design context." "All humans are X and Y".'

The irony persists that irrespective of the potential of the technology, game studios are commercial ventures and aren't necessarily interested in risk-taking, leaving that to a vibrant indie sector. This of course is in no way exclusive to games as a medium. It's long been true of Hollywood and many other mainstream storytelling industries. Nevertheless, practitioners from a wide variety of backgrounds see the potential in the medium. For Charlie Webb, game storytelling is a 'synthesis' of other kinds of writing: 'You've got long-term, scripted storytelling of soap operas,' he says, 'the emergent community-driven narratives of pro wrestling, you've got radio plays, there are branching, choose-your-own adventure tales.'

For Christy Dena, the power of games lies in responsive systems: 'I love how these efforts free us to create and experience with as much range as we have in life. I can gesture my hands to communicate with a character? Cool. I can have my complex decisions interact with a complex world? I can see, hear, and feel places in other dimensions? Nice.' The implications of these and other approaches to narrative are immense. As narrative director Karen Hunt says, every time there's an innovation in game storytelling we should see this as an innovation in *all* storytelling.

Antony Johnston suggests that games have extended what we understand as story: 'What games have always done is *expand the nature of storytelling*. Escape rooms, immersive theatre, interactive group experiences like *[Star Trek] Bridge Command* and theme park zones like *Galaxy's Edge* – they all stand on the shoulders of videogame storytelling (and TTRPGs, to an extent). A braver soul than I might even argue that without the past 40 years of innovation in interactive narrative driven by games, they wouldn't exist. The games industry continues to push the boundaries of what storytelling is and can be, especially in the indie space. That's where you'll find tomorrow's ideas being road-tested today.'

As we've seen, game storytellers are a varied bunch with different skillsets, experiences and approaches. Because projects differ so markedly, we have to be highly adaptable and flexible in our thinking, advocating for a creative vision but also interpreting and shaping other practitioners' perspectives into something coherent. Sometimes we're like novelists or screenwriters with a distinctive story to tell; sometimes we're more akin to dramaturgs or choreographers, inventing a scenario, facilitating the discovery of a story or enabling participants to co-create narratives in the worlds we've created. Often we're all of these things simultaneously. As we move further into an era in which content creation is no longer in the hands of the few, where new voices compete for attention, new and old storytelling skills will become ever more vital.

Some of the pleasures afforded by games are familiar from other storytelling media. Many more are unique to this new and constantly evolving artform. Games tell stories but they also enable millions of players to create their own stories. They are immersive and participatory, sometimes expertly curated, sometimes emergent and surprising. They offer singular stories and worlds for those that want to play on their own and all kinds of collaborative and competitive experiences for those that want to interact with other players, real or otherwise.

They can tell tales that are spatial and temporal and take us to imaginary realms that are exploratory and alive. They can remember the choices we made along the way, who we saved, who we killed and the path we took. They let us step into the shoes of other people, in other epochs and other places, and they let us inhabit all manner of extraordinary creatures, as well as all kinds of ordinary ones. They can reshape time and space, reinvigorate genres and create new ones. In this way, video games give us the most convincing template as to what will come next in terms of storytelling.

Games reinvent storytelling. In an epoch that's increasingly connected and non-linear, where the kinds of story we tell have never been more important, this is why they matter so much. Older storytelling forms will continue to flourish, newer ones will appear, and hybrids will continue to arise. The virtual and the real worlds will keep colliding, and all manner of extraordinary stories will emerge.

<PLAY AGAIN (Y/N)?>

COLIN HARVEY

Colin Harvey is an experienced game writer and narrative designer. He was previously a Narrative Director on Electronic Arts' new Battlefield game and Principal Writer on Saber's Turok: Origins (forthcoming). He was also co-writer and Senior Narrative Designer on Sony's acclaimed Virtual Reality thriller Blood and Truth (2019). His other video game work includes Sniper Elite 4 (2017) for Rebellion and the Splatter Royale DLC for Saber's Evil Dead (2023).

Outside of games he has written licensed tie-in material for Big Finish's Doctor Who and Highlander ranges, short fiction for Warhammer and comic stories for 2000AD and Commando. He was formerly an academic teaching and researching worldbuilding, interactive narrative, game storytelling and transmedia storytelling at institutions including King's College London, Bournemouth University, London South Bank University and Western Sydney University.

Colin possesses a PhD exploring the interrelationship of storytelling and play in video game media and is the author of Fantastic Transmedia (Palgrave 2015). In 2022 he wrote and presented 'The Origins of the Metaverse' for BBC Radio Four.

www.ingramcontent.com/pod-product-compliance
Lightning Source LLC
LaVergne TN
LVHW042123070326
832902LV00036B/555